GREATEST-EVER
SUSHI & JAPANESE
RECIPES

GREATEST-EVER
SUSHI & JAPANESE
RECIPES

THE AUTHENTIC TASTE OF JAPAN: 100 TIMELESS CLASSIC AND REGIONAL RECIPES SHOWN IN OVER 300 STUNNING PHOTOGRAPHS

EMI KAZUKO & YASUKO FUKUOKA

HERMES
HOUSE

This edition is published by Hermes House,
an imprint of Anness Publishing Ltd,
Hermes House,
88–89 Blackfriars Road,
London SE1 8HA
tel. 020 7401 2077; fax 020 7633 9499

www.hermeshouse.com; www.annesspublishing.com

If you like the images in this book and would like to
investigate using them for publishing, promotions or
advertising, please visit our website
www.practicalpictures.com for more information.

Publisher: Joanna Lorenz
Senior Managing Editor: Conor Kilgallon
Text: Emi Kazuko
Recipes: Yasuko Fukuoka
Photography: Craig Robertson (recipes) and Janine
Hosegood (reference section)
Food for photography: Julie Beresford, assisted by
Atsuko Console (recipe section); and Annabel Ford
(reference section)
Stylist: Helen Trent
Production Controller: Steve Lang
Design: The Bridgewater Book Company Ltd

ETHICAL TRADING POLICY
At Anness Publishing we believe that business should be
conducted in an ethical and ecologically sustainable
way, with respect for the environment and a proper
regard to the replacement of the natural resources
we employ.

As a publisher, we use a lot of wood pulp to make
high-quality paper for printing, and that wood
commonly comes from spruce trees. We are therefore
currently growing more than 750,000 trees in three
Scottish forest plantations: Berrymoss (130 hectares/320
acres), West Touxhill (125 hectares/305 acres) and
Deveron Forest (75 hectares/185 acres). The forests we
manage contain more than 3.5 times the number of
trees employed each year in making paper for the books
we manufacture.

Because of this ongoing ecological investment
programme, you, as our customer, can have the pleasure
and reassurance of knowing that a tree is being
cultivated on your behalf to naturally replace the
materials used to make the book you are holding.
Our forestry programme is run in accordance with the
UK Woodland Assurance Scheme (UKWAS) and will be
certified by the internationally recognized Forest
Stewardship Council (FSC). The FSC is a non-
government organization dedicated to promoting
responsible management of the world's forests.
Certification ensures forests are managed in an
environmentally sustainable and socially responsible
way. For further information about this scheme, go to
www.annesspublishing.com/trees

NOTES
For all recipes, quantities are given in both
metric and imperial measures and, where
appropriate, in standard cups and spoons. Follow
one set of measures, but not a mixture, because
they are not interchangeable.
Standard spoon and cup measures are level. 1 tsp
= 5ml, 1 tbsp = 15ml, 1 cup = 250ml/8fl oz.
Australian standard tablespoons are 20ml.
Australian readers should use 3 tsp in place of
1 tbsp for measuring small quantities.
American pints are 16fl oz/2 cups. American
readers should use 20fl oz/2.5 cups in place of
1 pint when measuring liquids.
Electric oven temperatures in this book are for
conventional ovens. When using a fan oven, the
temperature will probably need to be reduced
by about 10–20°C/20–40°F. Since ovens vary,
you should check with your manufacturer's
instruction book for guidance.
The nutritional analysis given for each recipe is
calculated per portion (i.e. serving or item),
unless otherwise stated. If the recipe gives a
range, such as Serves 4–6, then the nutritional
analysis will be for the smaller portion size, i.e.
6 servings. Measurements for sodium do not
include salt added to taste.
Medium (US large) eggs are used unless
otherwise stated.
Front cover shows Deep-Fried and Marinated
Small Fish – for recipe, see page 121.

Contents

Introduction

To many people, Japan is an exciting and exotic country, mixing tradition and modernity to striking effect. Its cuisine is no exception, and in many ways reflects Japanese culture. The minimalism in aesthetics, such as poetry and music, is also evident in the presentation of food.

FRESHNESS AND SIMPLICITY

One of the defining features of the Japanese cuisine is the relationship between food and nature. Whenever possible, food is eaten in as natural a state as possible, as this is considered the best, if not the only way to experience the true taste of food. This is at the heart of the Japanese philosophy of eating, so the fish and shellfish caught in the seas of Japan are often eaten raw, or lightly cured with vinegar or salt.

Fresh, seasonal agricultural products are only lightly cooked to preserve their bite and flavour, or they may be slightly salted.

How and what people cook is also highly influenced by the season and by local produce. Many regional dishes exist that have been inspired by food that has been produced locally.

Japanese cooking retains the fresh quality of vegetables and rarely mixes different food types. Sauces are served in separate dishes as dips. This contrasts with other cuisines that use long, slow cooking techniques, often with the addition of sauces and spices.

ARTISTIC PRESENTATION

The Japanese aesthetic regarding food and drink may be described in artistic terms, and Japanese cooking can be compared to the *ukiyo-e* woodblock prints. The beauty of the *ukiyo-e* style lies in its economy of line and simplicity, and it is this same elegant minimalism that is found in all good Japanese cooking.

The unique approach of Japanese chefs helped to inspire French chefs in the 1970s to develop nouvelle cuisine, in which food was artistically arranged on the plate. However, nouvelle cuisine became notorious for its overemphasis on presentation rather than the size of the serving, forgetting the essential fact that Japanese meals consist of several, not just a few, small dishes.

ABOVE: *How a dish of* sashimi *is arranged is as important as the freshness of the fish.*

ABOVE: *Fresh seasonal vegetables are chosen and cooked with care.*

ABOVE: *A cooking technique called* tataki *is used to cook rare steak.*

CULTURAL DIFFERENCES

It is interesting to observe how Japan's food culture has developed differently to those of its neighbours, particularly China's. For instance, while many of the same herbs, spices, flavourings and sauces are used in both Chinese and Japanese cooking, the dishes produced by Japanese styles of cooking are quite different to the Chinese styles of cooking. Buddhism is also present in both countries, but in Japan it has led to the development of the tea ceremony and *cha-kaiseki*, the formal meal that is served with it, and these two elements – the tea ceremony and the formal meal – are unique to the Japanese cuisine.

USING THIS BOOK

As Japanese dishes are often served raw or only lightly cooked, careful selection and preparation of fresh ingredients is one of the most important aspects of Japanese cooking, and is also where a real part of the pleasure resides. No special knowledge is needed to make the recipes, and, apart from a few absolute essentials, such as a pair of chopsticks, most cooks will easily be able to prepare and cook Japanese recipes with minimal fuss using the kitchen equipment that they already possess.

The recipes in this book offer the best of local and national Japanese cuisine, from simple sushi appetizers and noodle dishes to delicious and filling hotpots and the most popular desserts. As they say in Japan, just heed what nature is offering and enjoy.

Sushi and rice

In Japanese cuisine, sushi means dishes that use su-meshi, a slightly sticky rice that is seasoned with vinegar before moulding. Many kinds of fish or vegetables are used in sushi dishes. Because rice is so popular in Japan, it is also shaped into rice balls, added to soups, or served with fish or meat dishes. Delicious recipes in this chapter include su-meshi in Tofu Bags and Red Rice Wrapped in Oak Leaves.

Hand-rolled sushi

This is a fun way to enjoy sushi. Called Temaki-zushi, *meaning hand-rolled, each guest rolls together individual fillings of fish and shellfish, vegetables and* su-meshi.

SERVES 4–6

2 quantities *su-meshi* (see page 171), made with 40ml/8 tsp caster (superfine) sugar

225g/8oz extremely fresh tuna steak

130g/4¹⁄₂oz smoked salmon

17cm/6¹⁄₂in Japanese cucumber or salad cucumber

8 raw king prawns (jumbo shrimp) or large tiger prawns, peeled

1 avocado

7.5ml/1¹⁄₂ tsp lemon juice

20 chives, trimmed and chopped into 6cm/2¹⁄₂in lengths

1 packet mustard and cress, roots cut off

6–8 shiso leaves, cut in half lengthways

TO SERVE

12 nori sheets, cut into four

mayonnaise

shoyu

45ml/3 tbsp wasabi paste from a tube, or the same amount of wasabi powder mixed with 15ml/1 tbsp water

gari

1 Put the *su-meshi* into a large serving bowl, then cover it with a damp dish towel.

2 Slice the tuna, with the grain, into 5mm/¹⁄₄in slices then into 1 x 6cm/¹⁄₂ x 2¹⁄₂in strips. Cut the salmon and cucumber into strips the same size as the tuna.

3 Insert bamboo skewers into the prawns, then boil in lightly salted water for 2 minutes. Drain and leave to cool. Remove the skewers and cut in half lengthways. Remove the vein.

4 Halve the avocado and remove the stone (pit). Cut into long strips. Sprinkle with the lemon juice.

5 Arrange the fish, shellfish, avocado and vegetables on a plate. Place the nori sheets on a few plates and put the mayonnaise into a bowl. Put the shoyu in individual bowls, and the wasabi paste in a dish. Heap the gari in a small bowl. Half-fill a glass with water and place four to six rice paddles inside.

6 Roll the sushi as follows: take a sheet of nori on the palm, scoop out 45ml/3 tbsp rice and spread it on the nori sheet. Spread some wasabi in the middle of the rice, then place a few strips of different fillings on top. Roll it up as a cone and dip into the shoyu. Have gari between rolls to refresh the mouth.

Nutritional information per portion: Energy 191kcal/797kJ; Protein 8.2g; Carbohydrate 21.3g, of which sugars 7.7g; Fat 8.2g, of which saturates 1.4g; Cholesterol 19mg; Calcium 26mg; Fibre 0.9g; Sodium 442mg.

Hand-moulded sushi

Originally developed in Tokyo as street finger food, Nigiri-zushi *is prepared with a selection of the freshest of fish and eaten within a few minutes of making.*

SERVES 4

4 raw king prawns (jumbo shrimp), head
    and shell removed, tails intact
4 scallops, white muscle only
425g/15oz assorted fresh seafood,
    skinned, cleaned and filleted
2 quantities *su-meshi*
15ml/1 tbsp rice vinegar, for moulding
45ml/3 tbsp wasabi paste from a tube, or
    the same amount of wasabi powder
    mixed with 15ml/1 tbsp water
salt
shoyu and gari, to serve

1 Insert a bamboo skewer into each prawn lengthways. Boil in salted water for 2 minutes. Drain and cool, then pull out the skewers. Cut open from the belly side but do not slice in two. Remove the vein and discard. Open out flat and place on a tray.

2 Slice the scallops horizontally in half, but not quite through. Place on the tray, cut-side down. Cut all the fish fillets into small pieces. Cover the tray, then chill.

3 Place the *su-meshi* in a bowl. Fill a bowl with water and the vinegar.

Wet your hand with the vinegared water. Scoop 25ml/1½ tbsp into your palm. Make a rectangular block with the *su-meshi*.

4 Put the *su-meshi* block on a damp board. Rub a little wasabi paste in the middle of a piece of topping. Put a *su-meshi* block on top of the fish slice and press it. Form your palm into a cup and shape the *nigiri-zushi* to a smooth mound. Place it on a tray. Repeat until all of the rice and toppings are used. Serve with shoyu. Eat a little gari between each sushi to refresh your mouth.

Nutritional information per portion: Energy 392kcal/1636kJ; Protein 29.3g; Carbohydrate 40.5g, of which sugars 0.2g; Fat 12.2g, of which saturates 2.1g; Cholesterol 77mg; Calcium 45mg; Fibre 0.1g; Sodium 86mg.

Jewel-box sushi

Chirashi *is the most common form of sushi eaten at home in Japan. A lacquered container is filled with* su-meshi, *and various colourful toppings are arranged on top.*

SERVES 4

2 eggs, beaten
vegetable oil, for frying
50g/2oz mangetouts (snow peas),
    trimmed
1 nori sheet
15ml/1 tbsp shoyu
15ml/1 tbsp wasabi paste from a tube, or
    the same amount of wasabi powder
    mixed with 10ml/2 tsp water
1¼ quantities *su-meshi* made with 40ml/
    8 tsp sugar
salt
30–60ml/2–4 tbsp ikura, to garnish

FOR THE FISH AND SHELLFISH TOPPINGS
115g/4oz very fresh tuna steak, skin
    removed
90g/3½oz fresh squid, body only,
    cleaned and boned
4 raw king prawns (jumbo shrimp), heads
    and shells removed, tails intact

FOR THE SHIITAKE
8 dried shiitake mushrooms, soaked in
    350ml/12fl oz/1½ cups water for
    4 hours, stalks removed
15ml/1 tbsp caster (superfine) sugar
60ml/4 tbsp mirin
45ml/3 tbsp shoyu

1 Slice the fresh tuna steak across the grain, so that it is cut into 7.5 x 4cm/ 3 x 1½in pieces, 5mm/¼in thick. Slice the fresh squid crossways into 5mm/¼in strips. Place both the tuna and squid on a tray, cover them and leave to chill.

2 Pour the shiitake soaking water into a pan, add the shiitake and bring to the boil. Skim the surface and reduce the heat. Cook for 20 minutes, then add the sugar. Reduce the heat and add the mirin and shoyu. Simmer until almost all the liquid has evaporated. Drain and slice thinly.

3 Boil the prawns in salted water for 2 minutes. Drain and cool. Cut open from the belly side but do not slice in two. Remove the black vein. Open out and add to the tray.

4 Beat the eggs and add a pinch of salt. Heat a little oil in a frying pan until it smokes. Wipe away the excess oil, tilt the pan and add enough egg to cover the bottom. Cook until the edge is dry and curling. Turn the omelette over. After 30 seconds, transfer to a board. Use the remaining egg mixture to make several more omelettes. Pile them up, roll then together into a tube and slice very thinly to make strands.

5 Par-boil the mangetouts for 2 minutes, then drain. Cut into 3mm/¹⁄₈in diagonal strips. Snip the nori into fine shreds. Mix with the shoyu and wasabi.

6 Divide half the *su-meshi* among four large rice bowls. Spread a quarter of the nori mixture over each bowl. Cover with the rest of the *su-meshi*. Flatten the surface with a wet spatula.

7 Sprinkle over egg strands to cover the surface. Arrange the tuna slices in a fan shape with a fan of shiitake on top. Place a prawn next to the tuna, and arrange the squid strips in a heap on the other side. Arrange the mangetouts and ikura on top.

Nutritional information per portion: Energy 384kcal/1609kJ; Protein 23.1g; Carbohydrate 57.3g, of which sugars 7g; Fat 5g, of which saturates 1.3g; Cholesterol 203mg; Calcium 61mg; Fibre 0.4g; Sodium 1191mg.

Marinated mackerel sushi

Fresh mackerel fillets are marinated, then packed into a mould with sushi rice to make Saba-zushi. Start preparations 8 hours in advance to allow the fish to absorb the salt.

MAKES ABOUT 12

500g/1¼lb mackerel, filleted
salt
rice vinegar
2cm/¾in fresh root ginger, peeled and
    finely grated, to garnish
shoyu, to serve

FOR THE *SU-MESHI* (VINEGARED RICE)
200g/7oz/1 cup Japanese short grain rice
40ml/8 tsp rice vinegar
20ml/4 tsp caster (superfine) sugar
5ml/1 tsp salt

1 Place the fillets skin side down in a flat dish, cover with a thick layer of salt, and leave to stand for at least 3–5 hours.

2 To make the *su-meshi*, put the rice in a large bowl and wash in several changes of water, until it runs clear. Tip into a sieve and leave to drain for 1 hour. Put the rice into a deep pan and add 250ml/8fl oz/1 cup water. Cover and bring to the boil. Reduce the heat and simmer for 12 minutes without lifting the lid. Remove from the heat and leave for 10 minutes.

3 Transfer the rice to a wet Japanese rice tub or large bowl. In a bowl, mix the vinegar, sugar and salt until dissolved. Add to the rice, fluffing it with a wet spatula. Cover with wet dish towels and cool.

4 Wipe the salt from the mackerel. Remove all remaining bones with tweezers. Lift the skin at the tail end of each fillet and peel towards the head end. Place the fillets in a dish, and pour in enough rice vinegar to cover the fish. Leave for 20 minutes, then drain and wipe dry.

5 Line a 25 x 7.5 x 4cm/10 x 3 x 1½in container with clear film (plastic wrap). Lay the fillets in the container, skinned side down, and fill the gaps with the remaining mackerel. Put the *su-meshi* into the container and press down. Cover with the clear film and place a weight on top. Leave overnight.

6 Slice the sushi into 2cm/¾in pieces. Garnish with ginger and serve with shoyu.

Nutritional information per portion: Energy 158kcal/659kJ; Protein 9g; Carbohydrate 15g, of which sugars 1.7g; Fat 6.8g, of which saturates 1.4g; Cholesterol 23mg; Calcium 9mg; Fibre 0g; Sodium 190mg.

Nori-rolled sushi

You will need a makisu (a sushi rolling mat) to make these sushi, called Nori-maki. *Both* Futo-maki *and* Hoso-maki *are served with some wasabi, gari and shoyu for dipping.*

Futo-maki (thick-rolled sushi)

MAKES 16 PIECES

2 nori sheets
350g/12oz/1¾ cups cooked rice with 45ml/
    3 tbsp rice vinegar added (*su-meshi*)

FOR THE OMELETTE

2 eggs, beaten
25ml/1½ tbsp second dashi stock, or the
    same amount of water and 5ml/1 tsp
    dashi-no-moto
10ml/2 tsp sake
2.5ml/½ tsp salt
vegetable oil, for frying

FOR THE FILLINGS

4 dried shiitake mushrooms, soaked overnight
120ml/4fl oz/½ cup water and 7.5ml/
    1½ tsp dashi-no-moto
15ml/1 tbsp shoyu
7.5ml/1½ tsp caster (superfine) sugar
5ml/1 tsp mirin
6 raw large prawns (shrimp), heads and shells
    removed, tails intact
4 asparagus spears, boiled for 1 minute
    in lightly salted water, and cooled
10 chives, about 23cm/9in long, ends trimmed

1 Mix the eggs, stock, sake and salt. Heat some oil in a frying pan. Add enough egg mixture to thinly cover the base. When just set, fold the omelette in half and wipe the pan with oil. With the first omelette still in the pan, repeat to make more omelettes. Place on top of one another to form one multi-layered omelette. Slide it onto a board. Cool, then cut into 1cm/½in wide strips.

2 Put the shiitake, dashi stock, shoyu, sugar and mirin in a pan. Bring to the boil, reduce the heat and cook for 20 minutes. Drain, discard the stalks, and slice the caps. Squeeze out liquid. Boil the prawns for 1 minute. Drain and cool. Remove the black vein.

3 Place a nori sheet at the front edge of the makisu. Scoop up half the *su-meshi* and spread it on the nori, leaving a margin on each side. Make a depression across the centre of the rice and fill with an omelette strip. Put half the asparagus and prawns on top. Add five chives, then half of the shiitake. Lift the makisu with your thumbs, press the fillings with your fingers, roll up, then roll on the board. Unwrap and make another roll. To serve, cut each into eight pieces.

Nutritional information per portion: Energy 107kcal/447kJ; Protein 3.8g; Carbohydrate 16.3g, of which sugars 1.3g; Fat 2.9g, of which saturates 0.6g; Cholesterol 52mg; Calcium 17mg; Fibre 0.2g; Sodium 112mg.

Hoso-maki (thin-rolled sushi)

MAKES 24 PIECES

2 nori sheets, cut in half crossways
1 quantity *su-meshi*
45ml/3 tbsp wasabi paste from a tube, or
   the same amount of wasabi powder
   mixed with 10ml/2 tsp water, plus
   extra for serving

FOR THE FILLINGS
90g/3½oz very fresh tuna steak
10cm/4in cucumber or 17cm/6½in
   Japanese cucumber
5ml/1 tsp roasted sesame seeds
6cm/2½in takuan, cut into 1cm/½in
   thick long strips

1 Cut the tuna with the grain into 1cm/½in wide strips. Cut the cucumber into 1cm/½in thick strips. Place the makisu on the work surface, then place a nori sheet on it horizontally, rough side up. Spread a quarter of the *su-meshi* over the nori, leaving a 1cm/½in margin on the side farthest from you. Press. Spread a little wasabi across the the rice and arrange tuna strips horizontally in a row across the middle. Cut off excess.

2 Roll up the makisu with both hands, wrapping the tuna in the middle and rolling away from the side closest to you. Hold the makisu and squeeze to firm the *nori-maki*. Unwrap the makisu, remove the rolled tuna *hoso-maki* and set aside. Repeat to make another one.

3 Repeat using only cucumber strips with the green skin on. Sprinkle sesame seeds on the cucumber before rolling. Repeat with the takuan strips, but omit the wasabi. Keep the sushi on a damp board, covered with clear film (plastic wrap) during preparation. To serve, cut each *hoso-maki* into six pieces. Wipe the knife with a dish towel dampened with rice vinegar after each cut.

Nutritional information per portion: Energy 23kcal/96kJ; Protein 0.5g; Carbohydrate 5g, of which sugars 0g; Fat 0g, of which saturates 0g; Cholesterol 0mg; Calcium 2mg; Fibre 0g; Sodium 0mg.

Su-meshi in tofu bags

Abura-age *(fried thin tofu)* is different to other tofu products. It can be opened up like a bag, and in this recipe it is served with soy sauce-based seasonings and filled with su-meshi.

SERVES 4

8 fresh abura-age or 275g/10oz can
    ready-to-use abura-age (contains
    16 halves)
900ml/1¹/₂ pints/3³/₄ cups second dashi
    stock, or the same amount of water
    and 10ml/2 tsp dashi-no-moto
90ml/6 tbsp caster (superfine) sugar

30ml/2 tbsp sake
70ml/4¹/₂ tbsp shoyu
generous 1 quantity *su-meshi*, made with
    40ml/8 tsp sugar
30ml/2 tbsp toasted white sesame seeds
gari, to garnish

1 Par-boil the fresh abura-age in rapidly boiling water for about 1 minute. Drain under running water and leave to cool. Squeeze the excess water out gently. Cut each sheet in half and carefully pull open the cut end to make bags. If you are using canned abura-age, drain the liquid.

2 Lay the abura-age bags in a large pan. Pour in the dashi stock to cover and bring to the boil. Reduce the heat and cover, then simmer for 20 minutes. Add the sugar in three batches during this time, shaking the pan to dissolve it. Simmer for a further 15 minutes.

3 Add the sake. Shake the pan again, and add the shoyu in three batches. Simmer until almost all the liquid has evaporated. Transfer the abura-age to a wide sieve and leave to drain.

4 Mix the *su-meshi* and sesame seeds in a wet mixing bowl. Wet your hands and take a little *su-meshi*. Shape it into a rectangular block. Open one abura-age bag and insert the block. Press the edges together to close the bag. Once all the bags have been filled, place them on a large serving plate with the bottom of the bag on top. Garnish with gari.

Nutritional information per portion: Energy 495kcal/2073kJ; Protein 20.5g; Carbohydrate 65.2g, of which sugars 34.5g; Fat 16.7g, of which saturates 0.6g; Cholesterol 0mg; Calcium 1093mg; Fibre 0.6g; Sodium 13mg.

Red rice wrapped in oak leaves

This sticky rice dish, Sekihan, *is cooked for special occasions and takes 8 hours to prepare. Edible kashiwa (oak) leaves are used when red rice is prepared for a boy-child's festival.*

SERVES 4

65g/2½oz/⅓ cup dried azuki beans
5ml/1 tsp salt
300g/11oz/1½ cups mochigome
50g/2oz/¼ cup Japanese short grain rice
12 kashiwa leaves (optional)

FOR THE *GOMA-SHIO*
45ml/3 tbsp sesame seeds (black sesame,
    if available)
5ml/1 tsp ground sea salt

1 Put the azuki beans in a pan and pour in 400ml/14fl oz/1⅔ cups plus 20ml/4 tsp water. Bring to the boil, reduce the heat and simmer, covered, for 20–30 minutes until the beans look swollen but are still firm. Drain and reserve the liquid, then add the salt. Return the beans to the pan.

2 Wash the two rices together. Drain in a sieve and leave for 30 minutes. Bring another 400ml/ 14fl oz/1⅔ cups plus 20ml/4 tsp water to the boil. Add to the beans and boil, then simmer for 30 minutes. Drain and add the liquid to the bowl with the reserved liquid. Cover the beans and cool. Add the rice to the bean liquid and soak for 4–5 hours. Drain the rice and reserve the liquid. Mix the beans into the rice.

3 Bring a steamer of water to the boil. Turn off the heat. Place a tall glass upside down in the centre. Pour the rice and beans into the steamer and pull the glass out. Steam on high for 10 minutes. Sprinkle the rice mixture with the reserved liquid from the bowl. Cover and repeat the process twice more at 10 minute intervals, then steam for 15 minutes more. Leave to stand for 10 minutes.

4 Make the *goma-shio*. Roast the sesame seeds and salt in a dry frying pan until the seeds start to pop. Cool, then put in a dish.

5 Wipe each kashiwa leaf with a wet dish towel. Scoop 120ml/4fl oz/½ cup of the rice mixture into a wet tea cup and press with wet fingers. Turn the cup upside down and shape the rice into a flat ball. Insert into a leaf folded in two. Repeat until all the leaves are used. Alternatively, transfer the red rice to a large bowl wiped with a wet towel. Serve with a sprinkle of *goma-shio*.

Nutritional information per portion: Energy 432kcal/1807kJ; Protein 12.4g; Carbohydrate 78.7g, of which sugars 0.5g; Fat 7.2g, of which saturates 1g; Cholesterol 0mg; Calcium 105mg; Fibre 2.2g; Sodium 496mg.

Lunch-box rice with three toppings

San-shoku Bento *is a typical* bento *(lunch box) menu for Japanese children. Colourful toppings and a variety of tastes hold their attention so they don't get bored.*

MAKES 4 LUNCH BOXES

275g/10oz/1½ cups Japanese short g
   rain rice cooked using 375ml/13fl oz/
   1²/₃ cups water, cooled
45ml/3 tbsp sesame seeds, toasted
salt
3 mangetouts (snow peas), to garnish

FOR THE *IRI-TAMAGO*
30ml/2 tbsp caster (superfine) sugar
5ml/1 tsp salt
3 large (US extra large) eggs, beaten

FOR THE *DENBU*
115g/4oz cod fillet, skinned and boned
20ml/4 tsp caster (superfine) sugar
5ml/1 tsp salt
5ml/1 tsp sake
2 drops of red vegetable colouring, diluted

FOR THE *TORI-SOBORO*
200g/7oz minced (ground) raw chicken
45ml/3 tbsp sake
15ml/1 tbsp caster (superfine) sugar

15ml/1 tbsp shoyu
15ml/1 tbsp water

1 To make the *iri-tamago*, add the sugar and salt to the eggs in a pan. Cook over a medium heat, stirring. When almost set, remove from the heat and stir until the egg is fine and slightly dry.

2 To make the *denbu*, cook the cod for 2 minutes in a pan of boiling water. Drain and dry well. Skin and remove all the bones. Put the cod and sugar into a clean pan, add the salt and sake, and cook over a low heat for 1 minute, stirring with a fork to flake the cod. Reduce the heat and sprinkle on the colouring. Stir for 15–20 minutes until the cod becomes fluffy and fibrous.

3 For the *tori-soboro*, put the chicken, sake, sugar, shoyu and water into a pan. Cook over a medium heat for 3 minutes, before reducing the heat and stirring until the liquid has almost evaporated.

4 Blanch the mangetouts for 3 minutes, then drain and slice. Mix the rice with the sesame seeds. Divide the rice among four lunch boxes. Flatten the surface with the back of a spoon.

5 Spoon a quarter of the cooked egg mixture into each box to cover a third of the rice. Cover the next third with a quarter of the *denbu* and the last section with a quarter of the chicken. Garnish each topping with the mangetout sticks.

Nutritional information per portion: Energy 515kcal/2160kJ; Protein 29.3g; Carbohydrate 72.3g, of which sugars 17.4g; Fat 11.8g, of which saturates 2.3g; Cholesterol 191mg; Calcium 125mg; Fibre 0.9g; Sodium 862mg.

Rice balls with four fillings

Onigiri, **the Japanese name for this dish, means hand-moulded rice. Japanese rice is ideal for making rice balls, which are filled here with salmon, mackerel, umeboshi and olives.**

SERVES 4

50g/2oz salmon fillet, skinned
3 umeboshi, 50g/2oz in total weight
45ml/3 tbsp sesame seeds
2.5ml/$^1/_2$ tsp mirin
50g/2oz smoked mackerel fillet
2 nori sheets, each cut into 8 strips

6 pitted black olives, wiped and finely chopped
fine salt
Japanese pickles, to serve

FOR THE RICE
450g/1lb/2$^1/_4$ cups Japanese short grain rice
550ml/18fl oz/2$^1/_2$ cups water

1 Wash the rice, drain and put into a pan. Add the water and leave for 30 minutes. Cover and bring to the boil. Reduce the heat and simmer for 12 minutes. When you hear a crackling noise remove from the heat and leave, covered, for 15 minutes. Stir with a wooden spatula and cool for 30 minutes. Salt the salmon and leave for 30 minutes. Stone (pit) the umeboshi then mash them slightly. Mix with 15ml/1 tbsp of the sesame seeds and the mirin to make a rough paste. Wash the salmon. Grill (broil) the salmon and smoked mackerel under a high heat. Remove the skin and flake the fish. Keep the salmon and mackerel pieces separate. Toast the remaining sesame seeds.

2 Put a teacup and tablespoons into a bowl of water. Put salt into a dish. Wipe a board with a wet dish towel. Remove the teacup and shake off excess water. Scoop 30ml/2 tbsp rice into the cup. Make a well in the centre and add a quarter of the salmon. Cover with 15ml/1 tbsp rice. Press well.

3 Wet your hands, then spread a little salt over your palms. Turn the rice in the teacup out into one hand and squeeze to make a dense, flat ball. Wrap the ball with a nori strip. Put on the board. Make three more, then make four balls using the mackerel and another four using the umeboshi paste.

4 Scoop about 45ml/3 tbsp rice into the teacup. Mix in a quarter of the olives. Press the rice with your fingers. Wet your hands with water and rub with salt and a quarter of the toasted sesame seeds. Turn the teacup on to one hand and shape the rice into a ball. This time, do not wrap with nori. Repeat, making three more. Serve one kind of each ball on a plate with Japanese pickles.

Nutritional information per portion: Energy 548kcal/2288kJ; Protein 15.4g; Carbohydrate 90.8g, of which sugars 1g; Fat 13g, of which saturates 2.1g; Cholesterol 19mg; Calcium 108mg; Fibre 1.3g; Sodium 243mg.

Compressed sushi with smoked salmon

This sushi, known as Oshi-zushi, dates back almost a thousand years. The earliest forms of sushi were made as a means of preserving fish. The cooked rice produced an acid that preserved the fish. Only the marinated fish was eaten and the rice was discarded.

MAKES ABOUT 12

175g/6oz smoked salmon, thickly sliced
15ml/1 tbsp sake
15ml/1 tbsp water
30ml/2 tbsp shoyu

1 quantity *su-meshi*
1 lemon, thinly sliced into
    6 x 3mm/^{1}/$_8$in rings, to garnish

1 Lay the smoked salmon on a chopping board and sprinkle with a mixture of the sake, water and shoyu. Leave for an hour, then wipe dry.

2 Wet a wooden Japanese sushi mould or line a 25 x 7.5 x 5cm/10 x 3 x 2in plastic container with a large sheet of clear film (plastic wrap), allowing the edges to hang over.

3 Spread half the smoked salmon to evenly cover the bottom of the mould or container. Add a quarter of the cooked rice and firmly press down with your hands dampened with rice vinegar until it is 1cm/^{1}/$_2$in thick. Add the rest of the salmon, and press the remaining rice on top.

4 Put the wet wooden lid on the mould, or cover the plastic container with the overhanging clear film. Place a weight, such as a heavy dinner plate, on top. Leave in a cool place overnight, or for at least 3 hours. If you keep it in the refrigerator, choose the least cool part.

5 Remove the compressed sushi from the mould or container and unwrap. Cut into 2cm/^{3}/$_4$in slices and serve on a Japanese lacquered tray or a large plate. Quarter the lemon rings. Garnish with two slices of lemon on top of each piece and serve.

Nutritional information per portion: Energy 68kcal/286kJ; Protein 4.7g; Carbohydrate 10.2g, of which sugars 0.2g; Fat 0.7g, of which saturates 0.1g; Cholesterol 5mg; Calcium 6mg; Fibre 0g; Sodium 452mg.

Brown rice and mushrooms in clear soup

This is a good and quick way of using up left-over rice. Short grain Japanese or Italian brown rice are best for this recipe.

SERVES 4

1 litre/1¾ pints/4 cups second dashi stock, or the same amount
    of water and 20ml/4 tsp dashi-no-moto
60ml/4 tbsp sake
5ml/1 tsp salt
60ml/4 tbsp shoyu
115g/4oz fresh shiitake mushrooms, thinly sliced
600g/1lb 6oz cooked brown rice
2 large (US extra large) eggs, beaten
30ml/2 tbsp chopped fresh chives

FOR THE GARNISH
15ml/1 tbsp sesame seeds
shichimi togarashi (seven-spice powder), optional

1 Mix the dashi stock, sake, salt and shoyu in a large pan. Bring to the boil, then add the sliced shiitake. Cook for 5 minutes over a medium heat.

2 Add the cooked rice and stir over a medium heat. Break up any large chunks, and thoroughly warm the rice.

3 Pour the eggs into the pan. Lower the heat and cover. Do not stir. Remove from the heat after 3 minutes and stand for 3 minutes more. Sprinkle in the chives. Serve garnished with sesame seeds and shichimi togarashi.

Nutritional information per portion: Energy 280kcal/1180kJ; Protein 8.4g; Carbohydrate 50g, of which sugars 2.4g; Fat 4.7g, of which saturates 1.3g; Cholesterol 95mg; Calcium 48mg; Fibre 2.1g; Sodium 1111mg.

Rice in green tea with salmon

This is a common Japanese snack to have after drinks. In the Kyoto region, offering this dish used to be a way of saying the party was over.

SERVES 4

150g/5oz salmon fillet
¼ nori sheet
250g/9oz/1¼ cups Japanese short grain rice cooked using
    350ml/12fl oz/1½ cups water
15ml/1 tbsp sencha leaves
5ml/1 tsp wasabi paste from a tube, or 5ml/1 tsp wasabi powder
    mixed with 1.5ml/¼ tsp water (optional)
20ml/4 tsp shoyu
salt

1 Salt the salmon and leave for 30 minutes. Wipe off the salt and grill (broil) for 5 minutes until cooked through. Remove the skin and bones, then flake the salmon.

2 Cut the nori into narrow strips. If the rice is warm, put equal amounts into individual bowls. If the rice is cold, put in a sieve and pour hot water over it to warm it up. Drain and pour into the bowls. Place the salmon on top.

3 Put the sencha leaves in a teapot. Pour 600ml/1 pint/ 2½ cups hot water into the teapot and wait for 45 seconds. Strain the tea gently and evenly over the top of the rice and salmon. Add some nori and wasabi, if using, to the top of the rice, then trickle shoyu over and serve.

Nutritional information per portion: Energy 296kcal/1238kJ; Protein 12.5g; Carbohydrate 50.7g, of which sugars 0.7g; Fat 4.5g, of which saturates 0.7g; Cholesterol 19mg; Calcium 22mg; Fibre 0g; Sodium 729mg.

Five ingredients rice

The Japanese love rice so much they invented many ways to enjoy it. Here, chicken and vegetables are cooked with short grain rice making a healthy light lunch dish called Kayaku-gohan.

SERVES 4

275g/10oz/1¹⁄₃ cups Japanese short
    grain rice
90g/3¹⁄₂oz carrot, peeled
2.5ml/¹⁄₂ tsp lemon juice
90g/3¹⁄₂oz gobo or canned bamboo
    shoots
225g/8oz oyster mushrooms
8 mitsuba sprigs, root part removed
350ml/12fl oz/1¹⁄₂ cups water and
    7.5ml/1¹⁄₂ tsp dashi-no-moto
    (stock granules)
150g/5oz chicken breast fillet, skinned,
    boned and cut into 2cm/³⁄₄in dice
30ml/2 tbsp shoyu
30ml/2 tbsp sake
25ml/1¹⁄₂ tbsp mirin
pinch of salt

1 Wash the rice in a bowl. Change the water until it is clear. Drain the rice in a sieve for 30 minutes.

2 Cut the carrot into 5mm/¹⁄₄in rounds, then cut into flowers.

3 Fill a bowl with water and add the lemon juice. Peel the gobo and slice with a knife as if sharpening a pencil. Leave for 15 minutes, then drain. If using canned bamboo shoots, slice into matchsticks.

4 Tear the mushrooms into thin strips. Chop the mitsuba sprigs into

2cm/³⁄₄in long pieces. Put them in a sieve and pour over hot water to wilt. Drain and set aside.

5 Heat the dashi stock and add the carrots and gobo or bamboo shoots. Bring to the boil and add the chicken. Remove any scum from the surface, and add the shoyu, sake, mirin and salt. Add the rice and mushrooms and cover. Bring back to the boil, wait 5 minutes, reduce the heat and simmer for 10 minutes. Remove from the heat, leave covered and stand for 15 minutes. Add the mitsuba and serve.

Nutritional information per portion: Energy 331kcal/1386kJ; Protein 16.2g; Carbohydrate 61.1g, of which sugars 5.6g; Fat 1.2g, of which saturates 0.2g; Cholesterol 26mg; Calcium 32mg; Fibre 1.5g; Sodium 567mg.

Chicken and egg on rice

This dish is called Oyako Don *which means a parent (the chicken) and a child (the egg). It is traditionally cooked in a don-buri, which is a deep, round ceramic bowl with a lid.*

SERVES 4

250g/9oz chicken thighs, skinned and boned

4 mitsuba sprigs or a handful of mustard and cress

300ml/½ pint/1¼ cups water and 25ml/1½ tbsp dashi-no-moto (stock granules)

30ml/2 tbsp caster (superfine) sugar

60ml/4 tbsp mirin

60ml/4 tbsp shoyu

2 small onions, sliced thinly lengthways

4 large (US extra large) eggs, beaten

275g/10oz/scant 1½ cups Japanese short grain rice cooked with 375ml/13fl oz/scant 1⅔ cups water

shichimi togarashi, to serve (optional)

1 Cut the chicken into 2cm/¾in square bitesize chunks. Remove the root part from the mitsuba, and chop into 2.5cm/1in lengths.

2 Pour the dashi stock, sugar, mirin and shoyu into a frying pan with a lid and bring to the boil. Add the onion slices and lay the chicken on top. Cook over a high heat for 5 minutes, shaking the pan frequently.

3 When the chicken is cooked, sprinkle with the mitsuba or mustard and cress.

4 Pour the beaten eggs over the chicken. Cover and wait for 30 seconds. Do not stir.

5 Remove from the heat and leave to stand for 1 minute. The egg should be just cooked but still soft, rather than set. The egg should not become a firm omelette.

6 Scoop the warm rice on to individual plates, then pour the soft eggs and chicken on to the rice. Serve with a little shichimi togarashi, if liked.

Nutritional information per portion: Energy 455kcal/1910kJ; Protein 25g; Carbohydrate 71.9g, of which sugars 16.9g; Fat 7.7g, of which saturates 2.1g; Cholesterol 256mg; Calcium 59mg; Fibre 0.1g; Sodium 1196mg.

Soups and noodles

In Japan, soups are usually eaten with or at the end of the meal. Japanese noodles are sometimes compared with Chinese ones, but apart from ramen noodles, the two are quite different. Japanese soup stocks are made with great care to set off the flavour of the noodles. Some noodles, such as buckwheat, have a delicate aroma, and can be eaten plain, served with just a simple dipping sauce.

Miso soup

Essential to any Japanese meal is a bowl of rice. Next is miso soup, served in a lacquered bowl.
Of the many variations, **Wakame To Tofu No Miso-shiru** *comes first.*

SERVES 4

5g/¹/₈oz dried wakame
¹/₂ x 225–285g/8–10¹/₄oz packet fresh
    soft tofu or long-life silken tofu
400ml/14fl oz/1²/₃ cups second dashi
    stock or the same amount of water
    and 5ml/1 tsp dashi-no-moto
45ml/3 tbsp miso
2 spring onions (scallions), finely chopped
shichimi togarashi or sansho (optional),
    to serve

1 Soak the wakame in a large bowl of cold water for 15 minutes.

2 Drain the wakame and chop into stamp-size pieces if using the long or broad type.

3 Cut the tofu into 1cm/¹/₂in strips, then cut horizontally through the strips. Cut the strips into squares.

4 Bring the dashi stock to the boil in a medium saucepan.

5 Put the miso in a cup and mix with 60ml/4 tbsp hot stock. Reduce the heat and pour two-thirds of the miso into the pan of stock.

6 Taste the soup and add more miso if required. Add the wakame and tofu and increase the heat. Just before the soup comes to the boil again, add the spring onions and remove from the heat. Do not boil. Serve sprinkled with shichimi togarashi or sansho, if liked.

Nutritional information per portion: Energy 89kcal/371kJ; Protein 12.1g; Carbohydrate 1.9g, of which sugars 1.7g; Fat 3.7g, of which saturates 1g; Cholesterol 32mg; Calcium 21mg; Fibre 0.6g; Sodium 1284mg.

Clear soup with seafood sticks

This delicate soup, called O-sumashi, which is often eaten with sushi, is very quick to make if you prepare the first dashi beforehand or if you use freeze-dried dashi-no-moto.

SERVES 4

**4 mitsuba sprigs or 4 chives and a few
    sprigs of mustard and cress**
4 seafood sticks
**400ml/14fl oz/1²/₃ cups first dashi
    stock, or the same amount of water
    and 5ml/1 tsp dashi-no-moto**
15ml/1 tbsp shoyu
7.5ml/1¹/₂ tsp salt
**grated rind of yuzu (optional),
    to garnish**

1 Cut off the root from the mitsuba, then cut 5cm/2in from the top, retaining both the long straw-like stem and the leaf.

2 Blanch the stems in hot water. If you use chives, choose those 10cm/4in in length and blanch them.

3 Take a seafood stick and carefully tie around the middle with a mitsuba stem or chive, holding it in place with a knot. Repeat to make four tied seafood sticks.

4 Loosen each end of a seafood stick to make it look like a tassel.

5 Place one seafood stick in each soup bowl. Add the four mitsuba leaves or mustard and cress.

6 Heat the dashi stock in a medium-sized pan and bring to the boil. Add shoyu and salt to taste. Pour the stock gently over the mitsuba and seafood stick. Sprinkle with grated yuzu rind, if using, and serve immediately.

Nutritional information per portion: Energy 30kcal/125kJ; Protein 5.4g; Carbohydrate 1g, of which sugars 0.9g; Fat 0.5g, of which saturates 0.1g; Cholesterol 23mg; Calcium 36mg; Fibre 0.2g; Sodium 877mg.

New Year's soup

The elaborate New Year's Day celebration brunch starts with a tiny glass of spiced warm sake, o-toso. *Then, this New Year's soup,* O-zoni, *and other festive dishes are served.*

SERVES 4

4 dried shiitake mushrooms

300g/11oz chicken thighs, bones removed and reserved

300g/11oz salmon fillet, skin on, scaled

30ml/2 tbsp sake

50g/2oz satoimo or Jerusalem artichokes, peeled

50g/2oz daikon, peeled

50g/2oz carrots, peeled

4 spring onions (scallions), white part only, trimmed

4 mitsuba sprigs, root part removed

1 yuzu or lime

4 large raw tiger prawns (jumbo shrimp), peeled, but with tails left on

30ml/2 tbsp shoyu

8 mochi (rice cake) slices

salt

1 Soak the dried shiitake overnight in 1 litre/1¾ pints/4 cups cold water. Remove the shiitake and pour the water into a pan. Bring to the boil, add the chicken bones, then reduce the heat to medium. Skim to remove scum. After 20 minutes, reduce the heat and simmer for 30 minutes until the liquid has reduced by a third. Strain into another pan.

2 Chop the chicken and salmon into small bitesize cubes. Par-boil in boiling water with 15ml/1 tbsp sake for 1 minute. Drain and wash.

3 Put the peeled satoimo in a pan and add enough water to cover. Add a pinch of salt and bring to the boil. Reduce the heat to medium, cook the satoimo for 15 minutes and drain.

4 Rinse and wipe the satoimo. Cut the satoimo, daikon and carrots into 1cm/½in cubes.

5 Discard the stalks from the shiitake, and slice the caps thinly. Chop the white part of the spring onions into 2.5cm/1in lengths.

6 Put the mitsuba into a sieve and pour hot water over them. Divide the leaves and stalk. Take a stalk and fold it into two and tie it in the middle to make a bow. Make four.

7 Cut the yuzu into four 3mm/⅛in thick round slices. Hollow out the inside to make rings. Add the remaining sake to the soup stock and bring to the boil. Add the daikon, carrot and shiitake, then reduce the heat to medium and cook for 15 minutes.

8 Put the prawns, satoimo or artichokes, spring onions, chicken and salmon into the pan. Wait for 5 minutes, then add the shoyu. Reduce the heat to low.

9 Cut the mochi in half crossways. Toast under a moderate preheated grill (broiler). Turn every minute until both sides are golden and the pieces have started to swell like a balloon; this will take about 5 minutes.

10 Quickly place the toasted mochi in individual soup bowls and pour the hot soup over the top. Arrange a mitsuba leaf in the centre of each bowl, put a yuzu or lime ring on top, and lay a mitsuba bow across. Serve immediately.

Nutritional information per portion: Energy 252kcal/1057kJ; Protein 36.4g; Carbohydrate 2.5g, of which sugars 2.3g; Fat 10.8g, of which saturates 2.1g; Cholesterol 165mg; Calcium 59mg; Fibre 1g; Sodium 857mg.

Miso soup with pork and vegetables

This is quite a rich and filling soup. Its Japanese name, Tanuki Jiru, *means raccoon soup for hunters, but as raccoons are not eaten nowadays, pork is used instead.*

SERVES 4

200g/7oz lean boneless pork
15cm/6in piece gobo or 1 parsnip
50g/2oz daikon
4 fresh shiitake mushrooms
1/2 konnyaku (yam cake) or 1/2 x
    225–285g/8–10¼oz packet tofu
a little sesame oil, for stir-frying

600ml/1 pint/2½ cups of water and
    10ml/2 tsp dashi-no-moto
    (stock granules)
70ml/4½ tbsp miso
2 spring onions (scallions), chopped
5ml/1 tsp sesame seeds

1 Press the meat down on a chopping board and slice horizontally into thin long strips. Cut the strips crossways into stamp-size pieces. Set aside.

2 Peel the gobo using a potato peeler, then cut diagonally into 1cm/½in thick slices. Quickly plunge the slices into a bowl of cold water to stop discolouring. If using parsnip, peel, cut in half lengthways, then cut into 1cm/½in thick half-moon-shaped slices. Peel and slice the daikon into 1.5cm/²⁄₃in thick discs. Cut the discs into 1.5cm/²⁄₃in cubes. Remove shiitake stalks and cut the caps into quarters.

3 Place the konnyaku in a pan of boiling water and cook for 1 minute. Drain and cool. Cut into quarters lengthways, then crossways into 3mm/⅛in thick pieces.

4 Heat a little sesame oil in a cast-iron pan until purple smoke rises. Stir-fry the pork, then add the tofu, if using, the konnyaku and all the vegetables except for the spring onions. When the colour of the meat has changed, add the stock. Bring to the boil over a medium heat and skim off the foam until the soups looks fairly clear. Reduce the heat, cover, and simmer for 15 minutes.

5 Put the miso in a bowl, and mix with 60ml/4 tbsp hot stock to make a smooth paste. Stir one-third of the miso into the soup. Add more miso to taste. Add the spring onion and remove from heat. Serve very hot in individual bowls sprinkled with sesame seeds.

Nutritional information per portion: Energy 89kcal/371kJ; Protein 12.1g; Carbohydrate 1.9g, of which sugars 1.7g; Fat 3.7g, of which saturates 1g; Cholesterol 32mg; Calcium 21mg; Fibre 0.6g; Sodium 1284mg.

Buckwheat noodles with dipping sauce

Cold soba noodles are often eaten in summer and served on a bamboo tray with a dipping sauce. The sauce enhances their flavour.

SERVES 4

4 spring onions (scallions), finely chopped
1/2 nori sheet, about 10cm/4in square
400g/14oz dried soba noodles
5ml/1 tsp wasabi paste from a tube, or
    5ml/1 tsp wasabi powder mixed with
    2.5ml/1/2 tsp water

FOR THE DIPPING SAUCE
30g/11/4oz kezuri-bushi
200ml/7fl oz/scant 1 cup shoyu
200ml/7fl oz/scant 1 cup mirin
750ml/11/4 pints/3 cups water

1 To make the dipping sauce, mix all the ingredients in a small pan. Bring to the boil, and cook for 2 minutes. Reduce the heat to medium, and cook for a further 2 minutes. Strain through muslin. Cool, then chill.

2 Soak the spring onions in ice-cold water in a bowl for 5 minutes. Drain and squeeze out the excess water. Toast the nori over a medium flame until dry and crisp, then cut it into short strips, 3mm/1/8in wide.

3 Heat 2 litres/31/2 pints/9 cups water in a large pan. Bring to the boil, then add the soba. Distribute the noodles evenly in the pan, and stir to prevent sticking. When the water is bubbling, pour in 50ml/2fl oz/1/4 cup cold water to lower the temperature. Repeat this process and cook according to the packet instructions, or about 5 minutes. To test if the noodles are ready, pick one out and cut it with your finger. It should be tender to the touch.

4 Put a large sieve under cold running water. Pour the cooked soba into the sieve, and wash with your hands. Rub the soba well to remove the starch; the soba should feel slightly elastic. Drain again.

5 Pour the dipping sauce into four cups. Put the wasabi and spring onions into individual dishes. Divide the soba among four plates or baskets. Sprinkle with nori strips and serve cold, with the sauce, wasabi and spring onions.

Nutritional information per portion: Energy 449kcal/1905kJ; Protein 12.1g; Carbohydrate 91.7g, of which sugars 17.9g; Fat 6.3g, of which saturates 0g; Cholesterol 0mg; Calcium 35mg; Fibre 3.1g; Sodium 360mg.

Soba noodles in hot soup with tempura

When you cook Japanese noodle dishes, everyone should be ready at the dinner table, because cooked noodles start to soften and lose their taste and texture quite quickly.

SERVES 4

400g/14oz dried soba noodles
1 spring onion (scallion), sliced
shichimi togarashi (optional)

FOR THE TEMPURA
16 medium raw tiger or king prawns
   (jumbo shrimp), heads and shell
   removed, tails intact
1 large (US extra large) egg, beaten
400ml/14fl oz/1²/₃ cups ice-cold water
200g/7oz/scant 2 cups plain
   (all-purpose) flour
vegetable oil, for deep-frying

FOR THE SOUP
150ml/¼ pint/²/₃ cup mirin
150ml/¼ pint/²/₃ cup shoyu
900ml/1½ pints/3¾ cups water
25g/1oz kezuri-bushi or 2 x 15g/½oz
   packets
15ml/1 tbsp caster (superfine) sugar
5ml/1 tsp salt
900ml/1½ pints/3¾ cups water and
   12.5ml/2½ tsp dashi-no-moto
   (stock granules)

1 To make the soup, put the mirin in a pan. Bring to the boil, then add the rest of the soup ingredients apart from the dashi. Bring back to the boil, then reduce the heat. Skim off the scum and simmer for 2 minutes. Strain the soup and put into a clean pan with the dashi stock.

2 Carefully remove the black vein from the prawns, then make 5 shallow cuts into each prawn's belly. Clip the tip of the tail and squeeze out any moisture.

3 To make the batter, mix the egg and water in a bowl. Sift in the flour and stir briefly; it should be fairly lumpy. Heat the oil in a wok to 180°C/350°F. Hold the tail of a prawn, dip it in the batter, then plunge it into the hot oil. Deep-fry two prawns at a time until crisp and golden. Drain on kitchen paper and keep warm.

4 Put the noodles in a large pan with at least 2 litres/3½ pints/9 cups rapidly boiling water, and stir frequently to stop them sticking. When the water foams, pour in 50ml/2floz/¼ cup cold water to lower the temperature. Repeat when the water foams again. Transfer the noodles to a sieve and wash under cold water.

5 Heat the soup. Warm the noodles with hot water, and divide among serving bowls. Place the prawns on the noodles and add the soup.

6 Sprinkle each bowl with sliced spring onion and some shichimi togarashi, if you like.

Nutritional information per portion: Energy 794kcal/3356kJ; Protein 28g; Carbohydrate 135g, of which sugars 22.9g; Fat 19.5g, of which saturates 1.8g; Cholesterol 145mg; Calcium 155mg; Fibre 4.5g; Sodium 3278mg.

Udon noodles with egg broth and ginger

In this dish, called Ankake Udon, the soup for the udon is thickened with cornflour and retains its heat for a long time. A perfect lunch for a freezing cold day.

SERVES 4

400g/14oz dried udon noodles
30ml/2 tbsp cornflour (cornstarch)
4 eggs, beaten
50g/2oz mustard and cress
2 spring onions (scallions), finely chopped
2.5cm/1in fresh root ginger, peeled and
   finely grated, to garnish

FOR THE SOUP
1 litre/1³/₄ pints/4 cups water
40g/1¹/₂oz kezuri-bushi
25ml/1¹/₂ tbsp mirin
25ml/1¹/₂ tbsp shoyu
7.5ml/1¹/₂ tsp salt

1 To make the soup, place the water and the soup ingredients in a pan and bring to the boil on a medium heat. Remove from the heat when it starts boiling. Stand for 1 minute, then strain through muslin (cheesecloth). Check the taste and add more salt if required.

2 Heat at least 2 litres/3¹/₂ pints/9 cups water in a pan, and cook the udon for 8 minutes or according to the packet instructions. Drain under cold water and wash off the starch with your hands. Leave the udon in the sieve.

3 Pour the soup into a large pan and bring to the boil. Blend the cornflour with 60ml/4 tbsp water. Reduce the heat to medium and gradually add the cornflour mixture to the hot soup. Stir constantly. The soup will thicken after a few minutes. Reduce the heat to low.

4 Mix the egg, mustard, and cress, and spring onions in a bowl. Stir the soup again to create a whirlpool. Pour the eggs slowly into the soup pan. Reheat the udon with hot water. Divide among individual bowls and pour the soup over the top. Garnish with the ginger and serve hot.

Nutritional information per portion: Energy 517kcal/2187kJ; Protein 19.5g; Carbohydrate 87.7g, of which sugars 7g; Fat 12.4g, of which saturates 1.7g; Cholesterol 190mg; Calcium 130mg; Fibre 3.2g; Sodium 1019mg.

Pot-cooked udon in miso soup

Udon is a white wheat noodle, popular in the south and west of Japan. It is eaten with various hot and cold sauces and soups. Here, the noodles are cooked in a clay pot with a rich miso soup.

SERVES 4

200g/7oz chicken breast fillet,
   boned and skinned

10ml/2 tsp sake

2 abura-age

900ml/1½ pints/3¾ cups water
   and 7.5ml/1½ tsp dashi-no-moto
   (stock granules)

6 large fresh shiitake mushrooms, stalks
   removed, quartered

4 spring onions (scallions), trimmed and
   chopped into 3mm/⅛in lengths

30ml/2 tbsp mirin

about 90g/3½oz aka-miso or
   hatcho-miso

300g/11oz dried udon noodles

4 eggs

shichimi togarashi (optional)

1 Cut the chicken into bitesize pieces. Sprinkle with sake and leave to marinate for 15 minutes. Put the abura-age in a sieve and rinse with hot water. Drain on kitchen paper and cut each abura-age into four squares.

2 To make the soup, heat the water and stock granules in a large pan. When it has come to the boil, add the chicken, shiitake mushrooms and abura-age and cook for 5 minutes. Remove from the heat and add the spring onions.

3 Put the mirin and miso into a small bowl. Scoop 30ml/2 tbsp soup from the pan and mix this in well. To cook the udon, boil at least 2 litres/3½ pints/9 cups water in a large pan. Cook the udon for 6 minutes and drain.

4 Put the udon in a flameproof clay pot or casserole. Mix the miso paste into the soup and check the taste. Add more miso if required. Ladle in enough soup to cover the udon, and arrange the soup ingredients on top of the udon. Put the soup on a medium heat and break an egg on top. When the soup bubbles, wait for 1 minute, then cover and remove from the heat. Leave to stand for 2 minutes. Serve with shichimi togarashi, if you like.

Nutritional information per portion: Energy 439kcal/1855kJ; Protein 28.8g; Carbohydrate 59.5g, of which sugars 3.9g; Fat 11.1g, of which saturates 1.8g; Cholesterol 225mg; Calcium 59mg; Fibre 2.9g; Sodium 1707mg.

Cold somen noodles

At the height of summer, Hiya Somen *– cold somen noodles served immersed in cold water with ice cubes and accompanied by sauces and relishes – are a refreshing meal.*

SERVES 4

300g/11oz dried somen noodles

FOR THE DIPPING SAUCE
105ml/7 tbsp mirin
2.5ml/¹/₂ tsp salt
105ml/7 tbsp shoyu
20g/³/₄oz kezuri-bushi
400ml/14fl oz/1²/₃ cups water

FOR THE RELISHES
2 spring onions (scallions), trimmed and
   finely chopped
2.5cm/1in fresh root ginger, peeled and
   finely grated

2 shiso leaves, finely chopped (optional)
30ml/2 tbsp toasted sesame seeds

FOR THE GARNISHES
10cm/4in cucumber
5ml/1 tsp salt
ice cubes or a block of ice
ice-cold water
115g/4oz cooked, peeled small prawns
   (shrimp)
orchid flowers or nasturtium flowers
   and leaves

1 To make the sauce, bring the mirin to the boil. Add the salt and shoyu and shake gently to mix. Add the kezuri-bushi and mix. Add the water and bring to the boil and cook for 3 minutes. Strain through muslin (cheesecloth) or a jelly bag. Cool, then chill for at least an hour before serving.

2 Prepare the garnish. Cut the cucumber in half and scoop out the seeds, then slice thinly. Sprinkle with the salt and leave for 20 minutes. Rinse in cold water and drain.

3 Bring at least 1.5 litres/2¹/₂ pints/6¹/₄ cups water to the boil. Meanwhile, untie the bundle of somen. Have ready 75ml/2¹/₂fl oz/¹/₃ cup cold water. Put the somen in the boiling water. When it foams, pour the glass of water in. When the water boils again, the somen are ready. Drain into a colander under cold running water, and rub the somen with your hands to remove the starch. Drain.

4 Put some ice cubes in the centre of a chilled glass bowl, and add the somen. Pour on enough ice-cold water to cover the somen, then arrange cucumber slices, prawns and flowers on top. Prepare all the relishes separately in small dishes. Divide one-third of the sauce among four cups. Put the remaining sauce in a jug (pitcher). Serve the noodles cold with the relishes.

Nutritional information per portion: Energy 445kcal/1885kJ; Protein 16.3g; Carbohydrate 79.2g, of which sugars 23.7g; Fat 9.2g, of which saturates 0.7g; Cholesterol 56mg; Calcium 109mg; Fibre 2.9g; Sodium 2420mg.

Tokyo-style ramen noodles in soup

Ramen is a hybrid Chinese noodle dish presented in a Japanese way, and there are many different regional variations featuring local specialities. This dish is a legendary Tokyo version.

SERVES 4

250g/9oz dried ramen noodles

FOR THE SOUP STOCK
4 spring onions (scallions)
7.5cm/3in fresh root ginger, quartered
raw bones from 2 chickens, washed
1 large onion, quartered
4 garlic cloves, peeled
1 large carrot, roughly chopped
1 egg shell
120ml/4fl oz/$\frac{1}{2}$ cup sake
about 60ml/4 tbsp shoyu
2.5ml/$\frac{1}{2}$ tsp salt

**FOR THE *CHA-SHU*
(POT-ROAST PORK)**
500g/1$\frac{1}{4}$lb pork shoulder, boned
30ml/2 tbsp vegetable oil
2 spring onions (scallions), chopped
2.5cm/1in fresh root ginger, peeled and sliced
15ml/1 tbsp sake
45ml/3 tbsp shoyu
15ml/1 tbsp caster (superfine) sugar

FOR THE TOPPINGS
2 hard-boiled (hard-cooked) eggs
150g/5oz menma, soaked for 30 minutes and
    drained
$\frac{1}{2}$ nori sheet, broken into pieces
2 spring onions (scallions), chopped
ground white pepper
sesame oil or chilli oil

1 To make the soup stock, bruise the spring onions and ginger. Pour 1.5 litres/2$\frac{1}{2}$ pints/6$\frac{1}{4}$ cups water into a wok and bring to the boil. Add the chicken bones and boil until the colour of the meat changes. Discard the water and wash the bones.

2 Bring another 2 litres/3$\frac{1}{2}$ pints/9 cups water to the boil. Add the bones and other soup stock ingredients, except for the shoyu and salt. Reduce the heat and simmer until the water has reduced by half, skimming off any scum. Strain into a bowl through a muslin- (cheesecloth-) lined sieve.

3 Make the *cha-shu*. Roll the meat up tightly, 8cm/3$\frac{1}{2}$in in diameter, and tie with string. Heat the oil to smoking point in the wok and add the chopped spring onions and ginger. Cook briefly, then add the meat. Turn often to brown the outside evenly.

4 Sprinkle with sake and add 400ml/14fl oz/1$\frac{2}{3}$ cups water, the shoyu and sugar. Boil, then reduce the heat to low and cover. Cook for 25–30 minutes, turning every 5 minutes. Remove from the heat.

5 Slice the pork into 12 fine slices. Shell and halve the boiled eggs, and sprinkle some salt according to taste on to the egg yolks to season.

6 Pour 1 litre/1¾ pints/4 cups soup stock from the bowl into a pan. Boil and add the shoyu and salt. Check the seasoning; add more shoyu if required.

7 Bring 2 litres/3½ pints/9 cups water to the boil. Cook the noodles according to their instructions. If the water bubbles, pour in 50ml/2fl oz/¼ cup cold water. Drain and divide among bowls.

8 Pour the soup over the noodles to cover. Arrange half a boiled egg, pork slices, menma and nori on top, and sprinkle with spring onions. Serve with pepper and sesame or chilli oil. Season to taste with a little salt, if you like.

Nutritional information per portion: Energy 359kcal/1503kJ; Protein 36.1g; Carbohydrate 19.8g, of which sugars 9.8g; Fat 15.4g, of which saturates 3.4g; Cholesterol 174mg; Calcium 248mg; Fibre 1.8g; Sodium 930mg.

Vegetable dishes

Because Japanese cooking is centred on vegetables, preparation and cooking techniques for them have been perfected to achieve the best flavours and textures. In this chapter, the inspiring combinations of vegetables, mushrooms and seaweed are typical of Japanese cooking. Although the recipes are based on vegetables, many also contain fish, chicken or meat.

Braised turnip with prawn and mangetout

Taki-awase is an elegant dish in which three colours – the pink of the prawns, the white of the turnips and the green of the mangetouts – resemble a lady's spring kimono.

SERVES 4

8 small turnips, peeled

600ml/1 pint/2½ cups second dashi stock, or the same amount of water and 7.5ml/1½ tsp dashi-no-moto

10ml/2 tsp shoyu (use the Japanese pale awakuchi soy sauce if available)

60ml/4 tbsp mirin

30ml/2 tbsp sake

16 medium raw tiger prawns (jumbo shrimp), heads and shells removed with tails intact

dash of rice vinegar

90g/3½oz mangetouts (snow peas)

5ml/1 tsp cornflour (cornstarch)

salt

1 Par-boil the turnips for 3 minutes. Drain, then place them side by side in a pan. Add the dashi stock and cover with a saucer to submerge the turnips. Bring to the boil, then add the shoyu, 5ml/1 tsp salt, the mirin and sake. Reduce the heat to low, cover and simmer for 30 minutes.

2 Insert a cocktail stick (toothpick) into the back of each prawn, and remove and discard the black vein. Blanch the prawns in boiling water with the vinegar until the colour just changes. Drain. Cook the mangetouts in lightly salted water for 3 minutes. Drain and set aside.

3 Remove the saucer from the turnips and add the prawns for 4 minutes to warm through. Remove the turnips, drain and place in bowls. Transfer the prawns to a small plate.

4 Mix the cornflour with 15ml/ 1 tbsp water and add to the pan that held the turnips. Increase the heat a little and shake the pan until the liquid thickens slightly.

5 Place the mangetouts on the turnips and arrange the prawns on top, then pour about 30ml/2 tbsp of the hot liquid from the pan into each bowl.

Nutritional information per portion: Energy 83kcal/ 351kJ; Protein 6.4g; Carbohydrate 12g, of which sugars 10.4g; Fat 0.6g, of which saturates 0g; Cholesterol 49mg; Calcium 92mg; Fibre 3.5g; Sodium 68mg.

Lightly boiled spinach with toasted sesame seeds

O-hitashi has been served as a side dish on Japanese dining tables for centuries. Seasonal green vegetables are simply blanched and cooled and formed into little towers.

SERVES 4

450g/1lb fresh spinach
30ml/2 tbsp shoyu
30ml/2 tbsp water
15ml/1 tbsp sesame seeds
salt

1 Blanch young spinach in lightly salted boiling water for 15 seconds. For Japanese-type spinach, hold the leafy part and slip the stems into the pan. After 15 seconds, drop in the leaves and cook for 20 seconds.

2 Drain and place the spinach under running water. Squeeze out all the excess water. Now what looked like a large amount of spinach has become a ball, roughly the size of an orange. Mix the shoyu and water, then pour on to the spinach. Mix well and leave to cool.

3 Meanwhile, put the sesame seeds in a dry frying pan and stir until they start to pop. Leave to cool.

4 Drain the spinach and squeeze out the excess sauce. Line up the spinach on a chopping board, then form into a log shape of 4cm/1¹/₂in in diameter. Squeeze again to make firm. Cut across into four cylinders.

5 Place the spinach cylinders on a large plate or individual dishes. Sprinkle with toasted sesame seeds and a little salt, to taste, and serve.

Nutritional information per portion: Energy 54kcal/222kJ; Protein 4.1g; Carbohydrate 2.5g, of which sugars 2.3g; Fat 3.1g, of which saturates 0.4g; Cholesterol 0mg; Calcium 218mg; Fibre 2.7g; Sodium 692mg.

Daikon and carrot salad

An essential dish for New Year celebrations, the bright colour combination of daikon and carrot is regarded as a symbol of happiness.

SERVES 4

20cm/8in daikon
2 carrots
5ml/1 tsp salt
45ml/3 tbsp caster (superfine) sugar
70ml/4¹/₂ tbsp rice vinegar
15ml/1 tbsp sesame seeds

1 Cut the daikon into three pieces, then thickly peel the skin. Peel the carrots and cut them into 5cm/2in pieces. Slice both vegetables thinly lengthways then crossways to make very thin matchsticks. Alternatively, shred them with a grater to achieve a similar effect.

2 Place the daikon and carrot in a bowl. Sprinkle with the salt and mix. Leave for 30 minutes, then drain and squeeze out the excess liquid. Transfer to another bowl.

3 Mix the sugar and vinegar together in a bowl. Stir until the sugar has dissolved. Pour over the daikon and carrot, and leave for at least a day, mixing two to three times.

4 To serve, mix the vegetables evenly and heap in the middle of a bowl. Sprinkle with sesame seeds and serve.

Nutritional information per portion: Energy 89kcal/373kJ; Protein 1.5g; Carbohydrate 16.2g, of which sugars 16g; Fat 2.5g, of which saturates 0.4g; Cholesterol 0mg; Calcium 55mg; Fibre 1.9g; Sodium 510mg.

Spinach with peanut sauce

Traditional Japanese cooking rarely uses fat or oil, and nuts have long been an important source of essential nutritional oils in the diet.

SERVES 4

450g/1lb spinach

FOR THE PEANUT SAUCE
50g/2oz/¹/₃ cup unsalted shelled peanuts
30ml/2 tbsp shoyu
7.5ml/1¹/₂ tsp caster (superfine) sugar
25ml/1¹/₂ tbsp second dashi stock, or the same amount
of warm water with a pinch of dashi-no-moto

1 First, make the peanut sauce. Grind the shelled peanuts in a suribachi or a mortar and pestle. Alternatively, use an electric grinder.

2 Transfer the crushed nuts to a small mixing bowl and stir in the shoyu, sugar and dashi stock. When well mixed, the sauce will look like runny peanut butter.

3 Blanch the spinach for 30 seconds in rapidly boiling water until the leaves are wilted. Drain and cool under running water for 30 seconds.

4 Drain again and lightly squeeze out the excess water with your hands. Add the peanut sauce to the spinach in a bowl and mix gently. Serve on individual plates.

Nutritional information per portion: Energy 111kcal/460kJ; Protein 6.7g; Carbohydrate 6.3g, of which sugars 5.3g; Fat 6.7g, of which saturates 1.2g; Cholesterol 0mg; Calcium 202mg; Fibre 3.1g; Sodium 959mg.

Slow-cooked daikon

Freshly dug daikon is very juicy, and it is praised as the king of winter vegetables in Japan. In this dish, known as Furo Fuki Daikon, *the daikon is cooked slowly and served with tangy miso sauce.*

SERVES 4

1kg/2¼lb daikon, cut into 4 x 5cm/2in thick discs and peeled
15ml/1 tbsp rice (any kind except fragrant Thai or basmati)
100ml/3fl oz/scant ½ cup hatcho miso
60ml/4 tbsp caster (superfine) sugar
120ml/4fl oz/½ cup mirin
20cm/8in square dried konbu
rind of ¼ yuzu, shaved with a zester, to serve (optional)

1 Shave the top and bottom edge of each daikon section. Plunge into cold water. Drain and place flat in a pan. Pour in enough water to come 3cm/1¼in above the daikon. Add the rice and put on a high heat. When it comes to the boil, lower the heat and cook for 30 minutes.

2 Mix the miso and sugar in a pan. Add the mirin, a little at a time. Heat the mixture, stirring. When the mixture thickens, turn the heat to low. Cook, stirring, until the miso sauce sticks to a spoon. Remove from the heat and keep warm.

3 When the daikon is cooked, scoop the daikon, one by one, on to a flat-bottomed sieve and rinse with water. Discard the water and rice in the pan and wash the pan. Wipe the konbu with a wet cloth, and place in the pan. Add the daikon, just cover with water and warm for 15 minutes.

4 Divide the daikon among the bowls. Scoop out a little of the daikon at the top, then pour 15–20ml/3–4 tsp of the miso sauce over each piece. Garnish with yuzu zest, if using.

Nutritional information per portion: Energy 147kcal/622kJ; Protein 2.5g; Carbohydrate 34.9g, of which sugars 31.8g; Fat 0.5g, of which saturates 0.3g; Cholesterol 0mg; Calcium 64mg; Fibre 2.3g; Sodium 919mg.

Kabocha squash with chicken sauce

In this dish, known as **Kabocha Tori-soboro Kake,** *the mild sweetness of kabocha, similar to that of sweet potato, goes very well with the rich meat sauce.*

SERVES 4

1 kabocha squash, about 500g/1¼lb
½ yuzu or lime
20g/¾oz mangetouts (snow peas)
salt

FOR THE CHICKEN SAUCE
100ml/3fl oz/scant ½ cup water
30ml/2 tbsp sake
300g/11oz lean chicken, minced (ground)
60ml/4 tbsp caster (superfine) sugar
60ml/4 tbsp shoyu
60ml/4 tbsp mirin

1 Halve the kabocha squash, then remove the seeds and fibre around the seeds. Halve the squash again to make four wedges. Trim the stalky end of each kabocha wedge.

2 Remove strips of the peel on each of the wedges, cutting off strips lengthways of about 1–2.5cm/ ½–1in wide. Chop each wedge into large bitesize pieces. Place them side by side in a pan. Pour in enough water to cover, then sprinkle with salt. Cover and cook for 5 minutes over a medium heat, then lower the heat and simmer for 15 minutes until tender. Remove from the heat, cover and leave for 5 minutes.

3 Slice the yuzu or lime into thin discs, then hollow out the inside of the skin to make rings of peel. Cover with clear film (plastic wrap) until needed. Blanch the mangetouts in lightly salted water. Drain and set aside.

4 To make the sauce, bring the water and sake to the boil. Add the chicken, and when the meat is browned, add the sugar, shoyu and the mirin. Stir the mixture with a hand whisk until the liquid has almost all evaporated. Put the kabocha on a plate, then pour over the sauce. Add the mangetouts and garnish with yuzu rings.

Nutritional information per portion: Energy 172kcal/728kJ; Protein 19.6g; Carbohydrate 20g, of which sugars 19.2g; Fat 1.1g, of which saturates 0.4g; Cholesterol 53mg; Calcium 53mg; Fibre 1.4g; Sodium 1115mg.

Broad beans, daikon and salmon roe

Sora-mame No Ae-mono *is a typical tsumami bar snack. This unusual combination of colours, flavours and textures makes it ideal company for a refreshing glass of cold sake in summer.*

SERVES 4

200g/7oz daikon, peeled

1 nori sheet

1kg/2¼lb broad (fava) beans in their
  pods, shelled

1.5ml/¼ tsp wasabi paste from tube or
  2.5ml/½ tsp wasabi powder mixed
  with 1.5ml/¼ tsp water

20ml/4 tsp shoyu

60ml/4 tbsp ikura

salt

1 Grate the daikon finely with a daikon grater, or use a food processor to chop it into fine shreds. Place the daikon in a sieve and let the juices drain.

2 Tear the nori with your hands into flakes about 1cm/½in square.

3 Cook the broad beans in rapidly boiling salted water for about 4 minutes. Drain and cool under running water. Remove the skins.

4 Mix the wasabi paste with the shoyu in a small bowl. Add the nori flakes, toasted if you wish, and skinned beans, and mix well.

5 Divide the beans among four individual small bowls, heap on the grated daikon, then spoon the ikura on top.

6 Serve this dish cold. Ask your guests to mix everything well just before eating.

Nutritional information per portion: Energy 79kcal/335kJ; Protein 7.4g; Carbohydrate 11.6g, of which sugars 2.5g; Fat 0.6g, of which saturates 0.2g; Cholesterol 0mg; Calcium 59mg; Fibre 6.2g; Sodium 369mg.

Cabbage "noodle" pancake

The origin of this pancake is said to go back to the days of rationing after World War II, when flour made up for the shortage of rice, and cabbage was used for bulk.

MAKES 8

400g/14oz/3½ cups plain
    (all-purpose) flour
200ml/7fl oz/scant 1 cup water
2 large (US extra large) eggs, beaten
pinch of salt
4 spring onions (scallions),
    roughly chopped
400g/14oz white cabbage, finely sliced
vegetable oil, for frying
Japanese o-konomi yaki sauce or
    Worcestershire sauce
English (hot) mustard
mayonnaise
kezuri-bushi
ao nori
beni-shoga, to serve

FOR THE TOPPINGS

225g/8oz pork chops, boned
225g/8oz raw prawns (shrimp), heads and
    shells removed
115g/4oz queen scallops

1 To prepare the topping, put the pork in the freezer for 1–2 hours, then wait until half defrosted. Slice the pork thinly and set aside.

2 To make the pancakes, mix the flour together with the water. Add the eggs and salt and blend together. Add the spring onions and a third of the cabbage, and mix well. Repeat until all of the cabbage is coated with batter.

3 Put a frying pan over a hight heat. When hot, oil the base. Remove from the heat when the oil smokes and wait until the smoke dies down. Reduce the heat to medium and return the pan to the heat.

4 Pour some of the mixture into the pan. Make a circle of 2.5cm/1in thick and 10cm/4in in diameter.

5 Sprinkle the pancake with one-eighth of the prawns and scallops. Lay some pork on top and press down with a tablespoon. When the edge of the pancake is cooked, turn over.

6 Stretch the pancake out to 15cm/6in in diameter, and half the thickness. After 2–3 minutes, turn over again. Add the seasonings and sauces to the side with the topping.

7 Put the pancake on a plate and keep warm while you make seven more. Serve hot with beni-shoga.

Nutritional information per portion: Energy 313kcal/1322kJ; Protein 21.4g; Carbohydrate 42g, of which sugars 3.3g; Fat 7.8g, of which saturates 1.5g; Cholesterol 127mg; Calcium 132mg; Fibre 2.7g; Sodium 122mg.

Steamed aubergine with sesame sauce

This autumn recipe, Nasu Rikyu-ni, *represents a typical Zen temple cooking style. Fresh seasonal vegetables are chosen and cooked with care. This dish is also delicious cold.*

SERVES 4

2 large aubergines (eggplants)
400ml/14fl oz/1²/₃ cups second dashi stock,
   or the same amount of water with 5ml/
   1 tsp dashi-no-moto
25ml/1¹/₂ tbsp caster (superfine) sugar
15ml/1 tbsp shoyu
15ml/1 tbsp sesame seeds, finely ground in a
   suribachi or mortar and pestle
15ml/1 tbsp sake
15ml/1 tbsp cornflour (cornstarch)
salt

FOR THE ACCOMPANYING VEGETABLES

130g/4¹/₂oz shimeji mushrooms
115g/4oz/³/₄ cup fine green beans
100ml/3fl oz/scant ¹/₂ cup water with
   5ml/1 tsp dashi-no-moto (stock granules)
25ml/1¹/₂ tbsp caster (superfine) sugar
15ml/1 tbsp sake
1.5ml/¹/₄ tsp salt
dash of shoyu

1 Peel the aubergines and cut in quarters lengthways. Prick all over with a skewer, then plunge into salted water for 30 minutes.

2 Drain and steam the aubergines in a steamer, or in a hot wok with a bamboo basket inside, for 20 minutes, or until soft.

3 Mix the dashi stock, sugar, shoyu and 1.5ml/¹/₄ tsp salt together in a pan. Transfer the aubergines to this pan, then cover and cook over a low heat for 15 minutes. Take a few tablespoonfuls of stock from the pan and mix with the ground sesame seeds. Add this mixture to the pan.

4 Mix the sake with the cornflour, add to the pan with the aubergines and stock and shake the pan gently, but quickly. When the sauce becomes quite thick, remove from the heat.

5 Prepare and cook the accompanying vegetables. Wash the mushrooms and cut off the hard base part. Separate the large block into smaller chunks. Trim the green beans and cut in half. Mix the stock with the sugar, sake, salt and shoyu in a shallow pan. Add the green beans and mushrooms and cook for 7 minutes until tender. Serve the aubergines with the accompanying vegetables.

Nutritional information per portion: Energy 79kcal/333kJ; Protein 2.9g; Carbohydrate 10.2g, of which sugars 9.6g; Fat 2.9g, of which saturates 0.5g; Cholesterol 0mg; Calcium 52mg; Fibre 3.3g; Sodium 272mg.

Carrot in sweet vinegar

In this refreshing side dish carrot strips are marinated in rice vinegar, shoyu and mirin. It makes a good accompaniment for oily foods.

SERVES 4

2 large carrots, peeled
5ml/1 tsp salt
30ml/2 tbsp sesame seeds

FOR THE SWEET VINEGAR MARINADE
75ml/5 tbsp rice vinegar
30ml/2 tbsp shoyu (use the pale awakuchi soy sauce if available)
45ml/3 tbsp mirin

1 Cut the carrots into thin matchsticks, 5cm/2in long. Put the carrots and salt into a bowl, and mix well. After 25 minutes, rinse the carrot in cold water, then drain.

2 In another bowl, mix together the marinade ingredients. Add the carrots, and marinate for 3 hours.

3 Put a small pan on a high heat, add the sesame seeds and toss constantly until the seeds start to pop. Remove from the heat and cool.

4 Chop the sesame seeds with a large, sharp knife on a large chopping board. Place the carrots in a bowl, sprinkle with the sesame seeds and serve cold.

Nutritional information per portion: Energy 110kcal/461kJ; Protein 2g; Carbohydrate 16.4g, of which sugars 16g; Fat 4.5g, of which saturates 0.7g; Cholesterol 0mg; Calcium 70mg; Fibre 1.8g; Sodium 1040mg.

Fried aubergine with miso sauce

Make sure the oil is smoking hot when adding the aubergine slices, so that they do not absorb too much oil.

SERVES 4

2 large aubergines (eggplants)
1–2 dried red chillies
45ml/3 tbsp sake
45ml/3 tbsp mirin
45ml/3 tbsp caster (superfine) sugar
30ml/2 tbsp shoyu
45ml/3 tbsp red miso (use either the dark red aka-miso or even darker hatcho-miso)
90ml/6 tbsp sesame oil
salt

1 Cut the aubergines into bitesize pieces and place in a colander, sprinkle with salt and leave for 30 minutes, then squeeze. Remove the seeds from the chillies and chop the chillies into rings.

2 Mix the sake, mirin, sugar and shoyu in a cup. In a separate bowl, mix the red miso with 45ml/3 tbsp water to make a loose paste.

3 Heat the oil in a large pan and add the chilli. When you see smoke, add the aubergine, and, using cooking hashi, stir-fry for 8 minutes until tender. Lower the heat.

4 Add the sake mixture, and stir for 2–3 minutes. If the sauce starts to burn, lower the heat. Add the miso paste to the pan and cook, stirring, for 2 minutes. Serve hot.

Nutritional information per portion: Energy 221kcal/916kJ; Protein 1.4g; Carbohydrate 13.7g, of which sugars 13.4g; Fat 16.9g, of which saturates 2.5g; Cholesterol 0mg; Calcium 20mg; Fibre 2g; Sodium 805mg.

Vegetarian tempura

In the hot Japanese summer, Zen monks eat deep-fried vegetables to get over the fatigue of hard training. Although tempura preparation needs a little effort, the result is worth it.

SERVES 4

15ml/1 tbsp lemon juice or rice vinegar

15cm/6in renkon, sliced

1/2 each sweet potato and aubergine (eggplant)

vegetable oil and sesame oil, for frying

4 shiso leaves

1 green (bell) pepper, seeded and cut
    lengthways into 2.5cm/1in wide strips

1/8 kabocha squash, cut into 5mm/1/4in thick
    half-ring shapes

4 green beans, trimmed

4 fresh shiitake mushrooms

4 okra, trimmed

1 onion, sliced into 5mm/1/4in rings

FOR THE BATTER

200ml/7fl oz/scant 1 cup ice-cold water

1 large (US extra large) egg, beaten

90g/3$\frac{1}{2}$oz/generous 3/4 cup sifted plain
    (all-purpose) flour, plus extra for dusting

2–3 ice cubes

FOR THE CONDIMENT

4cm/1$\frac{1}{2}$in piece fresh root ginger, grated

450g/1lb daikon, grated

FOR THE DIPPING SAUCE

400ml/14fl oz/1$\frac{2}{3}$ cups water with 10ml/2 tsp
    dashi-no-moto (stock granules)

100ml/3fl oz/scant 1/2 cup shoyu

100ml/3fl oz/scant 1/2 cup mirin

1 To make the dipping sauce, mix all the ingredients in a pan. Bring to the boil, then remove from the heat. Set aside.

2 Fill a bowl with water and add the lemon juice. Peel the renkon, then slice it and the sweet potato into 5mm/1/4in thick discs and plunge into the bowl to prevent discolouring. Before frying, drain and dry. Slice the aubergine horizontally into 5mm/1/4in thick slices, then halve them lengthways. Soak in cold water before frying. Drain and dry.

3 Line an egg cup with clear film (plastic wrap) and press 2.5ml/1/2 tsp grated ginger into the bottom, then put in 30ml/2 tbsp grated daikon. Press again and turn upside-down on to a small plate. Make four of these mounds.

4 To make the batter, pour the ice-cold water into a bowl, add the egg and mix. Add the flour and roughly fold in. Do not beat. The batter should be quite lumpy. Add the ice cubes. Add oil to come halfway up the depth of a wok or deep-fryer. Heat the oil until the temperature reaches 150°C/300°F.

5 Deep-fry the shiso leaves. Hold the stalk of one leaf in your hand and stroke the leaf across the surface of the batter mix, coating one side of the leaf. Slip it into the oil until it goes crisp and bright green. Leave to drain. Deep-fry the renkon and sweet potato in the same way.

6 Increase the temperature to 175°C/347°F. Lightly dust the rest of the vegetables with flour, dunk into the batter mix, then shake off the excess. Deep-fry two to three pieces at a time until crisp. Leave to drain.

7 Divide the dipping sauce among four bowls. Place with the condiment. Arrange the tempura on a large plate and serve.

Nutritional information per portion: Energy 432kcal/1803kJ; Protein 8.2g; Carbohydrate 47g, of which sugars 24.6g; Fat 24.8g, of which saturates 3.4g; Cholesterol 48mg; Calcium 147mg; Fibre 5.8g; Sodium 1827mg.

Bacon-rolled enokitake mushrooms

The Japanese name for this dish is Obimaki enoki: *an obi (belt or sash) is made from bacon and wrapped around enokitake mushrooms before grilling them.*

SERVES 4

450g/1lb fresh enokitake mushrooms
**6 rindless smoked streaky (fatty) bacon
    rashers (strips)**
**4 lemon wedges and ground white
    pepper, to serve**

1 Cut off the root part of each enokitake cluster 2cm/³⁄₄in from the end. Do not separate the stems. Cut the rashers in half lengthways.

2 Divide the enokitake into 12 bunches. Take one bunch, then place the middle of the enokitake near the edge of one bacon rasher.

3 Roll up the bunch of enokitake in the bacon. Slide the bacon slightly upwards at each roll to cover 4cm/1¹⁄₂in of the enokitake. Secure with a cocktail stick (toothpick). Repeat to make 11 more rolls.

4 Preheat the grill (broiler) to high. Place the enokitake rolls on an oiled wire rack. Grill (broil) both sides until the bacon is crisp and the enokitake start to burn. This takes about 10–13 minutes.

5 Remove the enokitake rolls and place on a board. Using a fork and knife, chop each roll in half in the middle of the bacon belt. Arrange the top part of the enokitake roll standing upright, the bottom part lying down next to it. Serve with a wedge of lemon and a small heap of ground white pepper.

Nutritional information per portion: Energy 118kcal/490kJ; Protein 8g; Carbohydrate 0.5g, of which sugars 0.2g; Fat 9.4g, of which saturates 3.2g; Cholesterol 24mg; Calcium 9mg; Fibre 1.3g; Sodium 478mg.

Slow-cooked shiitake with shoyu

*Shiitake cooked slowly are so rich and filling that some people call them "vegetarian steak".
This dish, known as Fukumé-ni, is a useful and flavourful addition to other dishes.*

SERVES 4

20 dried shiitake mushrooms
45ml/3 tbsp vegetable oil
30ml/2 tbsp shoyu
25ml/1½ tbsp caster (superfine) sugar
15ml/1 tbsp toasted sesame oil

1 Start soaking the shiitake the day before. Put them in a bowl almost full of water. Cover the shiitake with a plate to stop them floating. Leave to soak overnight.

2 Measure 120ml/4fl oz/½ cup liquid from the bowl. Drain the shiitake into a sieve. Remove and discard the stalks.

3 Heat the oil in a wok or a large pan. Stir-fry the shiitake over a high heat for 5 minutes, stirring.

4 Reduce the heat to low, then add the measured liquid, the shoyu and sugar. Cook until there is almost no moisture left. Add the sesame oil. Leave to cool, then slice and arrange the shiitake on a large plate.

Nutritional information per portion: Energy 133kcal/553kJ; Protein 1.2g; Carbohydrate 7.4g, of which sugars 7.2g;
Fat 11.2g, of which saturates 1.4g; Cholesterol 0mg; Calcium 8mg; Fibre 0.6g; Sodium 537mg.

New potatoes cooked in dashi stock

Nikkorogashi *is a simple yet scrumptious dish, involving little more than new season's potatoes and onion cooked in dashi stock. As the stock evaporates, the onion becomes meltingly soft and caramelized, making a wonderful sauce that coats the potatoes.*

SERVES 4

15ml/1 tbsp toasted sesame oil
1 small onion, thinly sliced
1kg/2¼lb baby new potatoes, unpeeled

200ml/7fl oz/scant 1 cup second dashi
   stock, or the same amount of water
   with 5ml/1 tsp dashi-no-moto
45ml/3 tbsp shoyu

1 Heat the sesame oil in a wok or large pan. Add the onion slices and stir-fry for 30 seconds, then add the potatoes. Stir constantly, using cooking hashi for ease, until all the potatoes are well coated in sesame oil.

2 Pour on the dashi stock and shoyu and reduce the heat to the lowest setting. Cover and cook for 15 minutes, turning the potatoes every 5 minutes so they are evenly cooked.

3 Uncover the wok or pan for a further 5 minutes to reduce the liquid. If there is already very little liquid remaining, remove the wok or pan from the heat, cover and leave to stand for 5 minutes. Check that the potatoes are cooked, then remove from the heat.

4 Transfer the potatoes and onions to a deep serving bowl. Pour the sauce over the top and serve the dish immediately.

Nutritional information per portion: Energy 210kcal/890kJ; Protein 4.8g; Carbohydrate 42.4g, of which sugars 4.9g; Fat 3.5g, of which saturates 0.7g; Cholesterol 0mg; Calcium 21mg; Fibre 2.7g; Sodium 829mg.

Hijiki seaweed and chicken

The taste of hijiki is somewhere between rice and vegetable. It goes well with meat or tofu products, especially when it's stir-fried with a little oil first.

SERVES 4

90g/3½oz dried hijiki seaweed
150g/5oz chicken breast fillet with skin
½ small carrot, about 5cm/2in
15ml/1 tbsp vegetable oil
100ml/3fl oz/scant ½ cup water plus
    1.5ml/¼ tsp dashi-no-moto
    (stock granules)
30ml/2 tbsp sake
30ml/2 tbsp caster (superfine) sugar
45ml/3 tbsp shoyu
a pinch of shichimi togarashi or cayenne
    pepper

1 Soak the hijiki for 30 minutes. When ready to cook, it is easily crushed between the fingers. Pour into a sieve and wash under running water. Drain.

2 Peel the skin from the chicken and par-boil the skin in boiling water for 1 minute, then drain. Shave off all the yellow fat from the skin. Discard the clear membrane between the fat and the skin. Cut the skin into thin strips 5mm/¼in wide and 2.5cm/1in long. Cut the meat into bitesize chunks. Peel and chop the carrot into long, narrow matchsticks.

3 Heat the oil in a wok and stir-fry the chicken skin for 5 minutes, or until golden. Add the chicken meat and keep stirring until the colour changes. Add the hijiki and carrot and stir-fry for a further minute. Add the remaining ingredients. Lower the heat and cook for 5 minutes.

4 Leave to stand for about 10 minutes. Serve in small individual bowls. Sprinkle with shichimi togarashi, or cayenne pepper, if preferred.

Nutritional information per portion: Energy 154kcal/643kJ; Protein 10g; Carbohydrate 10.4g, of which sugars 10.2g; Fat 8.3g, of which saturates 2g; Cholesterol 39mg; Calcium 76mg; Fibre 1.1g; Sodium 884mg.

Vegetables and salmon in a parcel

In this recipe, the vegetables and salmon are wrapped and steamed with sake in their own moisture. Arranging the fish and all the vegetables can be tricky but it's well worth the effort.

SERVES 4

600g/1lb 6oz salmon fillet, skinned
  and cut into bitesize pieces
30ml/2 tbsp sake
15ml/1 tbsp shoyu, plus extra to serve
  (optional)
8 fresh shiitake mushrooms,
  stalks removed
2.5cm/1in carrot
2 spring onions (scallions)
about 250g/9oz fresh shimeji
  mushrooms, cleaned and root removed
115g/4oz mangetouts (snow peas)
salt

1 Preheat the oven to 190°C/375°F/Gas 5. Marinate the salmon in the sake and shoyu for 15 minutes. Drain and reserve the marinade. Carve a slit on the top of each shiitake. Repeat from the other side to cut out a notch 4cm/1¹⁄₂in long, then rotate the shiitake 90 degrees and carve another notch to make a cross in the top. Slice the carrot thinly, then cut out 8–12 flower shapes. Slice the spring onions in half lengthways.

2 Cut four sheets of foil, each about 29 x 21cm/11¹⁄₂ x 8¹⁄₂in wide. Place the long side of one sheet facing towards you. Arrange the salmon and shimeji mushrooms in the centre, place a spring onion diagonally across them. Put two shiitake on top, three to four mangetouts and sprinkle with carrot flowers. Sprinkle the marinade and a pinch of salt over the top. Fold the two longer sides of the foil together, then fold the shorter sides to seal. Repeat to make four parcels.

3 Bake for 15–20 minutes. When the foil has expanded into a balloon it is ready. Serve unopened with a little extra shoyu, if required.

Nutritional information per portion: Energy 303kcal/1263kJ; Protein 33.2g; Carbohydrate 2.2g, of which sugars 1.8g; Fat 17g, of which saturates 3g; Cholesterol 75mg; Calcium 54mg; Fibre 1.7g; Sodium 341mg.

Deep-fried layered shiitake and scallops

In this dish, you can taste three kinds of softness: chewy shiitake, mashed naga-imo with miso, and succulent scallop. The mixture creates a moment of heaven in your mouth. If it's difficult to eat with chopsticks, feel free to use a knife and fork.

SERVES 4

4 scallops	cornflour (cornstarch), for dusting
8 large fresh shiitake mushrooms	vegetable oil, for deep-frying
225g/8oz naga-imo, unpeeled	2 eggs, beaten
20ml/4 tsp miso	salt
50g/2oz/1 cup fresh breadcrumbs	4 lemon wedges, to serve

1 Slice the scallops in two horizontally, then sprinkle with salt. Remove the stalks from the shiitake by cutting them off with a knife. Discard the stalks. Cut slits on the top of the shiitake to form a white cross. Sprinkle with salt.

2 Heat a steamer and steam the naga-imo for 10–15 minutes, or until soft. Test with a skewer. Leave to cool. Wait until the naga-imo is cool enough to handle. Skin, then mash the flesh in a bowl. Add the miso and mix well. Break the breadcrumbs down finely. Mix half into the mashed naga-imo, keeping the rest on a small plate.

3 Fill the underneath of the shiitake caps with a scoop of mashed naga-imo. Smooth down with the flat edge of a knife and dust the mash with cornflour. Add a little mash to a slice of scallop and place on top. Spread another 5ml/1 tsp mashed naga-imo on to the scallop and shape to cover. Repeat to make eight little mounds.

4 Heat the oil to 150°C/300°F. Place the beaten eggs in a shallow container. Dust the shiitake and scallop mounds with cornflour, then dip into the egg. Handle with care as the mash and scallop are quite soft. Coat well with the remaining breadcrumbs and deep-fry in the oil until golden. Drain well on kitchen paper. Serve hot on individual plates with a wedge of lemon.

Nutritional information per portion: Energy 221kcal/918kJ; Protein 11.2g; Carbohydrate 11.7g, of which sugars 1.5g; Fat 14.6g, of which saturates 2.3g; Cholesterol 107mg; Calcium 50mg; Fibre 1.1g; Sodium 183mg.

Wakame, prawns and cucumber in vinegar dressing

This salad-style dish, called Suno-mono, uses wakame seaweed, which is not only rich in minerals and B complex vitamins and vitamin C, but also makes your hair look shiny.

SERVES 4

10g/¼oz dried wakame

12 medium raw tiger prawns
    (jumbo shrimp), heads
    removed but tails intact

½ cucumber

salt

FOR THE DRESSING

60ml/4 tbsp rice vinegar

15ml/1 tbsp shoyu

7.5ml/1½ tsp caster (superfine) sugar

2.5cm/1in fresh root ginger, peeled and
    cut into thin strips, to garnish

1 Soak the wakame in cold water for 15 minutes until fully open. The wakame expands by three to five times its original size. Drain.

2 Peel the prawns, including the tails and remove the black vein. Boil the prawns in salted water until they curl up completely. Drain and cool.

3 Halve the cucumber lengthways. Peel away half of the green skin to make green and white stripes. Scoop out the centre with a tablespoon. Slice thinly. Sprinkle with 5ml/1 tsp salt. Leave for 15 minutes in a sieve.

4 Blanch the wakame briefly in boiling water. Drain and cool under cold water. Add to the cucumber in the sieve. Press the cucumber and wakame to remove excess liquid. Repeat this two to three times.

5 Mix the dressing ingredients together in a bowl. Stir well until the sugar has dissolved. Add the wakame and cucumber and mix.

6 Pile up in four small bowls. Lean the prawns against the heap. Garnish with ginger and serve the dish immediately.

Nutritional information per portion: Energy 39kcal/164kJ; Protein 6.8g; Carbohydrate 2.5g, of which sugars 2.4g; Fat 0.3g, of which saturates 0g; Cholesterol 73mg; Calcium 34mg; Fibre 0.1g; Sodium 339mg.

Assorted seaweed salad

Kaisou Salada *is an example of the Japanese idea of eating: look after your appetite and your health at the same time. Seaweed is rich in fibre and it has virtually no calories.*

SERVES 4

5g/¹⁄₈oz each dried wakame, dried arame
   and dried hijiki seaweeds
about 130g/4¹⁄₂oz enokitake mushrooms
2 spring onions (scallions)
a few ice cubes
¹⁄₂ cucumber, cut lengthways
250g/9oz mixed salad leaves

FOR THE MARINADE

15ml/1 tbsp rice vinegar
6.5ml/1¹⁄₄ tsp salt

FOR THE DRESSING

60ml/4 tbsp rice vinegar
7.5ml/1¹⁄₂ tsp toasted sesame oil
15ml/1 tbsp shoyu
15ml/1 tbsp water with a pinch of dashi-
   no-moto (stock granules)
2.5cm/1in piece fresh root ginger,
   finely grated

1 Soak the wakame for 10 minutes in a bowl of water and, in a separate bowl of water, soak the arame and hijiki for 30 minutes together.

2 Trim the hard end of the enokitake mushroom stalks, then cut the bunch of mushrooms in half and separate out the stems.

3 Cut the spring onions into thin, 4cm/1¹⁄₂in long strips, then soak the strips in cold water with a few ice cubes to make them curl up. Drain. Slice the cucumber into thin, half-moon shapes.

4 Cook the wakame and enokitake in boiling water for 2 minutes, then add the arame and hijiki for a few seconds. Immediately remove from the heat. Drain and transfer to a bowl. Sprinkle over the vinegar and salt while still warm. Chill in the refrigerator.

5 Mix the dressing ingredients together in a small bowl. Arrange the mixed salad leaves in a large serving bowl with the cucumber on top, then add the seaweed and enokitake mixture. Garnish with spring onion strips and serve immediately with the dressing.

Nutritional information per portion: Energy 36kcal/149kJ; Protein 2.2g; Carbohydrate 2.4g, of which sugars 2.3g; Fat 2g, of which saturates 0.3g; Cholesterol 0mg; Calcium 69mg; Fibre 1.7g; Sodium 307mg.

Daikon layered with smoked salmon

The original recipe calls for layered, salted sliced salmon and daikon, pickled in a wooden barrel for a long time. This modern version is less salty and far easier to make.

SERVES 4

10cm/4in daikon, about 6cm/2¹/₂in in diameter, peeled
10ml/2 tsp salt
5ml/1 tsp rice vinegar
5cm/2in square dashi-konbu, chopped into 1cm/¹/₂in strips
50g/2oz smoked salmon, thinly sliced
2.5ml/¹/₂ tsp white poppy seeds

1 Slice the daikon very thinly into rounds. Put in a shallow container, sprinkle with salt and vinegar, and add the snipped dashi-konbu. Mix and rub gently with the hands. Cover and leave in the refrigerator for 1 hour.

2 Drain in a sieve and squeeze out the excess liquid. If necessary, rinse with running water for 30 seconds, then drain and squeeze out again.

3 Cut the smoked salmon slices into 4cm/1¹/₂in squares. Take one slice of daikon, top with a salmon slice, then cover with another daikon slice. Repeat until all the salmon is used. Place in a shallow container, cover, then leave to pickle at room temperature for up to 1 day.

4 Arrange the daikon rounds on a serving plate and put a pinch of poppy seeds in the centre.

Nutritional information per portion: Energy 29kcal/122kJ; Protein 2.8g; Carbohydrate 0.5g, of which sugars 0.5g; Fat 1.8g, of which saturates 0.3g; Cholesterol 6mg; Calcium 12mg; Fibre 0.3g; Sodium 500mg.

Broccoli and cucumber pickled in miso

Broccoli stem is usually wasted because of the fibrous texture, but you will be surprised how tasty it is when pickled. In Yasai Miso Zuke, miso and garlic give a kick to its subtle flavour.

SERVES 4

3 broccoli stems (use the florets in another dish, if you wish)
2 Japanese or salad cucumbers, ends trimmed
200ml/7fl oz/scant 1 cup miso (any kind)
15ml/1 tbsp sake
1 garlic clove, crushed

1 Peel the broccoli stems and quarter them lengthways. Peel the cucumber every 5mm/¹/₄in to make green-and-white stripes. Cut the cucumber in half lengthways. Scoop out the centre with a teaspoon. Cut into 7.5cm/3in lengths.

2 Mix the miso, sake and garlic in a container with a lid. Remove half the miso mix. Lay some of the broccoli stems and cucumber in the container and push into the miso mix. Spread a little of the reserved miso over the top as well. Repeat this process to fill up the container. Cover and chill for 1–5 days.

3 Wash the vegetables under running water, then wipe with kitchen paper. Cut the broccoli pieces in half then slice into thin strips lengthways. Cut the cucumber into 5mm/¹/₄in thick half-moon slices. Serve cold.

Nutritional information per portion: Energy 54kcal/227kJ; Protein 5.6g; Carbohydrate 4.9g, of which sugars 3.8g; Fat 1g, of which saturates 0.2g; Cholesterol 0mg; Calcium 66mg; Fibre 2.9g; Sodium 1789mg.

Beans, tofu and eggs

The virtues of tofu as a nutrient could fill a book, and the uses of this wonder food are limitless. Tofu's essential blandness adapts to and absorbs a host of other flavours. Beans and eggs are equally versatile and are perfect for making even the simplest of dishes healthy and filling.

Cooked black-eyed beans

Traditionally, this dish was served in the coldest time of the year using only preserved food such as salted salmon and dried vegetables. Here, fresh salmon and vegetables are used instead.

SERVES 4

150g/5oz salmon fillet, boned and
   skinned
400g/14oz can black-eyed beans (peas)
   in brine
50g/2oz fresh shiitake mushrooms, stalks
   removed
50g/2oz carrot, peeled
50g/2oz daikon, peeled
5g/¹⁄₈oz dashi-konbu about 10cm/4in
   square
60ml/4 tbsp water
5ml/1 tsp caster (superfine) sugar
15ml/1 tbsp shoyu
7.5ml/1¹⁄₂ tsp mirin
salt
2.5cm/1in fresh root ginger, peeled and
   thinly sliced or grated, to garnish

1 Slice the salmon into 1cm/¹⁄₂in thick pieces. Salt the fillet and leave for 1 hour, then wash away the salt and cut it into 1cm/¹⁄₂in cubes.

2 Par-boil the fish in boiling water for 30 seconds, then drain and wash.

3 Slice the fresh ginger thinly lengthways, then stack the slices and cut into thin threads. Soak for 30 minutes, then drain well.

4 Drain the can of beans and tip the liquid into a medium pan. Set the beans and liquid aside.

5 Chop all the vegetables into 1cm/¹⁄₂in cubes. Wipe the dried konbu with a damp dish towel, then snip with scissors.

6 Add the salmon, vegetables and konbu to the bean liquid with the beans, water, sugar and 1.5ml/¹⁄₄ tsp salt. Bring to the boil. Reduce the heat. Simmer for 6 minutes or until the carrot is cooked. Add the shoyu.

7 Cook for 4 minutes. Add the mirin, then remove from the heat, mix and check the seasoning. Leave for 1 hour. Garnish with the ginger.

Nutritional information per portion: Energy 198kcal/834kJ; Protein 16.9g; Carbohydrate 22.8g, of which sugars 3.9g; Fat 5g, of which saturates 1g; Cholesterol 19mg; Calcium 37mg; Fibre 4.1g; Sodium 294mg.

Sweet azuki bean soup with mochi rice cake

Azuki beans are commonly used in traditional Japanese desserts. This sweet soup for winter is eaten between meals as a snack, but never after the meal as it is quite filling.

SERVES 4

130g/4¹/₂oz/²/₃ cup dried azuki beans
pinch of baking powder
130g/4¹/₂oz/scant ³/₄ cup caster
   (superfine) sugar
1.5ml/¹/₄ tsp salt
4 mochi

1 Soak the azuki beans overnight in 1 litre/1³/₄ pints/4 cups water. Pour the beans and soaking water into a large pan, then bring to the boil. Reduce the heat to medium-low. Add the baking powder. Cover and cook for about 30 minutes.

2 Add a further 1 litre/1³/₄ pints/ 4 cups water, and bring back to the boil. Reduce the heat to low, and cook for a further 30 minutes.

3 When the beans are ready, they should crush easily. If they are still hard, cook for another 20 minutes.

4 Divide the sugar into two. Add one half to the pan with the beans and stir. Cook for 3 minutes, then add the rest and wait for 3 minutes.

5 Add the salt and cook for another 3 minutes. Keep the soup warm.

6 Cut the mochi in half. Grill (broil) under a moderate heat until light golden brown and puffy. Turn several times.

7 Put two pieces of mochi into small bowls and pour the soup around them. Serve hot.

Nutritional information per portion: Energy 270kcal/1148kJ; Protein 12.4g; Carbohydrate 52g, of which sugars 35.1g; Fat 2.9g, of which saturates 0.5g; Cholesterol 0mg; Calcium 331mg; Fibre 2.7g; Sodium 10mg.

Stuffed and grilled thin tofu

In Japan, spring onions are thought to prevent colds, and this dish is made doubly effective by also including grated garlic.

SERVES 4

1 packet abura-age (2 abura-age per
    packet)

FOR THE FILLING

4 spring onions (scallions), trimmed
    and very finely chopped
about 15ml/1 tbsp shoyu
1 garlic clove, grated or crushed
30ml/2 tbsp lightly toasted sesame seeds

1 Put the abura-age in a sieve and pour hot water over to wash off excess oil. Drain and gently dry on kitchen paper.

2 Put one abura-age on a board and roll over several times with a rolling pin. Cut it in half and carefully open at the cut part to make two bags. Repeat the process with the remaining piece of abura-age.

3 Mix the spring onions, shoyu, garlic and sesame seeds in a small bowl. Check the seasoning and add more shoyu, if required.

4 Fill the bags with the filling. Grill (broil) for 3–4 minutes on each side until crisp and lightly browned.

5 Cut into four triangles and arrange on four small plates. Serve hot.

Nutritional information per portion: Energy 235kcal/976kJ; Protein 18.4g; Carbohydrate 2.1g, of which sugars 1.2g; Fat 17g, of which saturates 0.6g; Cholesterol 0mg; Calcium 1109mg; Fibre 0.8g; Sodium 278mg.

Deep-fried tofu in dashi soup

A creamy tofu block is deep-fried in a crisp thin batter, then soaked in hot broth. This tasty dish is typical in a Zen vegetarian menu.

SERVES 4

2 x 295g/10¾oz packets long-life soft
   or silken tofu, drained
vegetable oil, for deep-frying
30ml/2 tbsp plain (all-purpose) flour

FOR THE SAUCE
50ml/2fl oz/¼ cup shoyu
50ml/2fl oz/¼ cup mirin
pinch of salt
300ml/½ pint/1¼ cups second dashi
   stock, or the same amount of water
   and 7.5ml/1½ tsp dashi-no-moto

FOR THE GARNISH
2.5cm/1in fresh root ginger, peeled
   and finely grated
60ml/4 tbsp finely chopped chives

1 Wrap the tofu in 2–3 layers of kitchen paper. Set a chopping board, or large plate with a weight, on top to press the tofu, and leave for 30 minutes.

2 To make the sauce, place the shoyu, mirin, salt and dashi stock in a pan over a medium heat. Mix and cook for 5 minutes, then set aside.

3 Squeeze the ginger and make into four balls. Set aside. Unwrap the tofu and pat dry. Slice one tofu block into four squares each 2.5 x 6cm/1 x 2½in. Repeat with the other tofu block.

4 Heat the oil to 190°C/375°F. Dust the tofu with the flour and slide into the oil. Deep-fry until golden. Drain well on kitchen paper.

5 Arrange two tofu pieces in each bowl. Reheat the sauce and pour from the side of the bowl. Put a ginger ball on the tofu and sprinkle with chives. Serve.

Nutritional information per portion: Energy 40kcal/164kJ; Protein 3.9g; Carbohydrate 1.1g, of which sugars 0.9g; Fat 2.2g, of which saturates 0.4g; Cholesterol 24mg; Calcium 187mg; Fibre 0.3g; Sodium 380mg.

Deep-fried tofu balls

There are many variations of these delicious deep-fried tofu balls called hiryozu, *meaning flying dragon's head. This is one of the easiest to make.*

MAKES 16

2 x 285g/10¼oz packets tofu blocks
20g/¾oz carrot, peeled
40g/1½oz/1¼ cups green beans
2 large (US extra large) eggs, beaten
30ml/2 tbsp sake
10ml/2 tsp mirin
5ml/1 tsp salt
10ml/2 tsp shoyu
pinch of caster (superfine) sugar
vegetable oil, for deep-frying
4 chives, finely snipped, to garnish

FOR THE LIME SAUCE

45ml/3 tbsp shoyu
juice of ½ lime
5ml/1 tsp rice vinegar

TO SERVE

175g/6oz daikon, peeled
2 dried red chillies, halved and seeded

1 Drain the tofu and wrap in a clean dish towel. Set a plate with a weight on top and leave for 2 hours, or until the tofu loses most of its liquid.

2 Cut the daikon into thick slices. Make 3 holes in each slice and insert chilli pieces into the holes. Leave for 15 minutes, then grate.

3 To make the tofu balls, chop the carrot finely. Slice the beans finely. Cook both vegetables for 1 minute.

4 In a food processor, mix the tofu, eggs, sake, mirin, salt, shoyu and sugar until smooth.

5 Transfer the mixture to a bowl and mix in the carrot and beans. Fill a wok with oil 4cm/1½in deep, and heat to 185°C/365°F.

6 Wet your hands with a little oil. Shape 40ml/8 tsp tofu mixture into a ball. Deep-fry until crisp and golden and drain. Repeat with the remaining mixture. Sprinkle the tofu balls with chives. Put 30ml/2 tbsp grated daikon and chillies in each of four small bowls.

7 Mix the lime sauce ingredients in a serving bowl. Serve the balls with the lime sauce and grated daikon.

Nutritional information per portion: Energy 40kcal/164kJ; Protein 3.9g; Carbohydrate 1.1g, of which sugars 0.9g; Fat 2.2g, of which saturates 0.4g; Cholesterol 24mg; Calcium 187mg; Fibre 0.3g; Sodium 380mg.

Pan-fried tofu with caramelized sauce

Tofu in the West is often used as a meat substitute for vegetarians, as it was by Chinese Buddhist monks who first brought vegetarian cooking into Japan. They invented many delicious dishes.

SERVES 4

2 x 285g/10¼oz packets tofu blocks, drained
4 garlic cloves
10ml/2 tsp vegetable oil
50g/2oz/¼ cup butter, cut into 5 equal pieces
watercress, to garnish

FOR THE MARINADE

4 spring onions (scallions), finely chopped
60ml/4 tbsp sake
60ml/4 tbsp shoyu (tamari or sashimi soy sauce, if available)
60ml/4 tbsp mirin

1 Wrap the tofu in three layers of kitchen paper. Put a board on top as a weight and leave for 30 minutes.

2 Mix all the marinade ingredients and leave for 15 minutes.

3 Slice the garlic thinly. Heat the oil in a frying pan and fry the garlic until golden. Turn frequently to prevent sticking and burning. Scoop them out on to kitchen paper. Reserve the oil in the pan.

4 Slice the tofu blocks horizontally in half, then cut each half into four

pieces. Soak in the marinade for 15 minutes. Wipe off excess marinade Reserve the marinade.

5 Reheat the oil in the pan and add a piece of butter. When the oil starts sizzling, reduce the heat and add the tofu one by one. Cover and cook for about 5–8 minutes on each side.

6 Cook the marinade for 2 minutes. Arrange four pieces of tofu on each plate. Pour over the marinade mixture and top with butter. Sprinkle with garlic chips and garnish with watercress.

Nutritional information per portion: Energy 271kcal/1127kJ; Protein 12.7g; Carbohydrate 11.5g, of which sugars 10g; Fat 17.9g, of which saturates 7.4g; Cholesterol 27mg; Calcium 742mg; Fibre 0.4g; Sodium 1152mg.

Grilled vegetable sticks

For this tasty kebab-style dish, made with tofu, konnyaku and aubergine, you will need 40 bamboo skewers, soaked in water overnight to prevent them burning when grilled.

SERVES 4

1 x 285g/10¼oz packet tofu block
1 x 250g/9oz packet konnyaku
2 small aubergines (eggplants)
25ml/1½ tbsp toasted sesame oil

FOR THE YELLOW AND GREEN SAUCES
45ml/3 tbsp shiro-miso
15ml/1 tbsp caster (superfine) sugar
5 young spinach leaves
2.5ml/½ tsp sansho
salt

FOR THE RED SAUCE
15ml/1 tbsp aka-miso
5ml/1 tsp caster (superfine) sugar
5ml/1 tsp mirin

TO GARNISH
pinch of white poppy seeds
15ml/1 tbsp toasted sesame seeds

1 Drain the liquid from the tofu packet and wrap the tofu in three layers of kitchen paper. Set a chopping board on top to press out the remaining liquid. Leave for 30 minutes until the excess liquid has been absorbed by the kitchen paper. Cut into eight 7.5 x 2 x 1cm/3 x ¾ x ½in slices.

2 Drain the liquid from the konnyaku. Cut it in half and put in a small pan with enough water to cover. Bring to the boil and cook for about 5 minutes. Drain and cut it into eight 6 x 2 x 1cm/2½ x ¾ x ½in slices.

3 Cut the aubergines into two lengthways, then halve the thickness to make four flat slices. Soak in cold water for 15 minutes. Drain and pat dry. To make the yellow sauce, mix the shiro-miso and sugar in a pan, then cook over a low heat, stirring to dissolve the sugar. Remove from the heat. Place half the sauce in a small bowl.

4 Blanch the spinach leaves in rapidly boiling water with a pinch of salt for 30 seconds and drain, then cool under running water. Squeeze out the water and chop finely. Transfer to a mortar and pound to a paste using a pestle. Mix the paste and sansho pepper into the bowl of yellow sauce to make the green sauce.

5 Put all the red sauce ingredients in a small pan and cook over a low heat, stirring constantly, until the sugar has dissolved. Remove from the heat.

6 Pierce the slices of tofu, konnyaku and aubergine with two bamboo skewers each. Heat the grill (broiler) to high. Brush the aubergine slices with sesame oil and grill (broil) for 7–8 minutes each side. Turn several times.

7 Grill the konnyaku and tofu slices for 3–5 minutes each side, or until lightly browned. Remove them from the heat but keep the grill hot.

8 Spread the red miso sauce on the aubergine slices. Spread one side of the tofu slices with green sauce and one side of the konnyaku with the yellow miso sauce from the pan. Grill the slices for 1–2 minutes. Sprinkle the aubergines with poppy seeds. Sprinkle the konnyaku with sesame seeds and serve all together.

Nutritional information per portion: Energy 178kcal/742kJ; Protein 12.9g; Carbohydrate 9.3g, of which sugars 8.6g; Fat 10.2g, of which saturates 1.4g; Cholesterol 0mg; Calcium 761mg; Fibre 1.9g; Sodium 17mg.

Simmered tofu with vegetables

A typical Japanese dinner at home consists of a soup, three different dishes and a bowl of rice. One of the three dishes is always a simmered one like this.

SERVES 4

4 dried shiitake mushrooms
450g/1lb daikon, peeled
2 atsu-age, about 200g/7oz each
115g/4oz/³/₄ cup green beans, trimmed
   and cut in half
5ml/1 tsp rice (any except for fragrant
   Thai or white basmati)
115g/4oz carrot, peeled and cut into
   1cm/¹/₂in thick slices

300g/11oz baby potatoes, unpeeled
750ml/1¹/₄ pints/3 cups water and
   7.5ml/1¹/₂ tsp dashi-no-moto
   (stock granules)
30ml/2 tbsp caster (superfine) sugar
75ml/5 tbsp shoyu
45ml/3 tbsp sake
15ml/1 tbsp mirin

1 Soak the dried shiitake in 250ml/8fl oz/1 cup water for 2 hours. Drain and discard the liquid. Remove and discard the stalks. Slice the daikon into 1cm/¹/₂in discs. Shave the edge of the daikon discs to ensure they are evenly cooked. Plunge into cold water.

2 Put the atsu-age in a sieve, and wash off the excess oil with hot water. Drain and cut into pieces of about 2.5 x 5cm/1 x 2in. Boil the green beans for 2 minutes, then drain and cool. Cover the daikon with water in a pan and add the rice. Bring to the boil then reduce the heat to medium-low. Cook for 15 minutes, then drain. Discard the rice.

3 Put the atsu-age, mushrooms, carrot and potatoes into the pan with the daikon. Add the dashi, bring to the boil, then reduce the heat. Skim off any scum. Add the sugar, shoyu and sake, shaking the pan to mix thoroughly.

4 Cut baking parchment into a circle 1cm/¹/₂in smaller than the pan lid and place inside the pan. Cover with the lid and simmer for 30 minutes, or until the sauce has reduced by half. Add the green beans for 2 minutes so that they just warm through.

5 Remove the paper and add the mirin. Taste the sauce and adjust with shoyu if required. Remove from the heat. Arrange the ingredients on a serving plate. Pour over a little sauce, and serve warm or cold.

Nutritional information per portion: Energy 142kcal/597kJ; Protein 4.2g; Carbohydrate 27.6g, of which sugars 15.1g; Fat 0.9g, of which saturates 0.3g; Cholesterol 0mg; Calcium 92mg; Fibre 3.3g; Sodium 1406mg.

Savoury egg soup

This delicious custard-like soup is softer and runnier than a Western custard pudding. It contains tasty surprises, such as pink prawns and jade-green gingko nuts.

SERVES 4

8 gingko nuts, shelled (or canned)

4 medium raw tiger prawns (jumbo shrimp), peeled, heads and tails removed, and deveined

5cm/2in carrot, thinly sliced

4 mitsuba sprigs

75g/3oz chicken breast fillet, skinned

5ml/1 tsp sake

5ml/1 tsp shoyu

2 fresh shiitake mushrooms, thinly sliced, stalks discarded

salt

FOR THE CUSTARD

3 large (US extra large) eggs, beaten

500ml/17fl oz/generous 2 cups water and 2.5ml/$\frac{1}{2}$ tsp dashi-no-moto (stock granules)

15ml/1 tbsp sake

15ml/1 tbsp shoyu

2.5ml/$\frac{1}{2}$ tsp salt

1 Boil the gingko nuts for 5 minutes. Drain. Remove any skin. Blanch the prawns in hot water until they curl up. Drain and pat dry. Cut the carrot slices into maple-leaf shapes. Blanch and drain.

2 Cut off the mitsuba roots. Cut the stems 2.5cm/1in from the top and keep the leaves. Halve the stems and wilt in hot water. Tie two mitsuba stems together.

3 Dice the chicken, then marinate in the sake and shoyu for 15 minutes.

4 To make the custard, put all the ingredients in a bowl. Mix and strain into another bowl. Bring a steamer to the boil, then lower the heat.

5 Divide the chicken, shiitake, gingko nuts, prawns and carrots among four ramekins. Divide the egg mixture among the ramekins.

6 Put the mitsuba stems on top, and the leaves if you like, and then cover each ramekin with a piece of foil. Place them in the steamer on low for 15 minutes until set. Serve hot.

Nutritional information per portion: Energy 163kcal/681kJ; Protein 16g; Carbohydrate 2.4g, of which sugars 1g; Fat 9.7g, of which saturates 2.3g; Cholesterol 205mg; Calcium 48mg; Fibre 0.5g; Sodium 654mg.

Rolled omelette

Easier to make than it looks, all that is needed to make this light and sweet omelette is a sushi rolling mat, wrapped in clear film. Use a round or rectangular frying pan.

SERVES 4

45ml/3 tbsp second dashi stock, or the same amount of water and a pinch of dashi-no-moto
30ml/2 tbsp mirin
15ml/1 tbsp caster (superfine) sugar
5ml/1 tsp shoyu
5ml/1 tsp salt
6 large (US extra large) eggs, beaten
vegetable oil

FOR THE GARNISH
2.5cm/1in daikon
4 shiso leaves (optional)
shoyu

1 Warm the stock. Mix in the mirin, sugar, shoyu and salt. Add to the eggs and stir well. Heat an omelette pan over medium heat. Soak kitchen paper in oil and wipe the pan.

2 Pour in a quarter of the egg mixture and tilt the pan to coat it. When the egg starts to set, roll it up towards you with chopsticks.

3 Keeping the rolled omelette in the pan, push it away from you. Oil the empty part of the pan again. Pour one-third of the egg mixture in at the empty side. Lift up the first roll with chopsticks, so the egg mixture runs underneath. When half set, roll the omelette around the first roll.

4 Move the roll gently on to a sushi rolling mat covered with clear film (plastic wrap). Roll the omelette firmly into the roller mat. Stand for 5 minutes and repeat the process again to make another roll.

5 Grate the daikon with a grater. Squeeze out the juice.

6 Cut the rolled omelettes into 2.5cm/1in slices crossways.

7 Lay the shiso leaves, if using, on four small plates and place a few slices of the omelette on top. Put a small heap of grated daikon to one side and add a few drops of shoyu to the top.

Nutritional information per portion: Energy 205kcal/854kJ; Protein 9.5g; Carbohydrate 11.9g, of which sugars 11.9g; Fat 13.8g, of which saturates 3g; Cholesterol 285mg; Calcium 49mg; Fibre 0g; Sodium 686mg.

Fish and shellfish

There are numerous delicious fish dishes in the Japanese culinary tradition, including many using fish that is so fresh it does not require cooking. The very freshest shellfish and fish are used to make sashimi. Other favourite methods range from "cooking" the fresh fish in vinegar, to flavouring it with seaweed, or frying the fish in a batter to create the classic dish, tempura.

Seared swordfish with citrus dressing

Kajiki No Tataki Salad *is a good example of how the Japanese adopt new dishes from all over the world. Fresh fish is sliced thinly and seared or marinated, then served with salad and vegetables.*

SERVES 4

75g/3oz daikon, peeled
50g/2oz carrot, peeled
1 Japanese or salad cucumber
10ml/2 tsp vegetable oil
300g/11oz skinned fresh swordfish steak,
    cut against the grain
2 cartons mustard and cress
15ml/1 tbsp toasted sesame seeds

FOR THE DRESSING

105ml/7 tbsp shoyu
105ml/7 tbsp second dashi stock, or the
    same amount of water and 5ml/1 tsp
    dashi-no-moto
30ml/2 tbsp toasted sesame oil
juice of $\frac{1}{2}$ lime
rind of $\frac{1}{2}$ lime, shredded into thin strips

1 Make the vegetable garnishes first. Use a very sharp knife, mandolin or vegetable slicer with a julienne blade to make very thin (about 4cm/1$\frac{1}{2}$in long) strands of daikon, carrot and cucumber. Soak the daikon and carrot in ice-cold water for 5 minutes, then drain and chill.

2 Mix together all the ingredients for the dressing and stir, then chill.

3 Heat the oil in a frying pan until smoking hot. Sear the fish for 30 seconds on all sides. Plunge it into cold water to stop the cooking. Dry and wipe off as much oil as possible.

4 Cut the swordfish steak in half lengthways before slicing it into 5mm/$\frac{1}{4}$in thick pieces in the other direction, against the grain.

5 Arrange the fish slices into a ring on individual plates.

6 Mix the vegetable strands, mustard and cress and sesame seeds together. Fluff up with your hands, then shape them into a sphere. Gently place it in the centre of the plate, on top of the swordfish.

7 Pour the dressing around the plate's edge and serve immediately.

Nutritional information per portion: Energy 223kcal/925kJ; Protein 15.4g; Carbohydrate 3.6g, of which sugars 3.3g; Fat 16.4g, of which saturates 2.5g; Cholesterol 31mg; Calcium 46mg; Fibre 0.9g; Sodium 1975mg.

Marinated salmon with avocado

Use only the freshest of salmon for this delicious salad. The marinade of lemon and dashi-konbu "cooks" the salmon, which is then served with avocado, almonds, salad and a miso mayonnaise.

SERVES 4

250g/9oz very fresh salmon tail, skinned and filleted

juice of 1 lemon

10cm/4in dashi-konbu, wiped with a damp cloth and cut into 4 strips

1 ripe avocado

4 shiso leaves, stalks removed and cut in half lengthways

about 115g/4oz mixed leaves such as lamb's lettuce, frisée or rocket (arugula)

45ml/3 tbsp flaked (sliced) almonds, toasted in a dry frying pan until just slightly browned

FOR THE MISO MAYONNAISE

90ml/6 tbsp good-quality mayonnaise

15ml/1 tbsp shiro-miso

ground black pepper

1 Cut the first salmon fillet in half crossways at the tail end where the fillet is not wider than 4cm/1^1/$_2$in. Next, cut the wider part in half lengthways. Cut the other fillet in the same way.

2 Pour the lemon juice and two of the dashi-konbu pieces into a wide plastic container. Lay the salmon fillets in the base and sprinkle with the rest of the dashi-konbu.

3 Marinate for 15 minutes, then turn once and leave for a further 15 minutes. The salmon should change to a pink "cooked" colour. Remove the salmon from the marinade and wipe with kitchen paper.

4 Cut the salmon into 5mm/^{1}/$_4$in thick slices against the grain.

5 Halve the avocado and sprinkle with a little of the remaining marinade. Remove the avocado stone (pit) and skin, then slice to the same thickness as the salmon.

6 Mix the mayonnaise ingredients together. Spread 5ml/1 tsp on to the back of each of the shiso leaves, then mix the remainder with 15ml/1 tbsp of the marinade.

7 Arrange the salad on four plates. Top with the avocado, salmon, shiso leaves and almonds, and drizzle over the remaining miso mayonnaise.

Nutritional information per portion: Energy 422kcal/1745kJ; Protein 16g; Carbohydrate 2.1g, of which sugars 1.4g; Fat 38.9g, of which saturates 5.9g; Cholesterol 48mg; Calcium 53mg; Fibre 2g; Sodium 133mg.

Lemon sole and fresh oyster salad

Oysters, flavoured with a rice-vinegar dressing, taste wonderful with lemon sole sashimi. In Japan, there is no choice of fish on a menu – it depends on which fish was caught that day.

SERVES 4

1 very fresh lemon sole, skinned and filleted into 4 pieces
105ml/7 tbsp rice vinegar
dashi-konbu, in 4 pieces, big enough to cover the fillets
50g/2oz Japanese cucumber, trimmed, or salad cucumber with seeds removed
50g/2oz celery sticks, strings removed
450g/1lb large broad (fava) beans, podded
1 lime, 1/2 thinly sliced
60ml/4 tbsp walnut oil
seeds from 1/2 pomegranate
salt

FOR THE OYSTERS

15ml/1 tbsp rice vinegar
30ml/2 tbsp shoyu
15ml/1 tbsp sake
12 large fresh oysters, opened
25g/1oz daikon or radishes, peeled and very finely grated
8 chives

1 Sprinkle salt on the sole fillets. Cover and chill for an hour. Mix the rice vinegar and a similar amount of water in a bowl. Wash the fish fillets in the mixture, then drain. Cut each fillet in half lengthways.

2 Lay one piece of dashi-konbu on a work surface. Place a pair of sole fillets, skinned sides together, on to it, then lay another piece of konbu on top. Cover all the fillets like this and chill for 3 hours.

3 Halve the cucumber crossways and slice thinly lengthways. Slice diagonally into 2cm/3/4in wide pieces. Repeat for the celery. Sprinkle the cucumber with salt and leave for 30–60 minutes. Squeeze to remove moisture. Boil the beans for 15 minutes. Drain, cool, then peel off the skins. Sprinkle with salt. Mix the vinegar, shoyu and sake in a bowl. Slice the sole thinly.

4 Place the cucumber and celery in a mound in the centre of four plates. Lay lime slices on top. Garnish with chives. Place the oysters to one side of the cucumber, topped with broad beans, then season with 5ml/1 tsp of the vinegar and 10ml/2 tsp grated daikon. Arrange the sole on the other side and drizzle with walnut oil and lime juice. Add the pomegranate seeds and serve.

Nutritional information per portion: Energy 264kcal/1105kJ; Protein 22.7g; Carbohydrate 14.8g, of which sugars 1.9g; Fat 13.1g, of which saturates 1.3g; Cholesterol 56mg; Calcium 143mg; Fibre 7.6g; Sodium 295mg.

Scallops sashimi in mustard sauce

The Japanese name, Hotate Kobachi, *means "scallop in a little deep bowl". This is a typical serving size for lots of Japanese dishes as a meal usually consists of at least three dishes or more.*

SERVES 4

8 scallops or 16 queen scallops, cleaned and coral removed
¼ dried sheet chrysanthemum petals (sold as kiku nori) or a handful of edible flower petals such as yellow nasturtium
4 bunches of watercress, leaves only

FOR THE DRESSING
30ml/2 tbsp shoyu
5ml/1 tsp sake
10ml/2 tsp English (hot) mustard

1 Slice the scallops in three horizontally then cut in half crossways. If you use queen scallops, slice in two horizontally.

2 Put the dried chrysanthemum or the flower petals in a sieve. Pour hot water from a kettle all over, and leave to drain for a while. When cool, gently squeeze the excess water out. Set aside and repeat with the watercress.

3 Mix together all the ingredients for the dressing in a bowl. Add the scallops 5 minutes before serving and mix well without breaking them. Add the flower petals and watercress, then transfer to four small bowls. Serve cold. Add a little more shoyu, if required.

COOK'S TIP
Do not use chrysanthemums from your garden, as the edible species are different to the ornamental varieties. Fresh edible chrysanthemums and other edible flowers are often available at specialist Japanese stores, or look for dried ones in Asian stores.

Nutritional information per portion: Energy 62kcal/262kJ; Protein 10.5g; Carbohydrate 2.5g, of which sugars 1g; Fat 1g, of which saturates 0.3g; Cholesterol 19mg; Calcium 58mg; Fibre 0.4g; Sodium 852mg.

Sashimi moriawase

The arrangement of a dish of sashimi *is as important as the freshness of the fish. Choose two or five kinds of fish from a group and only use the freshest catch of the day.*

SERVES 4

500g/1¼lb total of fish from the 4 groups

GROUP A, SKINNED FILLETS
Maguro akami: lean tuna
Maguro toro: fatty tuna
Sake: salmon
Kajiki: swordfish
Tai: sea bream or red snapper
Suzuki: sea bass
Hamachi: yellowtail
Katsuo: skipjack tuna

GROUP B, SKINNED FILLETS
Hirame: flounder or sole
Karei: halibut or turbot

GROUP C
Ika: squid body, cleaned, boned and skinned
Tako: cooked octopus tentacles
Hotate-gai: scallop (the coral, black stomach and frill removed)

GROUP D
Aka-ebi: sweet prawns (shrimp), peeled, heads can be removed, tails intact

Uni: sea urchin
Ikura: salted salmon roe

TO SERVE
1 fresh daikon, peeled and cut into 6cm/2½in lengths
1 Japanese or salad cucumber
4 shiso leaves
2 limes, halved (optional)
45ml/3 tbsp wasabi paste from a tube, or the same amount of wasabi powder mixed with 20ml/4 tsp water
1 bottle tamari shoyu

1 Make the *tsuma* (the daikon strands). Slice the daikon thinly lengthways, then cut the slices into thin strips lengthways. Rinse, drain and chill.

2 Cut the cucumber into 3cm/1¼in lengths, then cut each cylinder in half lengthways. Place the cucumber on a board, flat side down. Make fine cuts across each piece, leaving the slices joined together at one side. Then, squeeze the cucumber together so that the slices fan out sideways. Set aside.

3 Slice the fish. Group A needs *hira giri*, a thick cut: trim the fillet into a long rectangular shape. Skin side up, cut into 1cm/½in thick slices with the grain.

4 Group B needs *usu zukuri*, very thin slices. Place the fillet horizontally to you on its skinned side. Hold the knife almost horizontally to the fillet and shave it very thinly across the grain.

5 Group C fish each require different cutting styles. Slice the octopus diagonally into 5mm/¼in thick ovals. Slice the scallops in half horizontally. If they are thicker than 4cm/1½in, slice into three.

6 Cut open the squid body and turn to lie on its skinned side, horizontally to you. Score lines 5mm/¼in apart over the surface, then cut into 5mm/¼in strips. Group D is all ready to arrange.

7 Arrange the sashimi creatively. First, take a handful of daikon and heap up on to the serving plate a large mound or several small mounds. Then, base your design on the following basic rules:

Group A and C: Put each slice of fish side by side like domino pieces and lay them on a shiso leaf.

Group B: Use the thin, soft slices to make a rose shape, or overlap the slices slightly, so that the texture of the plate can be seen through them.

Group D: Place the prawns by their tails, 2–3 at a time, in a bundle. If the sea urchins come tightly packed in a little box, try to get them out in one piece. The salmon roe can be heaped on thin cucumber slices or scooped into a lime case, made from a half lime, flesh removed. Fill the case with some daikon and place the roe on top.

8 Arrange the cucumber fans, heaped wasabi paste and shiso leaves to perfect your design. Serve immediately. Pour some shoyu into four dishes and mix in the wasabi. As the sauce is quite salty, only dip the edge of the *sashimi* into it.

Nutritional information per portion: Energy 265kcal/1101kJ; Protein 27g; Carbohydrate 5.7g, of which sugars 5.2g; Fat 15g, of which saturates 2.6g; Cholesterol 64mg; Calcium 61mg; Fibre 1.5g; Sodium 1061mg.

Turbot sashimi salad with wasabi

Eating sashimi, or raw fish, with traditional sauces disappeared when shoyu became popular in the 17th century. The use of sauces returned with the Western-inspired salad.

SERVES 4

ice cubes
400g/14oz very fresh thick turbot, skinned and filleted
300g/11oz mixed salad leaves
8 radishes, thinly sliced

FOR THE WASABI DRESSING
25g/1oz rocket (arugula) leaves
50g/2oz cucumber, chopped
90ml/6 tbsp rice vinegar
75ml/5 tbsp olive oil
5ml/1 tsp salt
15ml/1 tbsp wasabi paste, or the same amount of wasabi powder mixed with 7.5ml/1½ tsp water

1 For the dressing, roughly tear the rocket and mix with the cucumber and vinegar in a food processor. Pour into a bowl and add the rest of the dressing ingredients, except the wasabi. Check the seasoning. Chill.

2 Prepare a bowl of ice-cold water. Cut the turbot in half lengthways, then cut into 5mm/¼in thick slices crossways. Plunge the fish into the ice-cold water as you slice.

3 After 2 minutes or so, the fish slices will start to curl and become firm. Take out with a slotted spoon and drain on kitchen paper.

4 In a large serving bowl, mix the fish, the salad leaves and the radishes together.

5 Mix the wasabi into the dressing, add this to the salad and toss well. Serve immediately.

Nutritional information per portion: Energy 233kcal/969kJ; Protein 18.5g; Carbohydrate 1.8g, of which sugars 1.8g; Fat 16.9g, of which saturates 2.8g; Cholesterol 0mg; Calcium 77mg; Fibre 0.9g; Sodium 72mg.

Seafood salad with fruity dressing

Here, white fish is briefly seared, then served with prawns and salad tossed in an oil-free apricot and apple dressing. The fruit flavours make a delicate accompaniment to the fish.

SERVES 4

1 baby onion, sliced lengthways
lemon juice
400g/14oz very fresh sea bream or sea
     bass, filleted
30ml/2 tbsp sake
4 large king prawns (jumbo shrimp),
     heads and shells removed
about 400g/14oz mixed salad leaves

FOR THE FRUITY DRESSING

2 ripe apricots, skinned and stoned
     (pitted)
1/4 apple, peeled and cored
60ml/4 tbsp second dashi stock or the
     same amount of water and 5ml/1 tsp
     dashi-no-moto
10ml/2 tsp shoyu
salt and ground white pepper

1 Soak the onion in ice-cold water for 30 minutes. Drain. Bring a pan half-full of water to the boil. Add a dash of lemon juice and plunge the fish into it. Remove the fish after 30 seconds and cool under cold running water. Cut into 8mm/1/3in thick slices crossways.

2 Bring the sake to the boil, then add the king prawns. Cook for 1 minute, or until they turn pink.

3 Cool the prawns under cold running water and cut into 1cm/1/2in thick slices crossways.

4 Slice an apricot thinly and set aside. Purée the remaining dressing ingredients. Chill. Lay out some salad leaves on plates. Mix the fish, prawn, apricot and onion together, add the remaining leaves, then pour on the dressing and toss. Serve the dish immediately.

Nutritional information per portion: Energy 157kcal/662kJ; Protein 25g; Carbohydrate 5.3g, of which sugars 4.9g; Fat 3.2g, of which saturates 0.5g; Cholesterol 129mg; Calcium 186mg; Fibre 1.6g; Sodium 299mg.

Cubed and marinated raw tuna

When preparing big fish like tuna or swordfish for sashimi, *Japanese fishmongers cut them lengthways to make a long rectangular shape. However, cubes of tuna work well in this recipe.*

SERVES 4

400g/14oz very fresh tuna, skinned
1 carton mustard and cress (optional)
20ml/4 tsp wasabi paste from a tube, or the same amount of wasabi powder mixed with 10ml/2 tsp water
60ml/4 tbsp shoyu
8 spring onions (scallions), green part only, finely chopped
4 shiso leaves, cut into thin slivers lengthways

1 Cut the tuna into 2cm/$\frac{3}{4}$in cubes.

2 If using mustard and cress, tie into pretty bunches or arrange as a bed in four small serving bowls or individual plates.

3 Just 5–10 minutes before serving, blend the wasabi with the shoyu. Add the tuna and spring onions. Mix and marinate for 5 minutes. Divide among the bowls and add shiso leaves on top. Serve immediately.

Nutritional information per portion: Energy 153kcal/643kJ; Protein 24.5g; Carbohydrate 2.3g, of which sugars 2.1g; Fat 5.1g, of which saturates 1.3g; Cholesterol 29mg; Calcium 28mg; Fibre 0.4g; Sodium 806mg.

Spicy fried mackerel

This dish goes down very well with chilled Japanese lager beer. Called Saba Tatsuta Agge, *it is also excellent cold and is very good served with salad.*

SERVES 4

675g/1½lb mackerel, filleted
60ml/4 tbsp shoyu
60ml/4 tbsp sake
60ml/4 tbsp caster (superfine) sugar
1 garlic clove, crushed
2cm/¾in piece fresh root ginger, peeled
    and finely grated
2–3 shiso leaves, chopped into thin strips
    (optional)
cornflour (cornstarch), for dusting
vegetable oil, for deep-frying
1 lime, cut into thick wedges

1 Using a pair of tweezers, remove any remaining bones from the mackerel. Cut the fillets in half lengthways, then slice diagonally crossways into bitesize pieces.

2 Mix the shoyu, sake, sugar, garlic, grated ginger and shiso in a mixing bowl. Add the mackerel and leave to marinate for 20 minutes.

3 Drain and pat gently with kitchen paper. Dust the fillets with cornflour.

4 Heat plenty of oil in a wok or a deep-fryer. The temperature must be kept around 180°C/350°F. Deep-fry the fillets, a few pieces at a time, until a shiny brown colour. Drain on kitchen paper. Serve at once with the lime wedges.

Nutritional information per portion: Energy 580kcal/2414kJ; Protein 32.2g; Carbohydrate 24g, of which sugars 17g; Fat 38.2g, of which saturates 6.9g; Cholesterol 91mg; Calcium 31mg; Fibre 0g; Sodium 1181mg.

Deep-fried plaice

In this dish, called Karei Kara-age, *the flesh of the fish and also the skeleton is deep-fried to such crispness that you can eat the bones, tails and heads, if you like.*

SERVES 4

4 small plaice or flounder, about
     500–675g/1¼–1½lb total weight,
     gutted, not trimmed, and washed
60ml/4 tbsp cornflour (cornstarch)
vegetable oil, for deep-frying
salt

FOR THE CONDIMENT
130g/4½oz daikon, peeled
4 dried chillies, seeded
1 bunch of chives, finely chopped
     (to make 50ml/2fl oz/¼ cup)

FOR THE SAUCE
20ml/4 tsp rice vinegar
20ml/4 tsp shoyu

1 Put the fish on a board. Make deep cuts around the gills and across the tail. Cut through the skin from the head down to the tail along the centre of the fish. Slide the knife under the cut near the head and cut the fillet from the bone. Fold the fillet with your hand as you cut as if peeling the fillet from the bone. Keep the knife horizontal to the fish.

2 Repeat for the other half, then turn the fish over and do the same to get four fillets from each fish. Place in a dish and sprinkle with salt on both sides. Keep the bony skeletons.

3 Pierce the daikon with a skewer in four places to make holes, then insert the chillies. After 15 minutes grate finely. Squeeze out the moisture. Scoop a quarter of the grated daikon and chilli into an egg cup, then press with your fingers. Turn out the cup on to a plate. Make three more mounds.

4 Cut the fish fillets into four slices crossways and put into a plastic bag with the cornflour. Shake to coat. Heat the oil in a wok to 175°C/347°F. Deep-fry the fillets, two at a time, until golden brown.

5 Raise the temperature to 180°C/350°F. Dust the skeletons with cornflour and slide into the oil. Cook until golden, drain for 5 minutes, then fry again until crisp. Drain again and sprinkle with salt.

6 Mix the rice vinegar and shoyu and put in a bowl. Arrange the skeletons and fried fish on the plates. Put the daikon and chives to one side on each plate. Have small plates for the sauce. To eat, mix the condiment with the sauce and dip the fillets and bones into the sauce.

Nutritional information per portion: Energy 207kcal/862kJ; Protein 18.2g; Carbohydrate 11g, of which sugars 1.6g; Fat 10.2g, of which saturates 1.4g; Cholesterol 46mg; Calcium 68mg; Fibre 0.9g; Sodium 835mg.

Teppan yaki

Many Japanese homes have a portable gas cooker, a table griddle, or a table equipped with a recessed cooking surface. This is because the Japanese love cooking as they eat.

SERVES 4

275g/10oz monkfish tail

4 large scallops, cleaned and corals separated

250g/9oz squid body, cleaned and skinned

12 raw king or tiger prawns (jumbo shrimp), shells and heads removed, tails intact

115g/4oz/1/2 cup beansprouts, washed

1 red (bell) pepper, seeded and cut into 2.5cm/1in wide strips

8 fresh shiitake mushrooms, stalks removed

1 red onion, cut into 5mm/1/4in thick rounds

1 courgette (zucchini), cut into 1cm/1/2in thick rounds

3 garlic cloves, thinly sliced lengthways

vegetable oil, for frying

SAUCE A, RADISH AND CHILLI SAUCE

8 radishes, finely grated

1 dried chilli, seeded and crushed

15ml/1 tbsp toasted sesame oil

1/2 onion, finely chopped

90ml/6 tbsp shoyu

30ml/2 tbsp caster (superfine) sugar

45ml/3 tbsp toasted sesame seeds

30ml/2 tbsp unsweetened orange juice

SAUCE B, WASABI MAYONNAISE

105ml/7 tbsp mayonnaise

15ml/1 tbsp wasabi paste from a tube

5ml/1 tsp shoyu

1 Sauce A: Mix the radish, its juice and the chilli in a bowl. Heat the sesame oil in a frying pan and fry the onion until soft. Pour in the shoyu and add the sugar and sesame seeds, removing the pan from the heat just as it starts to boil. Tip into the bowl and add the orange juice. Stir and cool.

2 Sauce B: Mix the mayonnaise, wasabi and shoyu together in a bowl and set aside.

3 Cut the monkfish into large, bitesize, 5mm/1/4in thick slices. Cut the scallops in half horizontally. Make shallow criss-cross slits in the skinned side of the squid. Slice into 2.5 x 4cm/1 x 11/2in pieces.

4 Put the seafood on half a platter, and arrange the vegetables (apart from the garlic) on the other half. Put sauce A in a small dish. Put the wasabi mayonnaise in a bowl.

5 Heat the griddle and oil it. Fry the garlic until crisp then transfer to a dish and mix with sauces. Fry the ingredients as you eat, dipping into the sauce or serving with mayonnaise. Oil the griddle from time to time.

Nutritional information per portion: Energy 307kcal/1273kJ; Protein 17.4g; Carbohydrate 4.2g, of which sugars 4g; Fat 23.7g, of which saturates 3.6g; Cholesterol 83mg; Calcium 91mg; Fibre 0.2g; Sodium 961mg.

Marinated and grilled swordfish

In medieval times, Saikyo (the western capital of ancient Japan) had a very sophisticated culture. Many of the classic recipes of today are from this period. Kajiki Saikyo Yaki is one such example.

SERVES 4

4 x 175g/6oz swordfish steaks
2.5ml/¹⁄₂ tsp salt
300g/11oz saikyo or shiro-miso
45ml/3 tbsp sake

FOR THE ASPARAGUS
25ml/1¹⁄₂ tbsp shoyu
25ml/1¹⁄₂ tbsp sake
8 asparagus spears, the hard ends
    discarded, each spear cut into three

1 Place the swordfish in a container and sprinkle both sides with the salt. Leave for 2 hours, drain and wipe.

2 Mix the miso and sake and spread half in the bottom of the cleaned container. Cover with a sheet of muslin (cheesecloth) the size of a dish towel, folded in half, then open the fold. Place the swordfish on top, and cover with the muslin. Spread the rest of the miso mixture on the muslin so that the muslin touches the fish. Chill for 2 days.

3 Preheat the grill (broiler) to medium. Oil the wire rack and grill (broil) the fish for 8 minutes on each side, turning every 2 minutes.

4 Mix the shoyu and sake in a bowl. Grill the asparagus on each side for 2 minutes, then dip into the bowl. Return to the grill for 2 minutes more on each side. Dip into the sauce again and set aside.

5 Serve the steak on four serving plates. Garnish with the asparagus.

Nutritional information per portion: Energy 213kcal/893kJ; Protein 32.7g; Carbohydrate 2.5g, of which sugars 2.2g; Fat 7.3g, of which saturates 1.6g; Cholesterol 72mg; Calcium 16mg; Fibre 0.3g; Sodium 2008mg.

Paper-wrapped and steamed red snapper

Originally, this elegant dish featured a whole red snapper wrapped in layered Japanese hand-made paper soaked in sake and tied with ribbons. This version is a little easier.

SERVES 4

4 small red snapper fillets, no greater
than 18 x 6cm/7 x 2¹/₂in, or whole
snapper, 20cm/8in long, gutted but
head, tail and fins intact
8 asparagus spears, hard ends discarded,
stems sliced, and tips cut in half
lengthways
4 spring onions (scallions), sliced
60ml/4 tbsp sake
grated rind of ¹/₂ lime
¹/₂ lime, thinly sliced
5ml/1 tsp shoyu
salt

1 Salt the fish on both sides and chill for 20 minutes. Preheat the oven to 180°C/350°F/Gas 4.

2 Lay two pieces of greaseproof (waxed) paper, 38 x 30cm/15 x 12in, on a surface. Fold up a third of the paper and turn back 1cm/¹/₂in from one end to make a flap. Fold 1cm/¹/₂in in from the other end. Fold the top edge down over first flap. Interlock flaps to form a rectangle. At each end fold the top corners down diagonally, fold the bottom corners up to meet the opposite folded edge to make a triangle. Press flat. Repeat to make four parcels.

3 Par-boil the asparagus tips for 1 minute, then drain and set aside. Place the asparagus slices and spring onions inside the parcels. Sprinkle with salt and add the fish. Add salt, sake and lime rind. Close the parcels.

4 Pour hot water into a roasting pan fitted with a wire rack to 1cm/¹/₂in below the rack. Bake on the rack for 20 minutes. Open the parcels, add a lime slice, asparagus tips and shoyu.

Nutritional information per portion: Energy 110kcal/465kJ; Protein 20.6g; Carbohydrate 1g, of which sugars 0.9g; Fat 1.5g, of which saturates 0.3g; Cholesterol 37mg; Calcium 51mg; Fibre 0.6g; Sodium 79mg.

Seafood, chicken and vegetable hot-pot

This dish, called Yose Nabe, *is cooked and eaten at the table, traditionally using a clay pot. You can use a flameproof casserole and will need a portable table-top stove.*

SERVES 4

225g/8oz salmon, scaled and cut into
    5cm/2in thick steaks with bones
225g/8oz white fish (sea bream, cod,
    plaice or haddock), cleaned and scaled
    then chopped into 4 chunks
300g/11oz chicken thighs, cut into large
    bitesize chunks with bones
4 hakusai leaves, base part trimmed
115g/4oz spinach
1 large carrot, cut into 5mm/$\frac{1}{4}$in thick
    rounds or flower shapes
8 fresh shiitake mushrooms, stalks
    removed, or 150g/5oz oyster
    mushrooms, base trimmed
2 thin leeks, washed and cut diagonally
    into 5cm/2in lengths

285g/10$\frac{1}{4}$ oz packet tofu block, drained
    and cut into 16 cubes
salt

FOR THE HOT-POT LIQUID
12 x 6cm/4$\frac{1}{2}$ x 2$\frac{1}{2}$in dashi-konbu
1.2 litres/2 pints/5 cups water
120ml/4fl oz/$\frac{1}{2}$ cup sake

FOR THE CONDIMENTS
90g/3$\frac{1}{2}$oz daikon, peeled
1 dried chilli, halved and seeded
1 lemon, cut into 16 wedges
4 spring onions (scallions), chopped
2 x 5g/$\frac{1}{8}$oz packets kezuri-bushi
1 bottle shoyu

1 Arrange the fish and chicken thighs on a large platter. Boil plenty of water in a large pan and cook the hakusai leaves for 3 minutes. Drain and cool. Add a pinch of salt to the water and boil the spinach for 1 minute, then drain.

2 Squeeze the spinach and lay on a sushi rolling mat, then roll it up. Rest, then unwrap and take the cylinder out.

3 Lay the hakusai leaves next to each other on the mat. Put the cylinder in the middle and roll again. Leave for 5 minutes, unroll and cut into 5cm/2in long cylinders.

4 Transfer the hakusai cylinders to the platter along with the remaining vegetables and tofu. Lay the dashi-konbu on the base of the casserole. Mix the water and sake in a bowl.

5 Insert a metal skewer into the cut side of the daikon two to three times, and insert the chillies. Leave for 5 minutes, then grate. Drain and squeeze the liquid out. Shape the pink daikon into a mound and put in a bowl. Put all the other condiments into small bowls.

6 Fill the casserole with two-thirds of the water and sake mixture. Bring to the boil, then reduce the heat. Put the carrot, shiitake, chicken and salmon into the pot. When the colour of the meat and fish changes, add the rest of the ingredients in batches.

7 Guests pour soy sauce into small bowls, and squeeze in a little lemon juice, then mix with a condiment. Pick up the food with chopsticks and dip into the sauce. Cook more ingredients as you go, adding more water and sake as the stock reduces.

Nutritional information per portion: Energy 317kcal/1325kJ; Protein 45.9g; Carbohydrate 5.9g, of which sugars 5.1g; Fat 12.3g, of which saturates 2.2g; Cholesterol 133mg; Calcium 455mg; Fibre 2g; Sodium 1961mg.

Fish cakes and vegetables

Oden is a satisfying dish to make as you can buy assorted ready-made fish balls and fish cakes from Asian food stores. You will also need a large clay pot or casserole and a portable stove.

SERVES 4

30 x 7.5cm/12 x 3in dashi-konbu

675g/1½lb daikon, peeled and cut into
  4cm/1½in lengths

12–20 ready-made fish balls and cakes

1 konnyaku

1 atsu-age

8 small shiitake mushrooms, stalks
  removed

4 medium potatoes, unpeeled, soaked in a
  bowl of water

4 hard-boiled (hard-cooked) eggs, unshelled

285g/10¼oz packet tofu block, cut into
  8 cubes

English (hot) mustard, to serve

FOR THE SOUP STOCK

1.5 litres/2½ pints/6¼ cups second
  dashi stock, or the same amount of
  water and 10ml/2 tsp dashi-no-moto

75ml/5 tbsp sake

15ml/1 tbsp salt

40ml/8 tsp shoyu

1 Wrap the dashi-konbu in a wet dish towel for 5 minutes, or until soft enough to bend easily by hand without breaking. Snip it in half crossways, then cut each into four ribbons lengthways. Tie the centre of each "ribbon".

2 Slightly shave the edges of each of the daikon cylinders. Place all the fish balls and cakes, konnyaku and atsu-age in a large pan. Add enough hot water to cover, then drain.

3 Cut the konnyaku in quarters, then cut each quarter in half diagonally to make eight triangles. Cut large fish cakes in half. Put two shiitake mushrooms on to each of four bamboo skewers.

4 Mix all the ingredients for the soup stock, but only fill the pot or casserole by two-thirds. Add the daikon and potatoes and bring to the boil. Add the hard-boiled eggs. Reduce the heat to low and simmer for an hour, uncovered, skimming occasionally.

5 Increase the heat to medium and add the other ingredients. Cook, covered, for 30 minutes, then bring to the table cooker and keep warm on the lowest heat. Serve with mustard. Top up the pot with stock when it has reduced to half.

Nutritional information per portion: Energy 370kcal/1555kJ; Protein 37.1g; Carbohydrate 28.8g, of which sugars 5.8g; Fat 10.4g, of which saturates 2.4g; Cholesterol 236mg; Calcium 327mg; Fibre 3.1g; Sodium 1926mg.

Rolled sardines with plum paste

Japanese cooks seek to taste and express the season in their cooking. This dish is one of many recipes to celebrate the arrival of the harvest, when the sardine season peaks in autumn.

SERVES 4

8 sardines, cleaned and filleted

5ml/1 tsp salt

4 umeboshi, about 30g/1¼oz total
  weight (choose the soft type)

5ml/1 tsp sake

5ml/1 tsp toasted sesame seeds

16 shiso leaves, cut in half lengthways

1 lime, thinly sliced, the centre hollowed
  out to make rings, to garnish

1 Carefully cut the sardine fillets in half lengthways and place them side by side in a large, shallow container. Sprinkle with salt on both sides.

2 Remove the stones (pits) from the umeboshi and put the fruit in a small mixing bowl with the sake and toasted sesame seeds. With the back of a fork, mash the umeboshi, mixing well to form a smooth paste.

3 Wipe the sardine fillets with kitchen paper. With a butter knife, spread some umeboshi paste thinly on to one of the sardine fillets, then press some shiso leaves on top. Roll up the sardine starting from the tail and pierce with a wooden cocktail stick (toothpick). Repeat to make 16 rolled sardines.

4 Preheat the grill (broiler) to high. Lay a sheet of foil on a baking tray, and arrange the sardine rolls on this, spaced well apart to prevent sticking. Grill (broil) for 4–6 minutes on each side, or until golden brown, turning once.

5 Lay a few lime rings on four individual plates and arrange the rolled sardines alongside. Serve hot.

Nutritional information per portion: Energy 177kcal/740kJ; Protein 20.9g; Carbohydrate 0.7g, of which sugars 0.7g; Fat 9.9g, of which saturates 2.8g; Cholesterol 0mg; Calcium 94mg; Fibre 0.2g; Sodium 121mg.

Crab meat in vinegar

A refreshing tsumami *(a dish that accompanies alcoholic drinks). For the dressing, use a Japanese or Greek cucumber, if possible – they are smaller and contain less water than ordinary cucumbers.*

SERVES 4

1/2 red (bell) pepper, seeded
pinch of salt
275g/10oz cooked white crab meat, or
   2 x 165g/5¹/2oz canned white crab
   meat, drained
about 300g/11oz Japanese or salad
   cucumber

FOR THE VINEGAR MIXTURE
15ml/1 tbsp rice vinegar
10ml/2 tsp caster (superfine) sugar
10ml/2 tsp awakuchi shoyu

1 Slice the red pepper into thin strips lengthways. Sprinkle with a little salt and leave for about 15 minutes. Rinse well and drain.

2 For the vinegar mixture, combine the rice vinegar, sugar and awakuchi shoyu in a small bowl.

3 Loosen the crab meat with cooking chopsticks and mix it with the sliced red pepper in a mixing bowl. Divide among four small bowls.

4 If you use a salad cucumber, scoop out the seeds. Finely grate the cucumber with a fine-toothed grater or use a food processor. Drain in a sieve.

5 Mix the cucumber with the vinegar mixture, and pour a quarter on to the crab meat mixture in each bowl. Serve cold immediately, before the cucumber loses its colour.

Nutritional information per portion: Energy 82kcal/345kJ; Protein 13.3g; Carbohydrate 5.6g, of which sugars 5.4g; Fat 0.8g, of which saturates 0.1g; Cholesterol 50mg; Calcium 100mg; Fibre 0.9g; Sodium 560mg.

Tempura seafood

This quintessentially Japanese dish actually has its origins in the West, as tempura was introduced to Japan by Portuguese traders in the 17th century.

SERVES 4

8 large raw prawns (shrimp), heads and
    shells removed, tails intact, cleaned
130g/4^1/$_2$oz squid body, cleaned and
    skinned
115g/4oz whiting fillets
4 fresh shiitake mushrooms, stalks
    removed
8 okra
^{1}/$_8$ nori sheet, 5 x 4cm/2 x 1^1/$_2$in
20g/^{3}/$_4$oz dried harusame (a packet is
    a 150–250g/5–9oz mass)
vegetable oil and sesame oil, for
    deep-frying
plain (all-purpose) flour, for dusting
salt

FOR THE DIPPING SAUCE

400ml/14fl oz/1^2/$_3$ cups water mixed
    with 5ml/1 tsp dashi-no-moto
    (stock granules)
200ml/7fl oz/scant 1 cup shoyu
200ml/7fl oz/scant 1 cup mirin

FOR THE CONDIMENT

450g/1lb daikon, peeled
4cm/1^1/$_2$in fresh root ginger

FOR THE TEMPURA BATTER

ice-cold water
1 large (US extra large) egg, beaten
200g/7oz/2 cups plain flour, sifted
2–3 ice cubes

1 Make four x 3mm/^{1}/$_8$in deep cuts across the belly of the prawns. Snip the tips of the tails and squeeze out any liquid. Pat dry with kitchen paper.

2 Cut open the squid body. Lay flat, inside down, on a board, and make shallow criss-cross slits on one side. Cut into 2.5 x 6cm/1 x 2^1/$_2$in rectangular strips. Cut the whiting into similar-size strips.

3 Make two notched slits on the shiitake caps, in the form of a cross. Sprinkle your hands with salt and rub over the okra, then wash under running water.

4 Cut the nori into four strips lengthways. Loosen the noodles from the block and cut the ends to get a few strips. Make four bunches and tie them in the middle with a nori strip. Wet the end to fix.

5 In a pan, mix all the dipping sauce ingredients and bring to the boil, then set aside and keep warm.

6 Finely grate the daikon. Drain, then squeeze out excess water. Lay clear film (plastic wrap) over an egg cup and press 2.5ml/^{1}/$_2$ tsp of peeled and finely grated ginger into the base. Add 30ml/2 tbsp daikon. Press and invert on a plate. Make three more.

7 Half-fill a pan or wok with 3 parts vegetable oil to 1 part sesame oil. Bring to 175°C/347°F. Make the batter. Add enough water to the egg to make 150ml/¼ pint/⅔ cup, then pour into a large bowl. Add the flour and mix with chopsticks. Do not beat; leave the batter lumpy. Add some ice cubes later to keep the temperature cool.

8 Dip the okra into the batter and deep-fry until golden. Drain on a rack. Batter the underside of the shiitake. Deep-fry. Increase the heat a little, then fry the harusame by holding the nori tie with chopsticks and dipping them into the oil for a few seconds. Drain and sprinkle with salt.

9 Hold the tail of a prawn, dust with flour, then dip into the batter. Do not put batter on the tail. Slide the prawn into the hot oil very slowly. Deep-fry one to two prawns at a time until crisp.

10 Dust the whiting strips, dip into the batter, then deep-fry until golden. Wipe the squid strips well with kitchen paper, dust with flour, then dip in batter. Deep-fry until the batter is crisp.

11 Drain excess oil from the tempura on a wire rack for a few minutes, then arrange them on individual plates. Set the condiment alongside the tempura. Reheat the dipping sauce to warm through, then pour into four small bowls. Serve.

Nutritional information per portion: Energy 505kcal/2129kJ; Protein 28.3g; Carbohydrate 69.9g, of which sugars 26.2g; Fat 14.4g, of which saturates 2.1g; Cholesterol 231mg; Calcium 172mg; Fibre 2.8g; Sodium 3741mg.

Clams and spring onions with miso sauce

The Japanese are really fond of shellfish, and clams are among the most popular. In season, they become sweet and juicy, and are excellent with this sweet-and-sour dressing.

SERVES 4

900g/2lb carpet shell clams or cockles,
   or 300g/11oz can baby clams in brine,
   or 130g/4½oz cooked and shelled
   cockles
15ml/1 tbsp sake
8 spring onions (scallions), green and
   white parts separated, then chopped
   in half
10g/¼oz dried wakame

FOR THE *NUTA* DRESSING
60ml/4 tbsp shiro-miso
20ml/4 tsp caster (superfine) sugar
30ml/2 tbsp sake
15ml/1 tbsp rice vinegar
about 1.5ml/¼ tsp salt
7.5ml/1½ tsp English (hot) mustard
sprinkling of dashi-no-moto (if using
   canned shellfish)

1 If using fresh clams or cockles, wash the shells and discard any that remain open when tapped.

2 Put the clams or cockles in a pan with 1cm/½in water. Sprinkle with sake, cover and bring to the boil. Cook for 5 minutes, then stand for 2 minutes. Discard any closed shells. Drain and reserve the liquid. When the shells have cooled slightly, take out the meat from most of the shells.

3 Cook the white parts of the spring onions in boiling water, then add the green parts after 2 minutes. Cook for 4 minutes altogether. Drain well.

4 Mix the shiro miso, sugar, sake, vinegar and salt for the *nuta* dressing, in a small pan. Stir in 45ml/3 tbsp of the reserved clam liquid, or the same amount of water and dashi-no-moto. Stir constantly over medium heat. When the sugar has dissolved, add the mustard. Season then leave to cool.

5 Soak the wakame in a small bowl of water for 10 minutes. Drain and squeeze out excess moisture. Mix together the clams or cockles, onions, wakame and dressing. Divide the mixture among four serving bowls and serve cold.

Nutritional information per portion: Energy 114kcal/482kJ; Protein 12.8g; Carbohydrate 13.2g, of which sugars 11.6g; Fat 0.6g, of which saturates 0.2g; Cholesterol 50mg; Calcium 71mg; Fibre 0.3g; Sodium 1762mg.

Deep-fried small prawns and corn

This dish is called Kakiage, an inexpensive and informal style of tempura. This is only one of many versions and it is a good way of using up small quantities of vegetables.

SERVES 4

200g/7oz small cooked, peeled prawns (shrimp)
4–5 button (white) mushrooms
4 spring onions (scallions)
75g/3oz/½ cup canned, drained or frozen corn, thawed
30ml/2 tbsp frozen peas, thawed
vegetable oil, for deep-frying
chives, to garnish

FOR THE TEMPURA BATTER

300ml/½ pint/1¼ cups ice-cold water
2 eggs, beaten
150g/5oz/1¼ cups plain (all-purpose) flour
1.5ml/¼ tsp baking powder

FOR THE DIPPING SAUCE

400ml/14fl oz/1²/₃ cups water and 5ml/1 tsp dashi-no-moto (stock granules)
100ml/3fl oz/scant ½ cup shoyu
100ml/3fl oz/scant ½ cup mirin
15ml/1 tbsp chopped chives

1 Roughly chop half the prawns. Cut the mushrooms into small cubes. Slice the white part from the spring onions and chop this roughly.

2 To make the tempura batter, in a medium mixing bowl, mix the cold water and eggs. Add the flour and baking powder, and very roughly fold in with a pair of chopsticks or a fork. Do not beat. The batter should still be quite lumpy.

3 Heat plenty of oil in a wok or a deep-fryer to 170°C/338°F.

4 Mix the prawns and vegetables in the batter. Pour a quarter of the batter into a bowl, then drop into the oil. Using spoons, gather the scattered batter to form a fist-size ball. Deep-fry until golden. Repeat three times. Drain on kitchen paper.

5 In a small pan, mix all the liquid dipping sauce ingredients together and bring to the boil, then turn off the heat. Sprinkle with chives.

6 Garnish the *kakiage* with chives, and serve with the dipping sauce.

Nutritional information per portion: Energy 370kcal/1558kJ; Protein 17.8g; Carbohydrate 50.4g, of which sugars 17.7g; Fat 12.3g, of which saturates 2g; Cholesterol 193mg; Calcium 124mg; Fibre 2.1g; Sodium 1964mg.

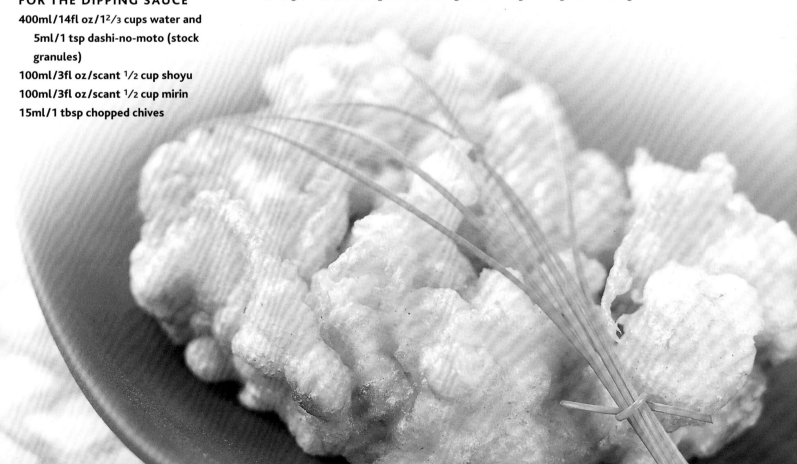

Fried prawn balls

When the moon waxes in September, the Japanese celebrate the arrival of autumn by making an offering to the moon, and have a feast. The dishes offered should all be round in shape.

MAKES ABOUT 14

150g/5oz raw prawns (shrimp), peeled
75ml/5 tbsp water and 2.5ml/¹⁄₂ tsp
   dashi-no-moto (stock granules)
1 large (US extra large) egg white,
   well beaten
30ml/2 tbsp sake
15ml/1 tbsp cornflour (cornstarch)
1.5ml/¹⁄₄ tsp salt
vegetable oil, for deep-frying

TO SERVE

25ml/1¹⁄₂ tbsp ground sea salt
2.5ml/¹⁄₂ tsp sansho
¹⁄₂ lemon, cut into 4 wedges

1 Mix the prawns, dashi stock, egg white, sake, cornflour and salt in a food processor, and process them until the mixture is smooth. Scrape from the sides and transfer to a small mixing bowl.

2 In a wok or small pan, heat the vegetable oil to 175°C/347°F. Take two dessertspoons and wet them with a little vegetable oil. Scoop about 30ml/2 tbsp of the prawn-ball paste into the spoons and form a small ball.

3 Carefully plunge the ball into the hot oil and deep-fry until lightly browned. Drain on a wire rack. Repeat this process, one ball at a time, until all the prawn-ball paste has been used. Mix the salt and sansho together on a plate.

4 Serve the fried prawn balls on a large platter or on four individual serving plates. Garnish with lemon wedges and serve hot with the sansho salt.

Nutritional information per portion: Energy 41kcal/170kJ; Protein 2.1g; Carbohydrate 1g, of which sugars 0g; Fat 3.2g, of which saturates 0.4g; Cholesterol 21mg; Calcium 9mg; Fibre 0g; Sodium 446mg.

Deep-fried and marinated small fish

*The influence of early Europeans, or **Nanban**, who first brought deep-frying to Japan a few hundred years ago, is still evident in this dish, known as **Kozakana Nanban-zuke**.*

SERVES 4

450g/1lb sprats (US small whitebait)
plain (all-purpose) flour, for dusting
1 small carrot
1/3 cucumber
2 spring onions (scallions)
4cm/1¹/₂in piece fresh root ginger, peeled
1 dried red chilli
75ml/5 tbsp rice vinegar
60ml/4 tbsp shoyu
15ml/1 tbsp mirin
30ml/2 tbsp sake
vegetable oil, for deep-frying

1 Wipe the sprats dry with kitchen paper, then put them in a small plastic bag with a handful of flour. Seal and shake vigorously to coat the fish.

2 Cut the carrot and cucumber into thin strips. Cut the spring onions into three, then slice into thin, lengthways strips. Slice the ginger into thin strips and rinse in cold water. Drain. Seed and chop the chilli into thin rings.

3 Mix the rice vinegar, shoyu, mirin and sake together to make a marinade. Add the chilli and all the sliced vegetables. Stir well using a pair of chopsticks.

4 Pour plenty of oil into a deep pan and heat to 180°C/350°F. Deep-fry the fish until they are golden brown. Drain on layered kitchen paper, then plunge them into the marinade. Leave to marinate for 1 hour, stirring occasionally.

5 Serve the fish cold in a shallow bowl and put the marinated vegetables on top. This dish will keep for about a week in the refrigerator.

Nutritional information per portion: Energy 307kcal/1273kJ; Protein 17.4g; Carbohydrate 4.2g, of which sugars 4g; Fat 23.7g, of which saturates 3.6g; Cholesterol 83mg; Calcium 91mg; Fibre 0.2g; Sodium 961mg.

Simmered squid and daikon

Ika To Daikon Ni *is a classic dish, the secret of which used to be handed down from mother to daughter. Nowadays, you are more likely to taste the real thing at restaurants.*

SERVES 4

**450g/1lb squid, cleaned, body and
  tentacles separated**
about 1kg/2¼lb daikon, peeled
**900ml/1½ pints/3¾ cups second dashi
  stock or the same amount of water
  and 5ml/1 tsp dashi-no-moto**
60ml/4 tbsp shoyu
45ml/3 tbsp sake
15ml/1 tbsp caster (superfine) sugar
30ml/2 tbsp mirin
grated rind of ½ yuzu or lime, to garnish

1 Separate the two triangular flaps from the squid body. Cut the body into 1cm/½in thick rings. Cut the triangular flaps into 1cm/½in strips. Finally, chop the tentacles into 4cm/1½in lengths.

2 Cut the daikon into 3cm/1¼in thick rounds and shave the edges of the sections with a sharp knife. Plunge the slices into cold water. Drain just before cooking.

3 Put the daikon and squid in a pan and pour on the stock. Bring to the boil, and cook for 5 minutes, skimming. Reduce the heat and add the shoyu, sake, sugar and mirin.

4 Cover with a circle of baking parchment and simmer for 45 minutes. Shake the pan occasionally. The liquid will reduce by almost a half. Leave for 5 minutes and serve hot with yuzu or lime rind.

Nutritional information per portion: Energy 185kcal/780kJ; Protein 19.6g; Carbohydrate 19.3g, of which sugars 17.8g; Fat 2.4g, of which saturates 0.7g; Cholesterol 253mg; Calcium 72mg; Fibre 2.3g; Sodium 1221mg.

Salmon teriyaki

Saké Teriyaki is a well-known Japanese dish, which uses a sweet and shiny sauce for marinating as well as for glazing the ingredients.

SERVES 4

4 small salmon fillets with skin on, each
    weighing about 150g/5oz
50g/2oz/¼ cup beansprouts, washed
50g/2oz mangetouts (snow peas), ends
    trimmed
20g/¾oz carrot, cut into thin strips
salt

FOR THE *TERIYAKI* SAUCE

45ml/3 tbsp shoyu
45ml/3 tbsp sake
45ml/3 tbsp mirin
15ml/1 tbsp plus 10ml/2 tsp caster
    (superfine) sugar

1 Mix all the ingredients for the sauce, except for the 10ml/2 tsp sugar, in a pan. Heat to dissolve the sugar. Remove and cool for an hour. Place the fish in a dish and pour over the sauce. Leave for 30 minutes.

2 Boil the vegetables in salted water. First add the beansprouts, then after for 1 minute add the mangetouts. Leave for 1 minute, then add the carrot strips. Drain and keep warm.

3 Preheat the grill (broiler) to medium. Take the salmon out of the sauce and pat dry. Reserve the sauce. Cook the salmon for 6 minutes, turning once, until golden on both sides.

4 Pour the sauce into the pan. Add the remaining sugar and heat until dissolved. Brush the salmon with the sauce, then grill until the surface of the fish bubbles. Turn over and repeat on the other side of the salmon.

5 Serve the vegetables with the salmon. Spoon over the rest of the sauce.

Nutritional information per portion: Energy 337kcal/1408kJ; Protein 31.6g; Carbohydrate 13g, of which sugars 12.5g; Fat 16.6g, of which saturates 2.9g; Cholesterol 75mg; Calcium 49mg; Fibre 0.6g; Sodium 872mg.

Meat and poultry

Most meat recipes in Japanese cooking use meat and poultry as a rich flavouring ingredient for vegetables and rice. Even in sukiyaki, the quintessential Japanese classic, there are plenty of accompanying vegetables. Sauces and stocks are also used to enhance the flavour of the dish.

Grilled chicken balls
cooked on bamboo skewers

These tasty chicken balls, called tsukune, are popular in yakitori bars and also are a favourite with children, because they can be eaten directly from the skewer.

SERVES 4

300g/11oz skinless chicken, minced (ground)
2 eggs
2.5ml/$^1/_2$ tsp salt
10ml/2 tsp plain (all-purpose) flour
10ml/2 tsp cornflour (cornstarch)
90ml/6 tbsp dried breadcrumbs
2.5cm/1in piece fresh root ginger, grated

FOR THE "*TARE*" *YAKITORI* SAUCE

60ml/4 tbsp sake
75ml/5 tbsp shoyu
15ml/1 tbsp mirin
15ml/1 tbsp caster (superfine) sugar
2.5ml/$^1/_2$ tsp cornflour (cornstarch) blended
    with 5ml/1 tsp water
shichimi togarashi or sansho, to garnish
    (optional)

1 Soak eight bamboo skewers overnight in water. Put all the ingredients for the chicken balls, except the ginger, in a food processor and blend well. Wet your hands and shape about a tablespoonful of the mixture into a small ball. Make a further 30–32 balls in the same way.

2 Squeeze the juice from the grated ginger into a bowl. Discard the pulp. Add the ginger juice to a pan of boiling water. Add the chicken balls, and boil for 7 minutes, or until the meat is brown and the balls float to the surface. Scoop out using a slotted spoon and drain on a plate covered with kitchen paper.

3 In a small pan, mix all the ingredients for the sauce, except for the cornflour liquid. Bring to the boil, then reduce the heat and simmer for 10 minutes, or until the sauce has slightly reduced. Add the cornflour liquid and stir until the sauce is thick. Transfer to a bowl.

4 Thread 3–4 balls on to each skewer. Cook under a medium grill (broiler). Turn them frequently for a few minutes, or until the balls start to brown. Brush with sauce and return to the heat. Repeat the process twice. Serve, sprinkled with shichimi togarashi or sansho, if you like.

Nutritional information per portion: Energy 332kcal/1397kJ; Protein 30.3g; Carbohydrate 29g, of which sugars 7.4g; Fat 9.7g, of which saturates 2.6g; Cholesterol 339mg; Calcium 84mg; Fibre 0.6g; Sodium 325mg.

Pot-cooked duck and green vegetables

Prepare the ingredients for this dish, Kamo Nabe, *beforehand, so that the cooking can be done at the table. Use a heavy pan or flameproof casserole with a portable stove.*

SERVES 4

4 duck breast fillets, about 800g/1³/4lb
　　total weight
8 large shiitake mushrooms, stalks
　　removed, a cross cut into each cap
2 leeks, trimmed and cut diagonally into
　　6cm/2¹/2in lengths
¹/2 hakusai, stalk part removed and cut
　　into 5cm/2in squares
500g/1¹/4lb shungiku or mizuna, root part
　　removed, cut in half crossways

FOR THE STOCK
raw bones from 1 chicken, washed
1 egg shell
200g/7oz/scant 1 cup short grain rice,
　　washed and drained

120ml/4fl oz/¹/2 cup sake
about 10ml/2 tsp coarse sea salt

FOR THE SAUCE
75ml/5 tbsp shoyu
30ml/2 tbsp sake
juice of 1 lime
8 white peppercorns, roughly crushed

FOR THE SOUP
130g/4¹/2oz Chinese egg noodles, cooked
　　and loosened
1 egg, beaten
1 bunch of chives, chopped
freshly ground white pepper

1 To make the stock, put the bones into a pan three-quarters full of water. Bring to the boil and drain when it reaches boiling point. Wash the pan and bones, then return to the pan with the same amount of water. Add the egg shell and bring to the boil. Simmer for 1 hour, skimming. Remove the bones and shell. Add the rice, sake and salt and simmer for 30 minutes. Set aside.

2 Heat a frying pan until just smoking. Remove from the heat and add the duck, skin side down. Sear until crisp. Turn over and sear the other side for 1 minute. Cool.

3 Wipe the duck fat with kitchen paper and cut the breast and skin into 5mm/¹/4in thick slices. Arrange on a plate with the vegetables.

4 Heat through the ingredients for the sauce and transfer to a bowl.

5 Bring the soup stock to the boil, then reduce to medium-low. Add half the shiitake and leeks. Wait for 5 minutes and put in half the stalk part of the hakusai. Add half the duck and cook for 1–2 minutes for rare or 5–8 minutes for well-done.

6 Each person prepares some duck and vegetables in a serving bowl and drizzles over a little sauce. Add the hakusai leaves, shungiku and mizuna to the stock as you eat, adjusting the heat as you go. When the stock is less than a quarter of the pot's volume, top up with 3 parts water to 1 part sake.

7 When the duck has been eaten, bring the reduced stock to the boil. Skim the oil from the surface, and reduce the heat to medium. Add the noodles, cook for 1–2 minutes and check the seasoning. Add more salt if required. Pour in the beaten egg and swirl in the stock. Cover, turn off the heat, then leave to stand for 1 minute. Decorate with the chopped chives and serve with ground pepper.

Nutritional information per portion: Energy 626kcal/2633kJ; Protein 52.3g; Carbohydrate 69.4g, of which sugars 6g; Fat 18.6g, of which saturates 4g; Cholesterol 277mg; Calcium 110mg; Fibre 4.3g; Sodium 1640mg.

Cubed chicken and vegetables

A popular Japanese cooking style simmers vegetables of different textures with a small amount of meat together in dashi stock. This chicken version is known as Iridori.

SERVES 4

2 chicken thighs, about 200g/7oz, boned,
   with skin remaining
1 large carrot, trimmed
1 konnyaku
300g/11oz satoimo or small potatoes
500g/1¼lb canned take-no-ko, drained
30ml/2 tbsp vegetable oil
300ml/½ pint/1¼ cups water and
   7.5ml/1½ tsp dashi-no-moto
   (stock granules)
salt

**FOR THE SIMMERING
SEASONINGS**
75ml/5 tbsp shoyu
30ml/2 tbsp sake
30ml/2 tbsp caster (superfine) sugar
30ml/2 tbsp mirin

1 Cut the chicken into bitesize pieces. Chop the carrot into 2cm/¾in triangular chunks.

2 Boil the konnyaku for 1 minute and drain. Cool, then slice it crossways into 5mm/¼in thick rectangular strips. Cut a 4cm/1½in slit down the centre of a strip without cutting the ends. Push the top of the strip through the slit to make a tie. Repeat with all the konnyaku.

3 Peel and halve the satoimo. Put the pieces in a colander and sprinkle with salt. Rub well and wash. Drain. If using, peel and halve the potatoes.

4 Halve the take-no-ko, then cut into the same shape as the carrot.

5 Heat the oil and stir-fry the chicken until the meat turns white. Add the carrot, konnyaku, satoimo and take-no-ko. Stir each time you add a new ingredient.

6 Add the dashi and bring to the boil. Cook for 3 minutes then reduce to medium-low. Add the seasonings, cover and simmer for 15 minutes until most of the liquid has evaporated. When the satoimo is soft, transfer the chicken and vegetables to a large bowl and serve.

Nutritional information per portion: Energy 302kcal/1266kJ; Protein 20g; Carbohydrate 27.8g, of which sugars 16g; Fat 12.1g, of which saturates 1.7g; Cholesterol 39mg; Calcium 659mg; Fibre 1.2g; Sodium 1388mg.

Sumo wrestler's hotpot

This filling hot-pot, called Chanko Nabe, *is probably responsible for the vast size of Sumo wrestlers, as it is their first meal of the day after 4–6 hours of morning exercise. You need a Japanese clay pot or heavy pan and a portable table stove or a plate warmer.*

SERVES 4–6

2 abura-age
1 bunch of shungiku or pak choi (bok choy), 200g/7oz, root part trimmed
1 large leek, trimmed
1 daikon, thickly peeled
1/2 hakusai
1 dashi-konbu, 4 x 10cm/1$\frac{1}{2}$ x 4in
350g/12oz chicken, boned and cut into large bitesize pieces
12 shiitake mushrooms, stalks removed, a cross cut into each cap
285g/10$\frac{1}{4}$oz packet tofu block, drained and cut into 8 cubes

FOR THE FISH BALLS
6 sardines, about 350g/12oz, cleaned and filleted

2.5cm/1in fresh root ginger, chopped
1 large (US extra large) egg
25ml/1$\frac{1}{2}$ tbsp miso (any except hatcho or aka)
20 chives, roughly chopped
30ml/2 tbsp plain (all-purpose) flour

FOR THE SOUP STOCK
550ml/18fl oz/2$\frac{1}{2}$ cups sake
550ml/18fl oz/2$\frac{1}{2}$ cups water
60ml/4 tbsp shoyu

FOR THE CITRUS PEPPER (OPTIONAL)
grated rind of 1 lime
10–12 white peppercorns

1 Make the fish balls by chopping all the ingredients. Transfer to a container, cover and set aside.

2 Blanch the abura-age for 30 seconds. Drain under running water and squeeze out the water. Cut each abura-age in half lengthways, then quarter crossways to make eight rectangles. Cut each rectangle in half diagonally to make two triangles, to give 32 triangles.

3 Cut the shungiku into 6cm/2$\frac{1}{2}$in lengths. Cut the leek diagonally in 2.5cm/1in thick oval shapes. Cut the daikon into 5mm/$\frac{1}{4}$in rounds. Cut the hakusai leaves into strips crossways, keeping the leaves and stalks separate. Grind the citrus pepper ingredients and set aside.

4 Lay the dashi-konbu on the base of the pan. Pour in the ingredients for the soup stock to fill half the pan, and bring to the boil on a high heat.

5 To cook the fish balls, reduce the heat to medium. Scoop up the fish-ball paste with a spoon and shape roughly like a rugby ball. Drop into the boiling stock. Repeat until all the paste is used. Skim frequently. Cook for 3 minutes.

6 Add the chicken, daikon, the stalks of the hakusai, the shiitake and leek, then the tofu and abura-age. Simmer for 12 minutes, or until the chicken is cooked. Add the soft parts of the hakusai and the shungiku and wait for 3 minutes. Remove from the heat.

7 Put the pan on the portable stove on the table, set at the lowest heat, or on a plate warmer. Serve small amounts of the ingredients in bowls. Guests help themselves from the pot. Sprinkle on citrus pepper, if you like.

COOK'S TIP
At the end of the meal there is a tasty, rich soup left in the pot. Add 200g/7oz cooked udon noodles into the remaining soup and bring to the boil again. After 2 minutes, serve the noodles in bowls with plenty of soup and chopped chives on top.

Nutritional information per portion: Energy 311kcal/1301kJ; Protein 38.4g; Carbohydrate 5.4g, of which sugars 4.2g; Fat 15.3g, of which saturates 1.4g; Cholesterol 73mg; Calcium 1099mg; Fibre 3g; Sodium 853mg.

Grilled skewered chicken

The Japanese always accompany alcoholic drinks with nibbles, which are generally called tsumami. *Grilled skewered chicken dipped in* yakitori *sauce is one of the most popular.*

SERVES 4

8 chicken thighs with skin, boned and cut into 2.5cm/1in cubes

8 large, thick spring onions (scallions), trimmed and cut into 2.5cm/1in sticks

FOR THE *YAKITORI* SAUCE
60ml/4 tbsp sake
75ml/5 tbsp shoyu
15ml/1 tbsp mirin
15ml/1 tbsp caster (superfine) sugar

TO SERVE
shichimi togarashi, sansho or lemon wedges

1 First, make the sauce. Mix all the ingredients together in a pan. Bring to the boil, then reduce the heat and simmer for 10 minutes, or until the sauce has thickened.

2 Preheat the grill (broiler) to high. Oil the wire rack and arrange the chicken cubes on it. Grill both sides of the chicken until the juices drip, then dip in the sauce and return to the rack. Grill for 30 seconds on each side, repeating the dipping process twice more. Keep warm.

3 Gently grill the spring onions until soft and slightly brown. Do not dip.

4 Thread about four pieces of the grilled chicken and three grilled spring onion pieces on to each of eight bamboo skewers. Make sure the chicken and spring onions are are evenly spaced on the skewers.

5 Arrange the skewers on a large serving platter and serve sprinkled with shichimi togarashi or sansho, or accompanied by lemon wedges.

Nutritional information per portion: Energy 165kcal/695kJ; Protein 22g; Carbohydrate 9g, of which sugars 8.8g; Fat 2.9g, of which saturates 0.8g; Cholesterol 105mg; Calcium 24mg; Fibre 0.4g; Sodium 1429mg.

Simmered beef slices and vegetables

This dish, Niku Jyaga, *is a typical home-cooked meal and is one of the traditional dishes referred to as "mother's speciality". It is easy to cook and you can use inexpensive cuts of beef.*

SERVES 4

250g/9oz beef fillet (or any cut), very
    thinly sliced
1 large onion
15ml/1 tbsp vegetable oil
450g/1lb small potatoes, halved then
    soaked in water
1 carrot, cut into 5mm/¼in rounds
45ml/3 tbsp frozen peas, defrosted and
    blanched for 1 minute

FOR THE SEASONINGS

30ml/2 tbsp caster (superfine) sugar
75ml/5 tbsp shoyu
15ml/1 tbsp mirin
15ml/1 tbsp sake

1 Cut the thinly sliced beef slices into 2cm/¾in wide strips, and slice the onion lengthways into 5mm/¼in pieces.

2 Heat the vegetable oil in a pan and lightly fry the beef and onion slices. When the colour of the meat changes, drain the potatoes and add to the pan.

3 Once the potatoes are coated with the oil in the pan, add the carrot. Pour in just enough water to cover, then bring to the boil, skimming a few times.

4 Boil vigorously for 2 minutes, then move the potatoes to the bottom of the pan and gather all the other ingredients to sit on top of them.

5 Reduce the heat to medium-low. Add the seasonings. Simmer for 20 minutes, partially covered, or until most of the liquid has evaporated.

6 Check if the potatoes are cooked. Add the peas and cook to heat through, then remove the pan from the heat. Serve the beef and vegetables immediately in four small serving bowls.

Nutritional information per portion: Energy 276kcal/1160kJ; Protein 17.8g; Carbohydrate 31.5g, of which sugars 13.2g; Fat 9.2g, of which saturates 2.9g; Cholesterol 36mg; Calcium 28mg; Fibre 2.3g; Sodium 1394mg.

Paper-thin sliced beef cooked in stock

The Japanese name for this dish, Shabu Shabu, *refers to "washing" the wafer-thin slices of beef in hot stock. You will need a portable stove to cook this meal at the table.*

SERVES 4

600g/1lb 6oz boneless beef sirloin
2 thin leeks, trimmed and cut into
    2 x 5cm/³⁄4 x 2in strips
4 spring onions (scallions), quartered
8 shiitake mushrooms, less stalks
175g/6oz oyster mushrooms, base part
    removed, torn into small pieces
¹⁄2 hakusai, base part removed and cut
    into 5cm/2in squares
300g/11oz shungiku, halved
275g/10oz tofu, halved then cut in
    2cm/³⁄4in thick slices crossways
10 x 6cm/4 x 2¹⁄2in dashi-konbu wiped
    with a damp cloth

FOR THE *PONZU*
juice of 1 lime made up to 120ml/
    4fl oz/¹⁄2 cup with lemon juice
50ml/2fl oz/¹⁄4 cup rice vinegar

120ml/4fl oz/¹⁄2 cup shoyu
20ml/4 tsp mirin
4 x 6cm/1¹⁄2 x 2¹⁄2in dashi-konbu
5g/¹⁄8oz kezuri-bushi

FOR THE *GOMA-DARE*
75g/3oz white sesame seeds
10ml/2 tsp caster (superfine) sugar
45ml/3 tbsp shoyu
15ml/1 tbsp sake
15ml/1 tbsp mirin
90ml/6 tbsp second dashi stock, or the
    same amount of water and 5ml/1 tsp
    dashi-no-moto

FOR THE CONDIMENTS
5–6cm/2–2¹⁄2in daikon, peeled
2 dried chillies, seeded and sliced
20 chives, finely chopped

1 Mix all the *ponzu* ingredients in a glass jar and leave overnight. Strain and keep the liquid in the jar.

2 Make the *goma-dare*. Roast the sesame seeds in a dry frying pan until the seeds pop, then grind to form a smooth paste. Add the sugar and grind, then add the other ingredients, mixing well. Pour 30ml/2 tbsp into each of four bowls, and put the rest in another bowl.

3 Prepare the condiments. Pierce the cut ends of the daikon four or five times with a skewer, then insert the chilli. Leave for 20 minutes, then grate the daikon. Divide the pink daikon among four small bowls. Put the chives in another bowl.

4 Cut the meat into 1–2mm/¹⁄16in thick slices, and place on a plate. Arrange the vegetables and tofu on another plate.

5 Fill a flameproof casserole three-quarters full of water and add the dashi-konbu. Bring everything to the table and heat the casserole.

6 Pour 45ml/3 tbsp *ponzu* into the grated daikon, and add the chives to the *goma-dare*. When the water comes to the boil, remove the konbu and reduce the heat to medium-low. Add a handful of each ingredient except the beef to the casserole.

7 Each guest picks up a slice of beef using chopsticks and holds it in the stock for 3–10 seconds. Dip the beef into one of the sauces and eat. Remove the vegetables and other ingredients as they cook, and eat with the dipping sauces. Skim the surface occasionally.

Nutritional information per portion: Energy 492kcal/2050kJ; Protein 46.7g; Carbohydrate 12.8g, of which sugars 11.6g; Fat 28.4g, of which saturates 7.8g; Cholesterol 87mg; Calcium 517mg; Fibre 3.7g; Sodium 3047mg.

Sliced seared beef

Japanese chefs use a cooking technique called tataki *to cook rare steak. They normally use a coal fire and sear a chunk of beef on long skewers, then plunge it into cold water to stop it cooking further. Use a wire mesh grill over the heat source to cook this way.*

SERVES 4

500g/1¼lb chunk of beef thigh (a long, thin chunk
   looks better than a thick, round chunk)
generous pinch of salt
10ml/2 tsp vegetable oil

15ml/1 tbsp caster (superfine) sugar
1 garlic clove, thinly sliced
1 small onion, thinly sliced
sansho

FOR THE MARINADE
200ml/7fl oz/scant 1 cup rice vinegar
70ml/4½ tbsp sake
135ml/4½fl oz/scant ⅔ cup shoyu

FOR THE GARNISH
6 shiso leaves and shiso flowers (if available)
about 15cm/6in Japanese or ordinary salad cucumber
½ lemon, thinly sliced
1 garlic clove, finely grated (optional)

1 Mix the marinade ingredients in a small pan and warm through until the sugar has dissolved. Remove from the heat and leave to cool. Sprinkle the beef with the salt and rub into the meat. Leave for 2–3 minutes, then rub the oil in evenly. Fill a large bowl with water. Heat a griddle. Sear the beef, turning until a depth of 5mm/¼in of the flesh is cooked. Immediately plunge the meat into the water for a few seconds. Wipe the meat and immerse fully in the marinade for 1 day.

2 Next day, slice the shiso leaves into thin strips. Slice the cucumber diagonally into oval shapes, then cut each oval into matchsticks. Remove the meat from the marinade. Strain the remaining marinade, reserving both the liquid and the marinated onion and garlic. Cut the beef into thin slices.

3 Heap the cucumber on a serving plate and put the onion and garlic on top. Arrange the beef leaning alongside. Or, if the slices are large enough, you could roll them. Fluff the shiso strips and put on top of the beef. Decorate with shiso flowers, if using.

4 To eat, take a few beef slices. Roll a slice with your choice of garnish, then dip it into the marinade. Add a little grated garlic, if you like.

Nutritional information per portion: Energy 258kcal/1079kJ; Protein 28.7g; Carbohydrate 9.8g, of which sugars 9.8g; Fat 11.7g, of which saturates 4.8g; Cholesterol 73mg; Calcium 20mg; Fibre 0.3g; Sodium 82mg.

Sukiyaki

You will need a sukiyaki pan or a shallow cast-iron pan, and a portable table stove to cook this traditional dish of beef and vegetables.

SERVES 4

600g/1lb 6oz well-marbled beef sirloin, without bone, sliced thinly
15ml/1 tbsp sake
1 packet shirataki noodles, about 200g/7oz, drained
10 spring onions (scallions), trimmed and quartered diagonally lengthways
2 large onions, cut into 8 slices lengthways
450g/1lb enokitake mushrooms, trimmed
12 shiitake mushrooms, stalks removed
300g/11oz shungiku, cut in half lengthways, or watercress

250–275g/9–10oz tofu, drained and cut into 8–12 large bitesize cubes
4–8 very fresh eggs, at room temperature
about 20g/³⁄₄oz beef fat

FOR THE *WARI-SHITA* SAUCE
75ml/5 tbsp second dashi stock, or the same amount of water and 5ml/1 tsp dashi-no-moto
75ml/5 tbsp shoyu
120ml/4fl oz/¹⁄₂ cup mirin
15ml/1 tbsp sake
15ml/1 tbsp caster (superfine) sugar

1 Arrange the beef on a large plate. Sprinkle with the sake. Par-boil the shirataki in rapidly boiling water for 2 minutes, then drain. Wash and cut into 5cm/2in lengths. Drain well. Heat all the ingredients for the *wari-shita* sauce over medium heat until the sugar has dissolved. Pour the sauce into a bowl.

2 On a tray, arrange the vegetables, shirataki and tofu. Break one egg into each of four small serving bowls. Start cooking when the guests are seated. Heat the pan on a table cooker until very hot, reduce the heat to medium, and add some beef fat. When it has melted, add the spring onions and onion slices. Increase the heat and stir-fry for 2 minutes, or until the onions are soft. The guests should now start to beat the egg in their bowls.

3 Add a quarter of the *wari-shita* sauce to the pan. When it starts to bubble, add a quarter of the vegetables, tofu and shirataki. Add four slices of beef to the pan. As they change colour, remove them immediately from the pan and dip into the egg. Cook the vegetables and other ingredients in the same way. Add more sauce when it is reduced in the pan.

Nutritional information per portion: Energy 868kcal/3633kJ; Protein 71.5g; Carbohydrate 51.7g, of which sugars 11.1g; Fat 43.2g, of which saturates 13.1g; Cholesterol 662mg; Calcium 605mg; Fibre 6.5g; Sodium 1695mg.

Pan-fried pork

Created by a dinner lady at a Tokyo university in the 1970s, this is popular with youngsters.

SERVES 4

450g/1lb pork chops, boned and trimmed
15ml/1 tbsp vegetable oil
1 small onion, thinly sliced lengthways
50g/2oz/¼ cup beansprouts
50g/2oz mangetouts (snow peas), trimmed
salt

FOR THE MARINADE
15ml/1 tbsp shoyu
15ml/1 tbsp sake
15ml/1 tbsp mirin
4cm/1½in piece fresh root ginger,
    very finely grated, plus juice

1 Freeze the pork for 2 hours. Cut into 3mm/⅛in slices, then into 4cm/1½in wide strips.

2 Mix all the marinade ingredients together. Add the pork and marinate for 15 minutes.

3 Heat the oil in a frying pan. Add the onion and fry for 3 minutes. Take half the pork out from the marinade and add to the pan. Transfer the meat to a plate when its colour changes. Repeat with the rest of the meat. Reserve the marinade. Add the onions to the plate.

4 Pour the marinade into the pan and simmer until it has reduced by one-third. Add the beansprouts and mangetouts, then the pork and increase the heat to medium-high for 2 minutes. Serve.

Nutritional information per portion: Energy 176kcal/738kJ; Protein 25.2g; Carbohydrate 2.4g, of which sugars 1.7g; Fat 7.4g, of which saturates 1.9g; Cholesterol 71mg; Calcium 20mg; Fibre 0.7g; Sodium 258mg.

Deep-fried pork fillet

Known as Ton-katsu, *some Japanese restaurants serve just this one dish.*

SERVES 4

4 pork loin chops or cutlets, boned
plain (all-purpose) flour, to dust
vegetable oil, for deep-frying
2 eggs, beaten
50g/2oz/1 cup dried white breadcrumbs
1 white cabbage, finely sliced
salt and ready-ground mixed pepper
prepared English (hot) mustard, to serve
Japanese pickles, to serve

FOR THE *TON-KATSU* SAUCE
60ml/4 tbsp Worcestershire sauce
30ml/2 tbsp good-quality tomato ketchup
5ml/1 tsp shoyu

1 Make a few cuts horizontally across the fat of the meat. Rub seasoning into the meat and dust with flour, shaking off any excess. Heat the oil in a deep-fryer or pan to 180°C/350°F.

2 Dip the meat in the eggs, then coat with breadcrumbs. Deep-fry two pieces at a time for 8–10 minutes until golden brown. Drain on kitchen paper.

3 Put the cabbage on four plates. Cut the pork crossways into 2cm/¾in thick strips and place on the cabbage.

4 For the *ton-katsu* sauce, mix the Worcestershire sauce, ketchup and shoyu in a jug (pitcher). Serve the pork immediately, with the sauce, mustard and pickles.

Nutritional information per portion: Energy 385kcal/1607kJ; Protein 30.9g; Carbohydrate 19.3g, of which sugars 9.6g; Fat 21g, of which saturates 4.2g; Cholesterol 253mg; Calcium 131mg; Fibre 2.5g; Sodium 633mg.

Roasted and marinated pork

Yuan, *a sauce made from sake, shoyu, mirin and citrus fruit, is often used to marinate ingredients either before or after cooking. If possible, leave the meat to marinate overnight.*

SERVES 4

600g/1lb 6oz pork fillet (tenderloin)
1 garlic clove, crushed
generous pinch of salt
4 spring onions (scallions), trimmed,
    white part only
10g/¼oz dried wakame, soaked in water
    for 20 minutes and drained
10cm/4in celery stick, trimmed and cut in
    half crossways
1 carton mustard and cress

FOR THE *YUAN* SAUCE
105ml/7 tbsp shoyu
45ml/3 tbsp sake
60ml/4 tbsp mirin
1 lime, sliced into thin rings

1 Preheat the oven to 200°C/400°F/Gas 6. Rub the pork with the garlic and salt. Leave for 15 minutes.

2 Roast the pork for 20 minutes, then turn it over and reduce the temperature to 180°C/350°F/Gas 4. Cook for a further 20 minutes.

3 Mix the sauce ingredients. Transfer the pork to the sauce and marinate for 2 hours, or overnight. Finely shred the spring onions. Soak in ice-cold water. When the shreds curl up, drain and gather them into a loose ball.

4 Cut the drained wakame into 2.5cm/1in squares or narrow strips. Slice the celery very thinly lengthways. Soak it in a bowl of cold water, then drain and gather it together in a loose ball as before.

5 Remove the pork from the marinade and wipe with kitchen paper. Slice the pork very thinly.

6 Strain the marinade into a small jug (pitcher) or bowl. Arrange the sliced pork on a large serving platter with all the vegetables around it and serve cold with the *yuan* sauce.

Nutritional information per portion: Energy 241kcal/1015kJ; Protein 33.4g; Carbohydrate 10.6g, of which sugars 10.3g; Fat 6.2g, of which saturates 2.1g; Cholesterol 95mg; Calcium 33mg; Fibre 0.4g; Sodium 1983mg.

Desserts and baking

Glutinous rice, azuki beans, squash, sweet

potatoes and sugar are the most commonly

used ingredients in Japanese desserts;

dairy foods are rarely used. It is not

customary in Japan to have a dessert after

a meal, so the dishes here are eaten as

an accompaniment to Japanese tea.

Green tea ice cream

In the past, the Japanese did not follow a meal with dessert, apart from some fruit. This custom is changing and many Japanese restaurants offer light desserts such as sorbet or ice cream.

SERVES 4

**500ml/17fl oz carton good-quality
    vanilla ice cream**
15ml/1 tbsp matcha
**15ml/1 tbsp lukewarm water from
    the kettle**

1 Soften the ice cream in the refrigerator for 20–30 minutes.

2 Mix the matcha powder and lukewarm water to a smooth paste.

3 Put half the ice cream into a mixing bowl. Add the matcha liquid and mix with a rubber spatula.

4 Add the rest of the ice cream. You can stop mixing when the ice cream looks a marbled dark green and white, or continue mixing until the ice cream is a uniform pale green. Put the bowl into the freezer.

5 After 1 hour, the ice cream is ready. Scoop into bowls to serve.

Nutritional information per portion: Energy 269kcal/1120kJ; Protein 4.9g; Carbohydrate 21.1g, of which sugars 21g; Fat 18.9g, of which saturates 11.3g; Cholesterol 0mg; Calcium 126mg; Fibre 0g; Sodium 75mg.

Sweet pancake

In Japan, the sweet bean paste is traditionally sandwiched between two pancakes to resemble a little gong. Alternatively, the pancakes can be folded to make a half gong.

MAKES 6–8

65g/2¹⁄₂oz/5 tbsp caster (superfine) sugar
3 large (US extra large) eggs, beaten
15ml/1 tbsp maple syrup or golden (light corn) syrup
185g/6¹⁄₂oz/1²⁄₃ cups plain (all-purpose) flour, sifted
5ml/1 tsp bicarbonate of soda (baking soda)
150ml/¹⁄₄ pint/²⁄₃ cup water
vegetable oil, for frying

FOR THE SWEET BEAN PASTE

250g/9oz canned azuki beans
40g/1¹⁄₂oz/3 tbsp caster sugar
pinch of salt

1 To make the bean paste, put the beans and their liquid into a pan, then heat over a medium heat. Add the sugar gradually and stir. Cook until the liquid has almost evaporated and the beans are mushy. Add the salt, remove from the heat, stir for 1 minute, then cool.

2 Mix the sugar, eggs and syrup until the sugar has dissolved, then add the flour to make a smooth batter. Cover. Leave for 20 minutes.

3 Mix together the bicarbonate of soda and water in a cup and mix into the batter.

4 Heat a little oil in a frying pan until hot. Remove from the heat and wipe with kitchen paper. Return to a medium heat and ladle some batter into the centre. Make a pancake about 13cm/5in in diameter and 5mm/¹⁄₄in thick. Cook for 2–3 minutes on each side until golden brown. Make 11–15 pancakes.

5 Take one pancake and spread about 30ml/2 tbsp of the bean paste in the middle leaving about 2.5cm/1in around the edge. Cover with another pancake. Repeat until all the pancakes are used. Serve warm or cold.

Nutritional information per portion: Energy 222kcal/941kJ; Protein 7.2g; Carbohydrate 38.9g, of which sugars 15.8g; Fat 5.3g, of which saturates 1g; Cholesterol 71mg; Calcium 106mg; Fibre 1.8g; Sodium 117mg.

Sweet azuki bean paste jelly

In this summery dessert, a dark red kanten and sweet bean cube is captured in a clear kanten jelly. It resembles a small stone trapped in a block of mountain ice.

SERVES 12

200g/7oz can azuki beans, drained
40g/1¹/₂oz/3 tbsp caster (superfine)
   sugar

FOR THE KANTEN JELLY
2 x 5g/¹/₈oz sachets powdered kanten
100g/3³/₄oz/¹/₂ cup caster sugar
rind of ¹/₄ orange in one piece

1 Tip the beans into a pan over a medium heat. When steam begins to rise, reduce the heat to low. Add the sugar one-third at a time, stirring until the sugar has dissolved and the moisture evaporated. Remove from the heat.

2 Pour 450ml/³/₄ pint/scant 2 cups water into a pan, and mix with one kanten sachet. Stir until dissolved, then add 40g/1¹/₂oz of the sugar and the orange rind. Bring to the boil and cook for 2 minutes, stirring until the sugar has dissolved. Remove from the heat and discard the orange rind.

3 Transfer 250ml/8fl oz/1 cup of the hot liquid into a 15 x 10cm/6 x 4in container. Leave to set.

4 Add the bean paste to the kanten liquid, and mix. Move the pan on to a wet dish towel and keep stirring for 8 minutes. Pour the bean liquid into an 18 x 7.5 x 2cm/7 x 3 x ³/₄in container and leave for 1 hour at room temperature, then 1 hour in the refrigerator. Turn upside down on a board covered with kitchen paper. Leave for 1 minute, then cut into 12 rectangular pieces.

5 Line 12 ramekins with clear film (plastic wrap). With a fork, cut the set kanten block into 12 squares. Put one square in each ramekin, then place a bean and kanten cube on top of each.

6 Pour 450ml/³/₄ pint/scant 2 cups water into a pan and mix with the remaining kanten sachet. Bring to the boil, add the remaining sugar, then stir until dissolved. Boil for a further 2 minutes, and remove from the heat. Place the pan on a wet dish towel to cool and stir for 5 minutes, or until the liquid starts to thicken.

7 Ladle the liquid into the ramekins. Twist the clear film at the top. Chill for at least 1 hour. Carefully remove the ramekins and clear film and serve cold.

Nutritional information per portion: Energy 65kcal/278kJ; Protein 1.5g; Carbohydrate 15.5g, of which sugars 12.4g; Fat 0.1g, of which saturates 0g; Cholesterol 0mg; Calcium 10mg; Fibre 0.6g; Sodium 2mg.

Kabocha squash cake

Yokan (cake) is a very sweet dessert often made with azuki beans, to be eaten at tea time with green tea. In this version kabocha squash is used instead of azuki and the cake is served with fruit.

SERVES 4

1 x 350g/12oz kabocha squash
30ml/2 tbsp plain (all-purpose) flour
15ml/1 tbsp cornflour (cornstarch)
10ml/2 tsp caster (superfine) sugar
1.5ml/¼ tsp salt
1.5ml/¼ tsp ground cinnamon
25ml/1½ tbsp water
2 egg yolks, beaten

TO SERVE

½ nashi, peeled, trimmed and sliced
   thinly lengthways
½ kaki, peeled, trimmed and sliced
   thinly lengthways (optional)

1 Cut off the hard part from the top and bottom of the kabocha, then cut it into three to four wedges. Scoop out the seeds. Cut into chunks. Steam the kabocha for about 15 minutes over a medium heat. Check if a chopstick can be pushed into the centre easily. Remove and leave, covered, for 5 minutes.

2 Remove the skin from the kabocha. Mash the flesh and push it through a sieve using a wooden spoon, or use a food processor. Transfer the flesh to a bowl, add the rest of the cake ingredients, and mix well.

3 Roll out the makisu sushi mat as if making a sushi roll. Wet some muslin (cheesecloth) slightly with water and lay it on the mat. Spread the kabocha mixture evenly. Hold the nearest end and roll up the makisu to the other end. Close both outer ends by rolling up or folding the muslin over. Put the rolled kabocha in the makisu back into the steamer for 5 minutes. Remove from the heat and leave to set for 5 minutes.

4 Open the makisu when the roll has cooled down. Cut the cake into 2.5cm/1in thick slices and serve cold with the nashi and kaki, if using.

Nutritional information per portion: Energy 91kcal/382kJ; Protein 2.8g; Carbohydrate 13.8g, of which sugars 4.2g; Fat 3.1g, of which saturates 0.9g; Cholesterol 101mg; Calcium 50mg; Fibre 1.1g; Sodium 7mg.

Steamed cake with sweet potatoes and shiro miso

This soft steamed cake, known as Mushi-kasutera, *is not too sweet, and can be eaten like bread. The secret is a little miso.*

SERVES 4

200g/7oz/scant 2 cups plain (all-purpose) flour
140g/4³⁄₄oz/scant ³⁄₄ cup caster (superfine) sugar
45ml/3 tbsp sweetened condensed milk
4 eggs, beaten
40g/1¹⁄₂oz shiro miso
150g/5oz sweet potatoes, trimmed and peeled
10ml/2 tsp cream of tartar
2.5ml/¹⁄₂ tsp bicarbonate of soda (baking soda)
30ml/2 tbsp melted butter

1 Sift the flour and sugar into a bowl. In another bowl, beat the condensed milk, eggs and shiro miso until smooth. Add to the flour and mix. Leave for 1 hour.

2 Cut the sweet potatoes into 2cm/³⁄₄in dice. Cover with water. Drain just before using. Preheat the steamer, and line with muslin (cheesecloth).

3 Mix the cream of tartar and bicarbonate of soda with 15ml/1 tbsp water. Add to the cake mixture with the melted butter and two-thirds of the diced sweet potato. Pour the cake mixture into the steamer, then push the rest of the sweet potato on to the surface of the cake.

4 Steam the cake for 30 minutes, or until risen to a dome shape. Serve warm or cold, cut into wedges.

Nutritional information per portion: Energy 512kcal/2165kJ; Protein 12.9g; Carbohydrate 90.5g, of which sugars 46.5g; Fat 13.6g, of which saturates 6.3g; Cholesterol 210mg; Calcium 162mg; Fibre 2.5g; Sodium 862mg.

Sticky rice cake wrapped in sweet azuki bean paste

This tea-time snack, Ohagi, *is an absolute favourite among all ages in Japan. It is made on occasions such as birthdays and festivals.*

MAKES 12

150g/5oz glutinous rice
50g/2oz Japanese short grain rice
410g/14¹⁄₄oz can azuki beans (canned in water, with sugar and salt)
90g/3¹⁄₂oz/6¹⁄₂ tbsp caster (superfine) sugar
pinch of salt
camellia petals, to decorate (optional)

1 Wash the two kinds of rice in a sieve under cold running water, then drain. Leave for 1 hour to dry. Tip the rice into a casserole, and add 200ml/7fl oz/scant 1 cup water. Cover and bring to the boil. Reduce the heat and simmer for 15 minutes. Leave for 5 minutes. Remove the lid, cover with a towel and cool.

2 Pour the azuki beans into a pan. Over a medium heat, add the sugar one-third at a time, mixing after each addition. Reduce the heat and mash the beans. Add salt and heat to remove excess liquid. Cool.

3 Wet your hands. Shape the rice into 12 small balls. Spread 30ml/2 tbsp of the bean paste 5mm/¹⁄₄in thick in the centre of damp muslin (cheesecloth). Put a rice ball in the middle, then wrap up in the paste with the muslin. Repeat until all the rice balls are used. Decorate with camellia petals, if using.

Nutritional information per portion: Energy 128kcal/541kJ; Protein 4.3g; Carbohydrate 27.2g, of which sugars 8.2g; Fat 0.5g, of which saturates 0.1g; Cholesterol 0mg; Calcium 14mg; Fibre 1.2g; Sodium 3mg.

The guide to
Japanese cooking

This section looks at seasonal and regional food and the development of Japanese cuisine. There is information on all the different ingredients used in Japanese cooking, such as rice, noodles, tofu, mushrooms, seaweeds and fish; a section on ready-made sauces; and advice on preparation and cooking techniques.

Development of **Japanese cuisine**

The first traces of food to be found in Japan were in the remains of prehistoric settlements scattered across southern Japan. They suggest that even before 200BC the diet was varied and balanced. Rice was first introduced in the 2nd century BC and has become the foundation of the cuisine because it is served at at every meal.

RICE: A STAPLE FOOD FOR ALL
In Japan, rice is so important that the word for cooked rice, *gohan* or *meshi*, also means meal. It plays a major part in Japanese cooking.

Rice was probably introduced to Japan from South-east Asia, and the earliest evidence of crop production was found in village settlements dating from around the 2nd century BC to the 2nd century AD. Rice cultivation revolutionized life in the western region of Japan, and from there soon spread further east.

From the 8th to the 12th centuries, when aristocratic culture blossomed, rice became established as a staple food, cooked in various ways for the upper classes, although the majority of the population was dependent on lesser-quality grains such as millet. It was the popularity of rice that led to the development of other basic

ABOVE: *This colour woodblock print by Hiroshige (1797–1858) shows the communal nature of rice cultivation.*

accompaniments, such as seasonings and sauces, and of cooking techniques.

By the end of the 12th century the aristocratic society had been replaced by feudal warlords. Techniques of rice production rapidly improved under the feudal system and rice became fully available to the general public on a daily basis during the 13th century.

Because rice keeps well it was possible for people to use it for their daily food source rather than depend on less predictable crops, meats or catches of fish and shellfish. Rice became the staple food and Japanese cuisine developed around it.

THE IMPORTANCE OF SALT
With the development of rice cultivation, salt started to play a part

in the culinary scene. It was extracted from the sea and replaced the former source of salt: animals' intestines. However, due to scarcity and its poor storage qualities, salt was mixed with animal or plant fibres and proteins. The mixture, called *hishio*, was a nutritious, fermented food as well as a seasoning, and was one of the most important developments in Japanese culinary history. *Hishio* later developed into some of the most important Japanese foods, such as *miso* and *shoyu* (grain *hishio*), *shiokara* and *sushi* (meat *hishio*), and *tsukemono* pickles (grass *hishio*).

TEA AND SAKE
The idea of fermentation was developed to produce alcohol using barley, yam and glutinous rice. At first this was an alcoholic food rather than a liquid, but it was the origin of sake. The aristocratic class contributed to the establishment of eating etiquette, which subsequently influenced *cha-kaiseki*, the meal served at the tea ceremony, and later Japanese cuisine as a whole.

At the royal court, an increasing number of annual ceremonies and rituals were performed, including Shinto ceremonies (the indigenous religion), and these would be accompanied by food and sake. Sake was, and still is, regarded as a sacred liquid, and drinking it was believed to help cleanse the body of evil spirits. Eating and drinking became an important part of the procedures and cooking itself became a ritual.

Foreign influences

From the earliest times, China and Korea have exerted great influence over Japan. From AD630 to AD894, trade missions to China brought back cultural influences that were reflected in architecture, art and food, while in the 1600s, potters from Korea helped to establish Japan's porcelain industry.

THE IMPACT OF BUDDHISM

Japanese cooking is largely fish- and vegetable-based and if meat is included in a meal it is used sparingly and often cooked with vegetables. This can be traced back to the 6th century when Buddhism arrived via China, proclaiming animal slaughter and meat eating to be a sinful act. An Imperial ordinance issued in AD675 banned the eating of beef, horse, dog and chicken. However, the ban seems not to have been fully effective since another official ban had to be issued in AD752 to commemorate the opening of the eyes of the Great Buddha at Todaiji Temple in Nara. As part of that decree, it was forbidden to kill any creature for the whole year, and records show that fishermen were compensated for their loss of earnings with rice. Even with the bans it was not until the 9th–12th centuries that this philosophy spread from Buddhist monks to the upper classes and then to the wider public.

ABOVE: *Some Buddhist temples have restaurants on the premises, serving vegetarian food.*

At the end of the 12th century, Zen Buddhism, a strict sect of Buddhism, arrived from China and, with it, *shojin ryori*. This was originally simple vegan cooking performed by the monks as part of their severe training. It usually consisted of a bowl of rice, soup and one or two other dishes, but it now refers to a formal vegetarian meal. Many Japanese dishes may appear to be vegetarian but, in fact, vegetables are often cooked in dashi soup: a fish stock. Authentic *shojin ryori* should be purely vegan cooking.

Accompanying the Zen philosophical movement, Chinese foods and cooking techniques were introduced to Japan. One important arrival was tea, which became a drink favoured by Buddhists and the upper classes. This led to the development of *cha-kaiseki* (the meal served before the tea ceremony), which established the form of Japanese cuisine.

INFLUENCES THROUGH TRADE

Other foreigners, including the Spanish, Portuguese, Dutch and English also influenced Japan as trading with them progressed from the mid 16th century to the closure of the country in the early 17th century. Any dish or sauce with the name *Nanban* derives from this period. With trade, many new vegetables and fruits also arrived: watermelons, sugar cane, chillies, figs, potatoes and the kabocha squash. The Portuguese also brought the tomato to Japan, although initially only as a decorative plant, and the most famous foreign import of this period, tempura, was introduced by Portuguese Jesuits.

Meat-eating was reintroduced and became popular among Catholic feudal lords. Sweets (candy) and cakes also joined the league of foreign imports, and many still bear the names of their foreign origin, such as *kasutera* (from the Portuguese *castella*). Drinks such as shochu and red wine also arrived at this time and were regarded as *Nanban* drinks.

Seasonal food

The seasons in Japan last for about three months each, with each new season bringing different produce and a changing catch of fish from the seas. In Japanese cooking the idea persists strongly. There is a word for seasonal food, shun, *and it is always present in the Japanese mind.*

There is no doubt that the wealth of the seas as well as the variety of fresh local produce contributed to the development of a cuisine that is rich in regional specialities.

The following represent just a sample of Japan's rich selection of fish and vegetables, together with dishes that are typically made and eaten during a particular season.

SPRING

Vegetables such as peas, broad (fava) beans and mangetouts (snow peas) are crisp and tender in early spring. One speciality is fresh bamboo shoots that are cooked with rice. New ginger shoots are used for making vinegared ginger sticks for grilled fish and ginger slices to accompany sushi. It is also clam-picking time on beaches, and along the rivers anglers are blessed with masu trout. Japanese strawberries are also available in early spring.

SUMMER

Early in May the season's new katsuo (bonito or skipjack tuna) arrives, and *katsuo no tataki* (seared and sliced *katsuo sashimi* with herbs and spices) is cherished at this time of the year. Other fish such as aji (scad or horse mackerel), kajiki (swordfish), suzuki (sea bass) and maguro (big-eye tuna) are all in *shun*, and best eaten as *sashimi* (raw fish thinly sliced).

Ume (Japanese green apricots) become available from early June. Rakkyo (Japanese bulb vegetable), umeboshi (dried and salted ume) and umeshu (ume liqueur) are all prepared for the coming year, or in the case of umeshu, it is ready for consumption the following summer.

AUTUMN

In Japan, autumn never passes without eating grilled samma (saury). Salmon, mackerel and sea bream are also all in season. The king of mushrooms, matsutake, dominates during this season and is either cooked with rice or steamed in clear soup. Autumn is also a fruit season and in particular the beautiful Japanese persimmon, kaki, arrives in abundance.

WINTER

The most famous winter fish of all must be fugu. So poisonous is this fish (just a hint of its liver can prove fatal), that a special licence is required to handle it. *Fugu-chiri* (fugu hotpot) is the dish of the season. Shungiku (garland chrysanthemum) is a good accompaniment to hotpot dishes. The two popular Japanese vegetables, hakusai and daikon, are also at their best in winter and are pickled in bulk for the coming months.

LEFT: *Fresh produce such as fish, shellfish, meat and poultry and dried goods are all available at a local market in Tokyo.*

Regional food

The regional foods and dishes vary greatly from Hokkaido, the northern island, to Kyushu, the southern island.

HOKKAIDO

Most of the seafood comes from here. Hokkaido is the only place where sheep are reared, so *ghengis khan-nabe* (lamb barbecue) is a local speciality. Ramen noodles in miso soup was first developed in Sapporo, the capital of Hokkaido.

THE NORTH OF HONSHU

From Akita and Niigata through to Toyama facing the Sea of Japan is Japan's treasured rice belt, which produces some of the finest sake. The regional produce also includes various *sansai* (mountain vegetables) and the maitake mushroom of Akita.

TOKYO AND THE CENTRAL REGION

Japan's capital and the surrounding areas, known as Kanto, may no longer produce much agricultural produce but it is an excellent culinary centre for all regional foods and dishes. It has some of the finest restaurants in Japan, not only of Japanese cuisine but also of other cooking traditions.

Tokyo-style cooking tends to use a little more seasoning and shoyu than Osaka cuisine. *Nigiri-zushi* (finger sushi with a slice of raw fish on top) is just one of Tokyo's many specialities.

Shinshu, the central mountain region of Honshu island, is particularly well known for its soba, wasabi, grapes and for its wine. The eels from Lake Suwa are also famous, while Shizuoka, the coastal county facing the Pacific Ocean, produces tea and mikan (satsumas).

KANSAI AND THE WEST

An area of great importance in culinary matters, Kansai includes both Osaka and Kyoto. The old capital, Kyoto, is considered the birthplace of Japanese cuisine and Osaka is now the culinary heart of Japan. Specialities include udon and udon-suki (*shabu shabu*, meaning beef and vegetable hotpot, with udon noodles). Kansai produces the best *wagyu* (Japanese beef fed on beer).

SHIKOKU AND THE WEST

Fresh fish and shellfish are abundant all the year round in these two southern islands and *Tosa-no tataki*, which is lightly seared katsuo (skipjack tuna) *sashimi*, is a very famous speciality of Shikoku. Various different types of citrus fruits are also produced on these islands, while Kyushu island is the largest shiitake mushroom producer in Japan.

ABOVE: *Rows of mezashi, a popular daily snack throughout Japan.*

ABOVE: *A fruit stall in a Tokyo market displays a variety of seasonal produce.*

ABOVE: *Mushrooms grow in abundance and are an essential part of everyday food.*

Cooking and eating

The philosophy of Japanese cooking is to serve food that has retained as much of its natural flavour as possible. It is therefore essential to choose ingredients at their best – they should be very fresh and in their season. If the food needs to be cooked at all this is done for the minimum time possible.

PREPARATION AND COOKING METHODS

The most important aspect of Japanese cooking lies in the preparation. As the food is eaten with hashi (chopsticks), it needs to be cut into bitesize pieces. Vegetables of various shapes and textures are cooked to the correct crunchy softness so that they will be appetizing as well as attractive. Fresh fish is almost always filleted and often thinly sliced to eat raw as *sashimi*. Meats are also thinly sliced most of the time or else minced (ground) meat is used.

If the food, especially vegetables, is to be cooked, it is always very lightly done to retain crispness. Cooking methods include simmering, grilling (broiling), steaming and frying; roasting is not really part of the Japanese cuisine. Many fish and vegetable dishes involve griddling over a direct heat, but in modern houses this is not done due to the smoke produced, in which case pan-frying may be substituted. Japanese cooking also uses various pickling and marinating methods.

TYPICAL MEALS

The traditional Japanese breakfast is a substantial meal. It consists of a bowl of hot, freshly boiled rice, miso soup, thick omelette roll, pickled vegetables and grilled (broiled) small salted fish such as horse mackerel. Today, however, busy people, particularly the young, prefer Western-style ready-made foods such as bread, ham and cheese plus salad and fruits with tea or coffee.

BELOW: *Meal time at* ryokan, *a Japanese old-style inn. Each diner's food is served on an individual legged tray.*

For lunch, Japanese soba (buckwheat noodles), udon (flour noodles) and Chinese-style ramen (egg noodles) are very popular at home and in restaurants, while single-dish meals include a tonkatsu rice bowl, a *bento* (lunch) box or curry.

Dinner at home in Japan is a rather casual affair, with each member of the family having a bowl of rice and miso soup probably with an individual main dish of either fish or meat. Two or three other dishes such as simmered vegetables, marinated fish and pickles will be placed in the centre of the table for everyone to help themselves. Second servings of rice and soup are available, and fruit and green tea are always served to finish the meal.

MENU PLANNING

A formal Japanese banquet will start with hors d'oeuvres, clear soup and *sashimi* (thinly sliced raw fish) followed in turn by a grilled dish, a steamed dish, a simmered dish and finally a deep-fried dish, accompanied by salads. The meal finishes with boiled rice, miso soup and pickles. All dishes are served individually on a tray. Fresh fruit and green tea usually end the lengthy banquet. Warmed sake is drunk throughout the meal until the rice is served.

At home a simpler traditional dinner will consist of individual bowls of soup and boiled rice with at least three main dishes, each one cooked differently: for example, *sashimi*, a grilled dish and a simmered dish. They are placed in the centre of the table for all the family to serve themselves.

For dinner parties at home, a standard menu consists of a plate of hors d'oeuvres to accompany drinks (when a toast may be made) followed by a first course, the main dish and then bowls of rice and soup with some pickles. Sake or grape wine is not served after the rice has arrived. Fruit and green tea end the meal.

ABOVE: *Eating out in Tokyo's Ginza district is popular with many Japanese.*

DRINK

There have been many attempts in the West to find out which wine goes best with Japanese food, and some food and wine experts even claim Champagne best suits the cuisine. However, nothing really matches the mellow, delicate flavour of sake because it does not override the subtle nature of Japanese cuisine. Moreover, while wine may have been developed to complement the food, it was the other way round with sake.

The Japanese drink lager beer more than any other drink and often start a meal with a glass of ice-cold lager. The lager is usually followed by sake, which is drunk cold in summer and warm in winter, or by shochu (a very alcoholic rough sake). A popular way of drinking shochu is to dilute it with hot water and add an umeboshi (dried salted Japanese apricot) to it.

Equipment

The most important aspect of Japanese cooking is preparation, cutting in particular, so Japanese kitchens are equipped with a battery of delicate utensils to ensure fresh ingredients will not be spoilt or damaged. Natural materials such as wood, bamboo or earthenware and stoneware are preferred since they provide a gentle touch on fresh ingredients and absorb extra moisture.

If your kitchen is well equipped with a few basic essential tools, such as a variety of sharp knives and a cutting board, along with a good selection of Western utensils, you really do not need to add anything special to cook Japanese food. Nevertheless, some traditional Japanese utensils, such as the grater, would be useful additions. Many of the utensils shown here are now available at high-quality kitchenware shops, as well as at specialist Japanese shops.

KNIVES

For the Japanese, knives are the cook's heart and soul; professional chefs must have their own and they move with them from job to job. There are well over 20 types of knives used in a professional kitchen, but an ordinary household set is not too different from that of a very good Western one, with the exception of a special

Japanese cutting styles

Ingredients need to be cut into sizes and shapes suitable for eating with hashi (chopsticks). There are a number of cutting shapes that can be used in Japanese cooking, and each has its own specific name. Some examples of different cutting shapes are: sengiri (shreds); wagiri (rounds); arare (dice); hangetsu (half-moons); tanzaku (oblong and thin); sainome (cubes); sasagaki (shavings); and hanagiri (flowers). The hyoshigi (clapper shape) cut is rectangular and thick, and is suitable for fairly dense vegetables. To achieve the correct shape, the appropriate knife must be used.

BELOW: *Japanese knives, from front, vegetable knife, sashimi knife, cleaver and all-purpose knife. These knives are all made from one piece of carbonized steel with the maker's name engraved on the blade shoulder.*

Wagiri

Sengiri

Hyoshigi

sashimi knife, which is about 30cm/ 12in long with a 2.5cm/1in wide sharp blade.

Many Japanese knives have a single sharp edge on one side of the blade only so they are thinner than most Western equivalents. A standard set of knives consists of a thin blade for vegetables; a cleaver for large fish, meat and poultry; a *sashimi* knife for slicing fish; and a small knife for peeling and chopping. Look for the maker's name on the blade shoulder as a sign of quality before buying.

SHARPENING STONE
Maintaining well-sharpened knives is an important role of the cook, and Japanese chefs take as great care in selecting grinding stones as in choosing good knives. Natural stone is the best quality and professionals sharpen knives using three stones with varying

ABOVE: *Porcelain and aluminium graters.*

degrees of density: coarse, medium and dense. However, if you do not carry out the sharpening process properly, you can easily spoil knives, so many people in Japan use professional sharpeners.

KATSUO-BUSHI SHAVER
A block of dried skipjack tuna is one of the very basic foodstuffs found in Japanese cooking, since its flakes are the main ingredients for making dashi stock, and the sound made by housewives shaving katsuo-bushi traditionally greeted families most mornings. Today,

however, flakes in packets are popularly used. The shaver comprises a plane on top of a box and the shaved flakes drop through into a drawer underneath.

GRATER
If you are going to choose just one Japanese utensil, the oroshi-gane or daikon-oroshi (fine-toothed daikon grater) is definitely the one. There are various types and materials vary, including aluminium and porcelain, but they are all basically a flat surface with numerous fine spikes on it.

The most convenient grater is made of aluminium and has a small curved base at the end of the spikes, a useful feature that catches the juice that may be exuded during grating. Japanese cooking uses a lot of grated daikon and fresh root ginger, and both the grated flesh and the juice are used in the recipes. Most graters usually have an area with finer spikes for grating spices such as wasabi.

LEFT: *Shaver and block of katsuo-bushi (dried skipjack tuna).*

CUTTING BOARD

If you cut ingredients properly you are assured of success in Japanese cooking, and the cutting board becomes your stage. The Japanese word for chef, *itamae*, means literally "before the board", and no Japanese cooking is done without a board. Boards should be washed thoroughly after use and different ingredients, particularly raw fish and meat, should never be placed on a board at the same time. Use coloured boards for different ingredients: red for meat, blue for fish and green for vegetables.

BAMBOO WHISK

When preparing tea for the Japanese tea ceremony, matcha, a high-grade, bright light green powdered tea, is whisked with this special bamboo utensil, rather than brewed in a pot.

GRINDER AND PESTLE

The Japanese suribachi and surikogi (grinder and wooden pestle) grind to finer granules or paste than their Western counterparts, the mortar and pestle. The suribachi is made of clay in the shape of a large pudding bowl, with numerous sharp ridges on the inside surface so that ingredients as diverse as sesame seeds and minced (ground) meat or prawns can be ground into a paste. It then becomes a mixing bowl. A food processor may be easier for grinding larger ingredients, but small items, such as sesame seeds, are best prepared by hand using a suribachi and surikogi.

COOKING HASHI

Once mastered, hashi (chopsticks) will become an indispensable tool in the kitchen as well as on the table. From beating eggs to turning over smaller items of food in a frying pan, a pair of hashi is more convenient than a fork. Cooking hashi range in lengths from 25cm/10in to over 35cm/14in, and a pair may be tied together so that one won't become lost. The longest one for deep-frying keeps your hand away from hot oil.

WIRE-MESH GRILL

Japanese cooking was developed using wood and charcoal as fuel, so grilling over a fire – wood, charcoal or now, commonly, gas – is the usual cooking method. This simple, round wire mesh, called yakiami, is placed over the fire on which fish, meat or vegetables, or even tofu, are cooked. It is a very useful piece of everyday equipment, but the standard metal oven shelf will also serve the purpose.

SKEWERS

Metal and bamboo skewers make grilling easier and prevent food from breaking into bits while cooking. They are also useful for checking how food is cooking without making obvious holes in it. Skewers come in various sizes.

BELOW: *A bamboo whisk is used to prepare the tea during the traditional tea ceremony.*

BOTTOM: *Metal and bamboo skewers come in a variety of sizes.*

BELOW: *Suribachi (grinder) and surikogi (wooden pestle).*

When food is served on the skewer, such as *yakitori* (grilled chicken) or *dengaku* (grilled tofu), bamboo is used, since it not only looks better but is also easier to handle than hot metal. Small flat bamboo skewers are useful for soft ingredients such as tofu, preventing them from slipping during cooking.

STRAINER

The Japanese mesh strainer, or zaru, which is made of bamboo or stainless steel is extremely effective, as it can be used to strain even tiny grains of rice and very fine noodles.

PAN AND DROP-IN LID

The traditional Japanese pan, made of aluminium or copper, often has a finely indented surface so that it does not become too hot too quickly and so that the heat spreads evenly over the pan. A one-handled pan, called yukihira, will be useful for Japanese as well as other styles of cooking. Drop-in lids are very handy when you are cooking delicate ingredients, such as vegetables or tofu, which you do not want to move about in the pan. The light touch of the wooden lid, placed directly on the food in the pan, keeps it still on the base.

STEAMER

The Japanese use a steamer as often as Westerners use an oven. It is an ideal utensil for gently cooking fresh ingredients in a way that will not diminish their nutritional content or damage their shape. The traditional Japanese steamer does not look any different from the ones now commonly available in the West except that it comes with a removable base pierced with holes, which is perched in the pan. Choose the widest type that you can find.

If you do not have a steamer, it is possible to improvise with a wok and trivet. Place the trivet in the wok, fill the wok one-third full of water and bring to the boil. Place the food in a heatproof bowl on the trivet, cover the wok with the dome-shaped lid and steam the food until it is cooked.

SIEVE

Uragoshi, the Japanese sieve, consists of a wooden round frame 20cm/8in in diameter and 7.5cm/3in deep, with very fine horsehair, stainless steel or nylon mesh. It is used to sift flours and to strain wet food, by placing it upside down on a plate and pushing the food through the mesh with a wooden spatula. Horsehair is prone to splitting when too dry, so soak the sieve in water before use except when sifting. After use wash carefully, and remove the mesh from the frame and store separately. For stainless steel and nylon mesh, dry thoroughly.

OMELETTE PAN

Tamago-yaki-nabe (the Japanese omelette pan) is only used for making *tamagoyaki* (rolled omelette). There are many sizes and shapes, but the best one is made of copper, plated inside with tin. Though handy, the straight-sided pan can be replaced by a frying pan. Carefully trim the edges of the cooked egg to make a rectangular shape.

RIGHT: *Traditional Japanese pan with a wooden drop-in lid used when cooking delicate ingredients, such as tofu.*

RIGHT: *A Japanese omelette pan used to make rolled omelettes.*

Utensils for rice

Rice is the staple grain of Asia, which is over half the world's population. In Japan, evidence of its production dates back to the 2nd century BC. It is not exaggerating to say that rice is at the heart of Japanese cuisine. Not surprisingly, there are utensils designed for the cooking and use of rice.

RICE COOKER

Traditionally in Japan rice was cooked over a real fire, usually wood, in an o'kama, a cast-iron pot with a round base and a tutu-like skirt around the pot that kept the heat to the lower part of the pan. Once cooked, the rice was transferred to an o'hitsu, a deep wooden container with a lid, from which the rice was served. This process has now been replaced by the electric cooker, which can keep the rice warm all day. The older generation, however, still yearns for, and much prefers rice that has been cooked over a wood fire, and the ultimate aim of electric rice cooker manufacturers is to appeal to this market and to recreate the taste of wood-fire cooked rice as closely as possible.

RICE KEEPER

The wooden o'hitsu used to be an object every household possessed, but since the introduction of electric rice cookers, which cook and keep rice warm in the one unit, it is more often simply a fashionable addition to modern kitchens or dining rooms. After cooking, rice is transferred to

BELOW LEFT: *Electric rice cookers are useful as they keep the rice hot all day.*

BELOW RIGHT: *A sushi tub is used to mix cooked rice with vinegar for sushi.*

it and, after serving, the remaining rice is kept in it. The wood may not keep the rice warm all day as the electric cooker does, but it does absorb extra moisture and keeps the rice pleasantly moist.

RIGHT: *Lacquered and wooden spatulas.*

SPATULA

Héra or shamoji (the wooden spatula) is probably the most indispensable utensil in a Japanese household. It is often used as a symbol representing the entire household (at such occasions as housewives' protests against rising household costs). There are now many types of Japanese rice spatulas, including bare wood or lacquered ones. The spatula is used for aerating cooked rice and also for pressing wet food through a sieve on to a plate.

SUSHI TUB

Handai, or hangiri (the sushi tub), is used to mix cooked rice with the vinegar mixture for sushi making. It is almost always made of Japanese cypress wood, which has the right porosity to absorb extra moisture. Soak the tub thoroughly in cold water before use. Just before mixing sushi rice, drain off the water well and wipe the tub with a cloth dampened with the vinegar mixture to avoid making the rice watery. After use, wash well with water and air-dry before putting away.

If you make sushi regularly a wooden tub is very useful, not only for mixing rice but also for serving. An ordinary large mixing bowl may not absorb moisture as a Japanese sushi tub does but it is certainly an acceptable substitute if you make sushi rice only occasionally.

SUSHI MAT

Makisu (a bamboo stick mat) is increasingly found in many Western households due to the popularity of sushi. It is a necessary item for making *nori-maki* (nori-rolled sushi),

ABOVE: *Sushi mats are made with flat or round bamboo sticks.*

but is also used for other purposes, such as squeezing water out of cooked salad vegetables before they are dressed. There are basically two types of makisu: one, measuring about 22 x 20cm/9 x 8in, and made of bamboo sticks with a pale green, shiny, flat side, is for sushi rolling; the other, a little larger in size, which has triangular or round bamboo sticks threaded together, is for making a pattern of lines on the roll, as when preparing *tamagoyaki* (thick egg omelette). After use, carefully wash away any food stuck between the sticks, wipe and leave to dry completely before storing.

WOODEN MOULD

The rectangular wooden mould is for making *oshi zushi*, pressed sushi. This, like the sushi tub, should be soaked well in water before use. Wet the mould before packing with fish and *su-meshi*. Cover with the lid and press tightly or place a weight such as a book on it. Other moulds are also used to shape cooked rice for party canapés or children's lunch boxes.

METAL MOULD

This double-layered mould is a very useful tool for setting mousse or tofu as well as liquids such as kanten, a gelling agent made from seaweed.

BELOW: *Wooden sushi mould.*

BELOW: *Wooden sushi mould for shaping rice into individual canapés.*

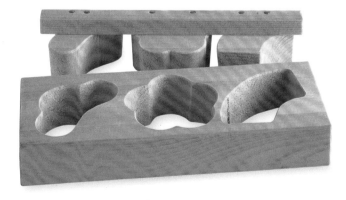

Rice

Since prehistoric times rice has been grown and eaten in Japan, and because of its rich content of vegetable protein, carbohydrate, vitamins and minerals, it quickly became popular. Numerous by-products such as sake, mirin, vinegar and miso have also been derived from rice.

URUCHIMAI

The short grain Japanese variety, *Oryza sativa japonica*, as opposed to the neighbouring South-east Asian countries' long grain, *jawa* and *indica*, was developed over the centuries to suit the climate as well as the taste of the Japanese people. Once cooked, it becomes quite tender and moist but firm enough to retain a little crunchiness. There are over 300 different types of short grain rice grown all over Japan in water-filled paddy fields; brand names such as Koshihikari and Sasanisiki are among the most popular.

GENMAI

There are degrees of polishing in rice production, and genmai, brown rice, is the least polished type. It retains its bran and germ and only the husk is removed. It is the most nutritious rice, and is high in fibre, but it takes a lot longer to cook than white rice and is very chewy. Genmai is widely available at health food stores and Asian stores.

MOCHIGOME

This short, opaque grain, also known as glutinous rice, makes a very sticky, dense rice when cooked. It has a high sugar content and is often steamed rather than boiled, then pounded to make mochi (rice cakes) and senbei (rice biscuits). Mochigome is also an important ingredient for making mirin (sweet rice wine), which is used only in cooking. It is an ingredient in many Japanese sauces such as teriyaki.

BELOW: *Some popular examples of Japanese short grain rice, clockwise from left, Kahomai, Maruyu, Minori, Kokuho, Mochigome and Nishiki.*

ABOVE: *Genmai, brown rice.*

Preparation and cooking

When cooking Japanese rice it is imperative that it is washed first in cold water and then left to drain, ideally for an hour but at least for 30 minutes. If time is limited, soak the rice for 10–15 minutes in plenty of water, then drain. When the rice is well moistened it will turn a soft opaque colour. Generally, 200g/7oz/1 cup rice is needed for two people.

The width, depth and material of the pan used will also make a difference to the end result. One of the best ways to get consistently good results is to use an electric rice-cooker.

Mochigome (glutinous rice) should be soaked overnight then steamed for 35–40 minutes. A bamboo steamer is best so that the grains can be spread thinly. If boiling, use 20 per cent of mochigome in a mix with ordinary rice.

Genmai should also be soaked for a few hours, ideally overnight; it should then be boiled with twice as much water and cooked for three times as long as ordinary rice.

Making sushi rice

Su-meshi (vinegared rice) is the base for all kinds of sushi and the rice must be correctly cooked. As a guide, to make *hoso-maki* (thin nori-rolled sushi), 350g/12oz/1¾ cups short grain rice should make six rolls (about 36 pieces), which is enough for four to six people.

1 Cook the rice following the method below. For extra flavour, add a 5cm/2in square of konbu (dried kelp) to the pan, removing before the water reaches boiling point.

2 In a measuring cup, mix 45ml/ 3 tbsp Japanese rice vinegar (or white wine vinegar), 37.5ml/7½ tsp sugar and 10ml/2 tsp sea salt to the rice. Stir well until they have dissolved.

3 Transfer the cooked rice to a wet wooden sushi tub or a large mixing bowl, and sprinkle the vinegar mixture evenly over the rice. Using a wooden spatula, fold the vinegar mixture into the rice; do not stir. Leave to cool before using to make sushi. Top sushi chefs spend years perfecting the techniques for making sushi rice.

Cooking Japanese rice

1 Wash the rice thoroughly in cold water, changing the water several times until the water runs clear, then drain the rice in a fine mesh strainer and set aside for 1 hour.

2 Put the rice in a deep pan and add 15 per cent more cold water than rice (for 200g/7oz/1 cup rice you will need about 250ml/8fl oz/1 cup water). The water level should not be more than a third from the base of the pan.

3 Cover the pan with a tight-fitting lid, then place over a high heat and bring to the boil; this may take 5 minutes. Turn the heat to the lowest setting and leave to simmer gently for 10–13 minutes, or until all the water has been absorbed.

4 Remove the pan from the heat and set aside, still covered with the lid, for about 10–15 minutes before serving.

Shaping Japanese rice

When making individual *su-meshi* blocks don't worry if the blocks don't look very neat. To make them perfectly requires at least two years' practice in a sushi restaurant kitchen.

To shape Japanese rice, make everything wet – from your hands to the mould, if using – and keep the work surface tidy at all times. Use both hands to squeeze the rice into a densely packed shape.

Using moulds

When making moulded sushi, one option is to use small plastic moulds, which are easily available. Otherwise line an eggcup with clear film (plastic wrap), push a topping in, add a dab of wasabi paste, then fill with *su-meshi*. Seal the end with the clear film and press with your fingers. When ready, remove from the eggcup and unwrap from the clear film.

Storage

Rice tastes best when newly harvested, and then it gradually deteriorates. Although it keeps for a long time, it is best eaten as soon as possible. Transfer raw rice to an earthenware, ceramic or plastic container with a lid and keep it in an airy, cool place away from direct sunlight. Keep rice perfectly dry; if the moisture content creeps up, the rice will soon turn mouldy. In the West rice is powdered with preservatives, hence its longevity.

Mochi with cheese and nori seaweed

This quick and easy snack is a tasty introduction to mochi.

1 Slice some Cheddar cheese a little smaller than the mochi cakes and about 5mm/¼in thick.

2 Grill (broil) the mochi cakes on each side under a medium heat for 2–3 minutes, turning them frequently to prevent burning. While the grilled mochi are still hot, make a horizontal slit at the side of each one and insert a cheese slice.

3 Cut an 18–20cm/7–8in nori sheet into four to eight pieces and wrap one piece around each of the mochi cakes before serving with a little shoyu.

ABOVE: *Shiratama flour is mainly used for making wagashi (Japanese cakes) and sweet dumplings for desserts.*

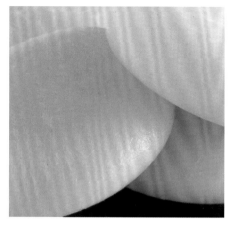

ABOVE: *Mochi (rice cakes), made from mochigome rice, are traditional fare for New Year's Day.*

ABOVE: *Nuka (rice bran) is most valued for its strong flavour and is a good base for pickling vegetables.*

RICE PRODUCTS

It is no surprise that the Japanese have developed various products out of rice and that these, in turn, have found a secure place in Japanese cooking.

Shiratama

This flour is comprised mostly of starch taken from mochigome (glutinous rice), which is first soaked in water, then sieved and dried. Shiratama is mostly used to make wagashi, which are Japanese cakes, and sweet dumplings.

Mochi

The main product of mochigome (glutinous rice) is mochi (rice cakes). Mochi cakes were once made by hand. The cooked rice was pounded until smooth, then shape and dried into a block then cut into shapes and fried, grilled (broiled) or boiled. Mochi can be made at home, but excellent ready-made cakes are available.

Domyoji

Mochigome rice is finely crushed to produce this flour, which is generally used for making wagashi (Japanese traditional cakes) and sometimes for cooking, usually in steamed dishes.

Nuka

This rice bran is traditionally used for pickling vegetables. The rice bran is first lightly roasted to bring out its flavour, then mixed with brine to make a mash, which ferments and makes a unique pickling base.

BELOW: *Sticky red rice is served in fresh edible oak leaves.*

Noodles

Certainly among the most popular foods in Japan, noodles are one of the oldest, most widely eaten foods in all of South-east Asia, if not in the world. Noodle stores are dotted along every high street all over Japan and Japanese noodles are also becoming very popular in the West.

SOMEN

These are very fine noodles which are made from wheat, but the dough is stretched with the help of vegetable oil to make very thin strips and then air-dried. There are two regions famous for their exceptional somen in Japan – Miwa in Nara and Ibo in Himeji – and the somen they produce takes only 1 minute to cook so a meal can be ready in a matter of minutes.

SOBA

This uniquely Japanese noodle is made of buckwheat flour mixed with ordinary wheat flour (which acts as a smoothing, binding agent). The colour of soba noodles ranges from dark brownish grey to light beige, and there is even a green-coloured soba, called *chasoba*, to which powdered tea has been added. The finest soba comes from Shinshu, the mountain area of central Japan. Fresh soba is available in Japan and most of the good soba shops make their own every day. It's also common to see a *soba-ya* (noodle store) every 10 yards or so on any high street in Japan, serving fresh soba, and other popular noodles. Cold soba noodles are often eaten in summer and served on a bamboo tray with a dipping sauce. The Japanese love the taste of the noodles themselves; the sauce enhances their flavour. Outside of Japan, prepacked dried soba is sold in bundles of fine strands at larger supermarkets and Asian stores, and is also available in packet form.

LEFT: *Dried somen noodles are available in packet form or in bundles.*

RIGHT: *Fine buckwheat soba noodles and green chasoba noodles, which get their distinctive colouring from the addition of powdered tea.*

UDON

This is a thick wheat noodle, which is eaten all over the world and probably has the longest history of all the noodles. To make udon, wheat flour is mixed with salted water to make a dough, then rolled out and thinly sliced. Fresh, raw udon is available in Japan but in the West it is usually either dried or cooked and frozen to be sold in packets.

Dried udon will keep for a few months if sealed in the packet and stored in a cool place. If using fresh udon then store in the refrigerator for a few days.

Cooking dried noodles

Dried noodles keep for months in an airtight container, so are ideal to keep in the store cupboard if you need a meal that is quick and easy to cook.

1 Bring plenty of water to the boil in a large pan and add the noodles. For each person use about 115g/4oz dried noodles cooked in at least 600ml/1 pint/2^{1}/$_{2}$ cups water.

2 Cook the noodles over a medium heat following the instructions on the packet. It normally takes up to 5–6 minutes for soba, 10–13 minutes for udon, 1–3 minutes for somen and hiyamugi, and 5–8 minutes for ramen. Lower the heat if the water boils over.

3 When the noodles are half transparent, they are done. Remove the pan from the heat, drain well and wash off all the outer starch under cold running water. Drain again and serve the noodles in hot soup or with a dipping sauce.

BELOW LEFT: *Soba noodles from Shinshu, central Japan, are considered to be the finest of all soba noodles produced.*

BELOW: *Dried and fresh udon noodles.*

LEFT: *Usually white, these hiyamugi noodles have occasional brown and pale pink strands.*

HIYAMUGI

These thin, white noodles are made in the same way as udon but cut very thinly. They take about 5 minutes to cook and are eaten in hot soup or with a dipping sauce. Dried and bundled hiyamugi is available in packets at Asian supermarkets.

RAMEN

Literally meaning stretched noodle, ramen originated in China, and is made of wheat flour with added eggs and what the Japanese call *kansui*, alkali water. The chemical reaction between them makes the wheat dough smooth and stretchable to create very fine noodles. Pure, naturally formed *kansui* is now hard to obtain and is often substituted with bicarbonate of soda (baking soda). Ramen is eaten with other cooked food with or without soup. Ramen is available fresh, dried or frozen at large supermarkets and Asian stores.

CULINARY USES

All Japanese noodles can be cooked in hot dashi-based soup with a few added ingredients, or eaten cold with a dipping sauce. Somen is a useful ingredient because of its white, almost hair-like fineness and is often used in clear soups or as a garnish. Ramen is always cooked in hot meat-based soup or eaten cold.

RIGHT: *Instant ramen noodles are usually sold with a flavoured soup sachet.*

GENERAL PREPARATION AND COOKING TIPS

Whether fresh or dried, all noodles need to be boiled, and this should be done carefully to prevent them becoming too soft. Follow the instructions on the packet. Cut a strand in the middle to check the noodles are cooked. If the noodles are to be eaten in hot soup, boil them until they are still a little hard. If they are to be eaten cold, cook thoroughly. Once boiled, wash off the outer starch under cold running water.

Japanese noodles except ramen are eaten simply, either on their own or with a few added ingredients and rarely with meat. Ramen tends to be cooked with meat-based ingredients.

Making handmade udon

MAKES 675G/1¹/₂LB

1 Sift 225g/8oz/2 cups plain (all-purpose) flour into a mixing bowl and make a well in the centre.

2 Dissolve 15ml/1 tbsp salt in 150ml/¹/₄ pint/²/₃ cup water, then pour liquid into the well in the centre of the flour. Using a wooden spoon, gently fold in until the mixture becomes a firm dough.

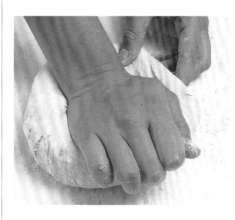

3 Turn the dough out on to a floured work surface and knead until it feels smooth but is still firm. Hit the dough hard with a fist at least 100 times to remove any air pockets. Cover with a damp cloth and leave for 2 hours.

4 Roll the dough out on a lightly floured work surface to make a rectangular sheet, 3mm/¹/₈in thick. Dust the pastry sheet lightly with flour, then fold one long side of pastry into the centre.

5 Carefully turn the pastry over, dust with flour again and fold the remaining third over the top. (If you look at the end of the folded dough, it will form an S-shape.) Fold the dough in half lengthways.

6 Using a sharp knife, cut the folded dough crossways into 3mm/¹/₈in thick strips. Separate the strands with your hands. The udon noodles can be frozen at this stage.

7 Bring plenty of water to the boil in a large, deep pan. Add the udon and cook for about 25–30 minutes, adding some cold water each time it starts to boil, until the noodles are thoroughly cooked but still slightly firm.

8 Drain the udon and wash well under cold running water to remove the outer starch from the noodles.

9 When you are ready to eat the udon noodles, you can either reheat them in a soup or quickly plunge them into a pan of boiling water. Drain the noodles well and serve with a dipping sauce of your choice.

COOK'S TIP

To check if the noodles are cooked, carefully cut a strip of udon and if the core of the cut face is turning from white to grey, then it's done.

To make a dipping sauce for cold udon, mix 2.5ml/¹/₂ tsp dashi, 45ml/3 tbsp shoyu and 15ml/1 tbsp mirin or 10ml/2 tsp sugar with 120ml/4fl oz/¹/₂ cup hot or cold water. Stir well and divide the sauce into individual serving cups. Serve with cold udon and some chopped spring onion and grated ginger.

Vegetables

In recent years an increasing number of exotic vegetables and fruits have been introduced to the West, and many Japanese varieties are now available, which makes cooking a lot easier.

As this style of cooking is largely vegetarian oriented, due to Buddhist traditions, the best way to wash, cut and cook each vegetable was painstakingly developed in order to retain its natural flavour and texture. The following are some of the typical vegetables eaten in Japan.

DAIKON

This long, white, dense vegetable, also known by the Indian name mooli, is a member of the radish family. Used widely in Japanese cooking, it is one of the oldest vegetables and its recorded use dates back to the 8th century. It is also one of the most versatile of vegetables: it can be cooked in soup, chopped for salad, shredded for a *sashimi* garnish or grated for use as a condiment. It is also made into *takuan*: bright yellow pickles often used for nori-rolled sushi.

As it is grown all over Japan all year round, there are numerous varieties with different shapes, sizes and hues. The one normally grown in the West (also most commonly available in Japan) is the green neck type, which has the fading pale-green part at the top of the main body.

Daikon keeps fairly well for a week or two in the fridge, but it is best used within three or four days.

Aroma and flavour

Daikon has an aroma similar to radish and a slightly pungent flavour which is not as bitter as radish. It can be eaten either cooked or uncooked, and is also useful for adding flavour when served as a condiment or in a dipping sauce. The raw texture is crunchy, and, when cooked, daikon becomes fairly soft but does not disintegrate.

Culinary uses

Daikon is used in Japanese cooking for its flavour and texture. If served raw, it is finely shredded and used as a crystal-white garnish for *sashimi*. The shreds mixed with carrot shreds make a good vinegared salad.

Daikon is also used for simmering in dishes with meat or poultry, since it withstands slow cooking, absorbs the flavour of other ingredients, and does not easily disintegrate. Various pickles are made with daikon, too.

Preparation and cooking

Select a firm daikon with a shiny, undamaged skin. When cut crossways, the cut surface should be smooth and watery. If the flesh has an opaque, snowflake-like spongy pattern, discard it. Always peel away the outer skin. Simmering daikon lets it absorb the flavour of other ingredients. When cutting daikon into slices or cylinders, shave off the top edges so that they will not cook first.

ABOVE: *Japanese cucumbers are smaller and thinner than Western varieties.*

BELOW: *Daikon, a member of the radish family, resembles a very large, long white carrot.*

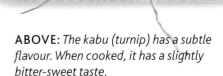

ABOVE: *The kabu (turnip) has a subtle flavour. When cooked, it has a slightly bitter-sweet taste.*

SATOIMO

This small, oval-shaped root is actually a potato, which originated in India. Satoimo is one of the oldest vegetables used in Japan and is also very popular in China. Underneath its hairy, striped, dark skin there is a unique slipperiness, which makes the vegetable very easy to peel. It is widely available at Asian food stores. If you cannot find satoimo, taro can be used as a substitute.

Aroma and flavour

Satoimo is a root vegetable that has a faint, potato-like aroma, but the flavour is much richer than ordinary potato and interestingly sweet and bitter at the same time. It also has a dense yet fluffy texture.

RIGHT: *Satoimo, a member of the potato family, has white flesh with a unique slippery coating under its hairy, striped skin.*

Culinary uses

Plain boiled or steamed satoimo, dipped in shoyu, is a popular snack in Japan. It is also an excellent vegetable to add to any simmered dishes, such as oden (a type of hotpot), and winter soups.

Preparation and cooking

To peel, boil the satoimo whole, then the hairy skin will come off easily. The flesh feels rather slimy; carefully wipe this film off with kitchen paper before using.

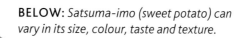

BELOW: *Satsuma-imo (sweet potato) can vary in its size, colour, taste and texture.*

SATSUMA-IMO

Originating in Central America, the sweet potato was introduced to Japan via Spain, the Philippines, China and Okinawa. It first arrived in Satsuma, the southernmost area of Japan, hence its Japanese name, meaning satsuma-potato.

There are numerous types of sweet potato even among the Japanese varieties. The colour of the skin varies from scarlet red to mauve, and the flesh varies from a rich yellow colour to dark mauve. The varieties available in the West are generally tougher and less sweet than Japanese ones. Sweet potato keeps for up to a week, if stored away from direct sunlight.

Aroma and flavour

It has a rich potato aroma and slightly sweet flavour.

Culinary uses

Sweet potato is most often used for simmered, steamed and fried dishes and is good for cooking on a barbecue. It can also be used as an ingredient in savoury cakes and desserts, and plain boiled or steamed satsuma-imo makes a tasty snack to accompany a drink, or it may be served with a selection of other nibbles (tsumami).

Preparation and cooking

As sweet potato contains a high percentage of water, it easily becomes over-soft and soggy if it is boiled. To avoid this, it is best to steam rather than boil sweet potato.

KABOCHA

This vegetable plays an essential part in Japanese cooking. Originally from Central America, this Japanese squash is the result of various crossbreedings over the last century. It has a dark green and ragged skin and is much smaller than Western squash varieties. The dense flesh is a rich yellow colour and, when boiled, becomes sweet and fluffy. Along with many other varieties of the squash family, it is now widely available.

Salt-steamed kabocha chips
This is a very nutritious snack.

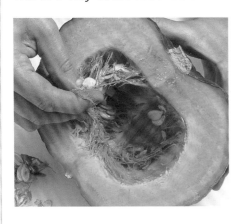

1 Lightly steam whole kabocha over a high heat for 5–6 minutes until the skin becomes soft enough to peel. Cut the kabocha in half, remove the seeds and scrape away the hard skin. Cut the flesh into bitesize chunks.

2 Return the chunks of kabocha to the steamer. Sprinkle with a pinch of coarse salt, cover and steam over a high heat for about 8–10 minutes. Remove from the pan and leave to stand for about 5 minutes.

Aroma and flavour
Kabocha has a mild chestnut aroma, and the flavour is also similar to, but not as sweet as, the chestnut. The texture is dense, similar to a moist sweet potato.

Culinary uses
To appreciate its delicate flavour, this vegetable is best simply steamed or boiled. It is also used for frying in tempura, as well as for simmering with other vegetables and chicken. The seeds are full of protein, and can be dry-roasted and eaten as a snack on their own or as a tasty accompaniment to drinks.

Preparation and cooking
This is a very hard vegetable and not easily cut. It is therefore advisable to lightly steam whole kabocha first in order to soften it slightly before cutting into large chunks. This is most easily done in a steamer, though a large pan will also suffice.

KURI

This Japanese variety of chestnut is grown throughout Japan and the southern Korean peninsula, and has a more triangular shape and smoother shell than the Chinese, European or American varieties. Kuri represents autumn and is a useful way to express the season in dishes for *kaiseki* (formal banquet) or tea-ceremony cooking. Apart from fresh kuri, peeled chestnuts are also available in cans, either cooked or uncooked.

Aroma and flavour
The transformation of kuri from its hard whitish raw state to a bright yellow jewel when cooked is quite striking. It is this golden yellow colour that makes it such a valued ingredient, along with its almost sesame-like aroma and subtly sweet, nutty flavour apparent in its cooked form.

ABOVE: *Kabocha has a dark and ragged green skin and the flesh can range from yellow to orange.*

Culinary uses

Kuri is one of the most useful and versatile ingredients found in Japanese cooking. It can be eaten just grilled (broiled) or boiled as a snack, or used as a means to express the season of autumn on hors d'oeuvres trays. It can also be mashed to make various sizes and shapes of sweet wagashi (Japanese cakes).

Kuri gohan (rice cooked with chestnuts) is one of the more popular dishes enjoyed by the Japanese each autumn. *Kuri kinton*, cooked and mashed kuri with added sugar made into a shiny sweet paste, is a much better version of ordinary kinto, which is made with mashed sweet potato and mirin, and is one of the many dishes eaten at the New Year's celebration meals.

Preparation and cooking

Fresh chestnuts must be soaked overnight before peeling. Make a slit in the shell before boiling or grilling (broiling) to make peeling easier. When peeling, remove the outer shell and the thin brown membrane attached to the flesh, otherwise it will taste bitter.

Storage

Whole chestnuts keep well for a few weeks. Once peeled, use immediately. Kuri are also available canned.

RIGHT:
Cooked sweet kuri (Japanese chestnuts).

Chestnut rice

With the golden colour of kuri (Japanese chestnuts) against the simple white of rice, this is a beautiful, as well as delicious, dish. Known as *Kuri gohan*, this is a well-loved traditional dish in Japan.

SERVES 4

**225g/8oz/generous 1 cup Japanese short
    grain rice**
**90g/3¹/₂oz fresh chestnuts, shelled
    and peeled, or 150g/5oz cooked,
    peeled chestnuts**
5ml/1 tsp sea salt
25ml/1¹/₂ tbsp sake or white wine
**10ml/2 tsp black sesame seeds,
    lightly toasted, to garnish**

1 Wash the rice, changing the water several times, until the water runs clear, then put the rice in a fine strainer, and leave for an hour.

2 Put the rice in a large, deep pan. If using fresh chestnuts, cut them in half and rinse in cold water. Drain the chestnuts and arrange them over the top of the rice.

3 Place the salt in a jug (pitcher) and pour in 300ml/¹/₂ pint/1¹/₄ cups water. Dissove the salt and add to the pan. Add some extra water, if it is necessary, to fully cover the rice and chestnuts. Pour in the sake or wine.

4 Cover and cook over a high heat for 5–8 minutes or until the mixture begins to bubble. Lower the heat and simmer for 10 minutes until the water is absorbed.

5 Leave to stand, still covered, for about 15 minutes, then gently mix the chestnuts into the rice. Try not to break up the chestnuts as you mix them in. Serve in individual rice bowls sprinkled with the black sesame seeds.

GINGKO NUT

The Japanese maple tree, *Icho*, bears the exquisite gingko nut, known as ginnan in Japan. It is a favourite delicacy and is traditionally served with sake. The word gingko or ginkgo is a corruption of ginkyo, another Japanese name for the maple tree. Gingko nut is available either fresh in its shell, shelled in packets, or shelled and cooked in cans or jars. A dried variety is also available.

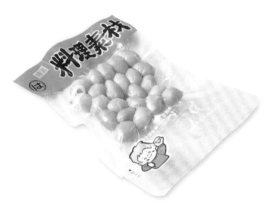

ABOVE: *Gingko nuts (here in a vacuum pack) are prized for their delicious flavour.*

Aroma and flavour

Gingko nut has very little aroma but has a fairly prominent milky flavour with a hint of bitterness, which adds vivid freshness to simmered dishes.

Culinary uses

Fried or lightly roasted gingko nuts sprinkled with salt are often served as an hors d'oeuvre. They can also be used for fried and simmered dishes, and in soups.

Preparation and cooking

To break the hard shell, place the nut with the join part vertically on a chopping board and bang on top with a rolling pin. The thin brown membrane should be removed, and the nuts blanched before use in any dish. The best method is to boil the nuts in just enough water to cover them and rub off the thin brown membrane with the back of a ladle. If dried gingko nuts are being used, they need to be soaked in water for several hours before use. Drain before adding to soups and simmered dishes.

HAKUSAI

Although its origin can be traced back to the Mediterranean, Chinese leaves (Chinese cabbage) is grown mainly in East Asia around China, the Korean peninsula and Japan. The Japanese variety, hakusai, meaning white vegetable, is a winter vegetable. It is larger and the outer leaves are greener than Chinese leaves, which is now widely available in the West.

Tightly wrapped, this vegetable will keep well in the fridge for quite a long time. A few leaves can be removed at a time for up to two weeks.

Aroma and flavour

Hakusai has a faint, fresh aroma and a very subtle cabbage flavour. The main quality of this vegetable is neither its aroma nor flavour but its crunchiness and versatility when cooked. As it absorbs the flavour of other ingredients, it is almost always cooked with meat, poultry, fish and other vegetables in a strong sauce.

Culinary uses

Salted hakusai is one of the usual dishes served to accompany plain cooked rice at the Japanese breakfast table. It is also used in simmered dishes, hotpots and steamed dishes: when cooked, the green part becomes more vivid and bright, and the white part translucent.

The straight, white trunk becomes flexible when cooked, so it can be rolled either on its own or with spinach, often with minced (ground) meat, poultry or fish stuffed inside, and then simmered.

Preparation and cooking

Trim the base, then separate the leaves and wash thoroughly. The white part is very crunchy when raw, but when cooked it quickly becomes soft and stringy and not very easy to chew. So, always cut the leaves crossways against the fibre into bitesize pieces.

ABOVE: *When purchasing hakusai (Chinese cabbage), choose densely clinging, tall round ones with curly green, crisp leaves.*

HORENSO

Originating in Western Asia, spinach can be classified into two main types: Eastern and Western. The Eastern variety was brought to Japan from China in the 16th century and commonly has a triangular, zigzag-edged leaf, which is pointed at the top, and a scarlet root. Western varieties have a rounder leaf.

Aroma and flavour

Japanese spinach has a rich grass aroma and a sweet flavour with a hint of bitterness, particularly in the soft lower stem.

Culinary uses

The most popular use for horenso in Japanese cooking is *ohitashi* (cooked salad with dashi stock). Lightly cooked spinach is also tossed with seed and nut dressings.

Preparation and cooking

Wash thoroughly before use as spinach grows touching the ground and earth gets inside the stems. Always lightly boil first, to get rid of the slight bitterness, except those young spinach leaves that can be used in a salad.

NEGI

This giant spring onion (scallion), which is 30–50cm/12–20in long and 1–2cm/^{1}/$_2$–^{3}/$_4$in in diameter, is a unique Japanese vegetable and, even in Japan, is generally available only in the Tokyo area and eastern Japan. It may look like a slim leek, but the texture is a lot more delicate, rather like that of the spring onion, and it does not have a hard core like the leek. Although the long white part in preference to the green part is mainly used for Japanese cooking, the mineral and vitamin contents are much greater in the green. It can be found in Asian supermarkets.

As with the spring onion, the green part starts to wilt and change colour within about two days even in the fridge but the main white part keeps fairly well for up to three days.

Aroma and flavour

Negi has a pungent aroma and also a strong onion flavour.

Culinary uses

In Japanese cooking this vegetable is mainly used finely chopped and added to sauces or soups as a herbal condiment. It gives a fresh, pungent final touch and a decorative look to plain shoyu or hot miso soup.

It is used for grilling (broiling), in particular with *yakitori* (skewered grilled chicken).

Preparation and cooking

Wash well and trim the base of the stem. Negi should be cooked lightly, as when it is overcooked it has an unpleasant slimy texture. For sauces and soups, it is normally very finely chopped. For hotpots, cut crossways diagonally. For grilling in recipes such as *yakitori*, cut straight across into 3–4cm/1^1/$_4$–1^1/$_2$in pieces.

BELOW: *At the top is horenso, a Japanese spinach, which is used in cooked salads. Negi (below) is a giant spring onion.*

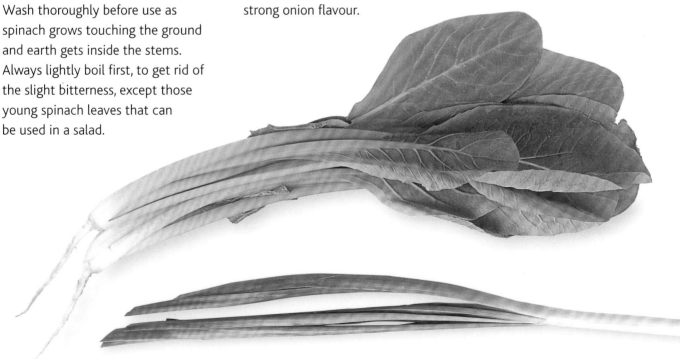

Making spring onion curls

The white part of a spring onion, finely shredded, is used to garnish *sashimi*; the curled shreds, which resemble silver hair, are a good alternative to daikon shreds.

1 Choose small, slim spring onions. Trim off most of the green leaves to leave a 7.5cm/3in length.

2 Shred the spring onions lengthways to within about 1cm/½in of the root end. Take care not to cut through the root completely.

3 Place the shredded spring onions in a small bowl of iced water and chill for 15–20 minutes, or until the shredded ends have curled.

RAKKYO

This bulb vegetable originated in the Himalayas and China. It grows in a bunch of six to seven small, thin oval-shaped bulbs, about 7.5cm/3in long. The body is milky white or with a faint purple hue.

It is picked young, with each bulb weighing 2–5g/¹⁄₁₆–¹⁄₈oz, but some grow to 10g/¹⁄₄oz after a year. Rakkyo is available in Japanese markets from late spring to early summer, when many households make rakkyo pickles to last throughout the year. When in season, it is available in Asian stores.

Like onions, the central core of rakkyo starts growing a green shoot after a while, and eventually the whole bulb dries out. It is best to pickle it immediately after its purchase.

Aroma and flavour

Rakkyo is the Japanese equivalent of garlic; eat just one and the odour will linger on your breath for the rest of the day. It has an intense onion smell with a hint of garlic. Apart from the smell, its flavour is too sharp to eat raw, but when pickled, the brine brings out the high sugar content, which makes it not only more palatable but an ideal addition to hot rice.

Culinary uses

Rakkyo is almost always pickled, either in brine, in sweet vinegar or marinated for a shorter time in shoyu. It is served with rice or Japanese curry.

Preparation and cooking

Trim the root and the top, and then wash the rakkyo under cold running water. If the rakkyo is young, pickle it immediately in brine; otherwise blanch quickly in boiling water and then marinate in shoyu. It will be ready to eat after a week. The longer rakkyo is marinated the milder the taste becomes, but the smell persists.

BELOW: *Rakkyo has a very intense flavour and is nearly always pickled, either in brine or vinegar, or marinated in shoyu and then served with rice.*

ABOVE: *Renkon's crunchy texture in cooked dishes is enjoyed by the Japanese.*

TAKENOKO

Bamboo shoot is one of the popular vegetables in South-east Asia and is widely available in cans. The Japanese cherish the fresh young shoots, which are inevitably a very seasonal delicacy, as they are only available from late spring to early summer.

The Japanese make use of the outer, hard brown barks for wrapping sushi or other rice-based lunches. Takenoko is also available pickled as *menma*, and cooked in jars and cans. It can also be found in a dried form in Asian supermarkets.

Aroma and flavour

Fresh takenoko has a very subtle, earthy aroma and a delicately bitter flavour, which improves with age. Whatever its age, the vegetable is capable of absorbing flavour from the sauce it is cooked with, while retaining its own taste.

Culinary uses

In Japanese cooking, takenoko is usually slowly simmered, so that its delicate flavour will not be spoiled. Simply cooked fresh bamboo shoots in dashi sauce is a popular dishes at Japanese restaurants. The young, tender shoot is also good for *takenoko gohan* (rice cooked with bamboo shoots); the older shoots are best for slow cooking with vegetables and chicken, or for stir-frying.

Preparation and cooking

The young shoot can be sliced into bitesize chunks and cooked at once, but older ones should be boiled first. For this use the milky water in which rice was washed, as the rice bran in the water reduces the shoot's bitterness. Canned bamboo shoots are ready cooked, so they just need to be rinsed and drained; dried bamboo shoots must be soaked in water before use.

LEFT AND BELOW: *Freshly peeled takenoko (left), takenoko bark (below left) and dried takenoko strips (below right) are three forms of the vegetable.*

RENKON

Although renkon refers specifically to the lotus root, the lotus plant itself has a long association with Buddhism and has long been a regular feature in temple ponds in Japan. The root has about four sections, and looks like a long, narrow balloon with a few knots. Although the outer skin is light beige, upon peeling it reveals a white, crispy flesh. Renkon has several vertical holes running through to the base.

Aroma and flavour

Renkon has very little aroma and flavour when raw.

Culinary uses

Renkon's crunchiness and unique pattern is appreciated in Japanese cuisine. It is used for tempura, sushi and for salads with vinegar dressing. It is always dressed or cooked with vinegar to bring out its sweetness.

Preparation and cooking

Trim the hard part from both ends and peel. Cut into rings. To avoid discoloration, plunge in vinegar and water. Cook in lightly acidulated boiling water. Do not use iron pans.

Fruit

From north to south, Japan covers vast latitudes and so is blessed with a variety of fruits, ranging from apples and pears in the north to various citrus fruits and the Japanese loquat in the south. Mikan, known as satsuma, is probably the most popular Japanese fruit in the West but kaki (persimmon) and nashi (pear) are also making their way into supermarkets in the West. The beautiful reddish colour of kaki makes it an attractive choice in cooking.

YUZU

Among the many varieties of citrus fruits used in Japanese cooking, yuzu, which has a sharp tangy flavour, is the most popular. It is about the size of a clementine with a firm, thick yellow skin and is in season throughout winter. Apart from culinary uses, yuzu is used in the bath in Japan; a hot citrus bath is good for your skin and for warming up your whole body. Yuzu is occasionally available in season from Japanese supermarkets, although lime can be substituted if yuzu cannot be found. A citrus flavouring called *ponzu* is made commercially to resemble the aroma of yuzu and is available in jars.

RIGHT: *Yuzu is about the size of a clementine and has a thick, yellow skin. Like a lemon, yuzu is too sour to eat alone. It is used to add a sharp piquant flavour to many dishes such as sauces and relishes.*

Aroma and flavour

Yuzu has a unique, sharp and strong, penetrating aroma, which makes it too sharp tasting to eat fresh. If a less tangy flavour is required, another fruit called sudachi would be chosen.

Culinary uses

Yuzu is mainly used for its exquisitely aromatic rind. Tiny pieces and slivers from the skin are scraped and used to garnish soups, salads, simmered dishes, pickles, relishes and desserts. Although the fruit is not edible, the juice can be used in salad dressings and dipping sauces. The whole outer skin, after the flesh has been removed, is often used as a cup in which to serve hors d'oeuvres.

Preparation and cooking

Using a very sharp knife, cut small pieces just before serving each time the yuzu is used. A few tiny pieces of the rind, up to 5mm/¼in in diameter, will be sufficient to garnish each dish.

FAR RIGHT: *Sudachi is a green fruit that resembles a lime. It is often used to garnish fish dishes such as sashimi. Lime can be used instead of sudachi.*

SUDACHI

This is another of the many varieties of citrus fruits used in Japanese cooking. Sudachi is a little smaller than yuzu, weighing 30–40g/1¼–1¼oz, and has a firm thick green skin and light yellow, moist flesh with relatively large seeds.

The juice of sudachi is not as sharp as that of yuzu, so it is used mainly to garnish *sashimi* (prepared fresh raw fish), and grilled (broiled) fish and hotpot dishes. The most notable combination, however, is with matsutake (pine mushroom) and the juice is always sprinkled over dishes such as lightly grilled matsutake or steamed matsutake teapot soup.

The rind is also finely grated and used as a flavouring for dipping condiments and sauces. Sudachi has a short season, appearing in late summer.

It is not well known in the wider world and is not normally available outside Japan. Sudachi has a zestier flavour and aroma than citrus fruits such as lime, or lemon, but either would make a good substitute.

APPLES

Originally from Central Asia, apples are some of the most common fruits grown all over the world: there are said to be more than 10,000 varieties. In Japan up to 1,500 types have existed in the country, though usually only about 20 varieties of apple are commercially grown. Modern varieties of apples are relatively new to Japan; they came from America in 1872. However, Japan has since developed many new varieties and is now exporting its own crossbreeds, such as Fuji, to the West. Japan has also developed varieties that contain what is called honey – a sweet, almost transparent part – found around the core. These types are not normally available outside of Japan.

Fuji is a cross between Kokko and Delicious and is regarded by some as one of the best apples in the world. It is juicy, yet the flesh is dense with a rich aroma and sweet flavour.

KAKI

Also known as Japanese persimmon, the kaki has been grown in Japan for centuries. There are as many as 800–1,000 varieties and those that are available in the West are normally fuyu or jiro. The kaki grows to about 10cm/4in in diameter and has a hard, smooth reddish orange skin and dense but crunchy flesh. It tastes very similar to Sharon fruit, one of the persimmon family. It has a regular, flower-like pattern at the core and can contain eight seeds although it is often seedless, which makes this fruit useful as a decorative garnish. Kaki fruit in a dish signifies autumn as its reddish colour is suggestive of autumn leaves. It is also used in dressed vegetable dishes and salads. There are some bitter varieties of kaki, which are not suitable for eating unprocessed and these are often dried like dates.

MIKAN

Known in the West as satsuma or mandarin, mikan grows in the warmer regions of Japan, particularly on the south and west coasts facing the Pacific Ocean. It is a winter fruit, which is one of the most juicy and sweetest of orange varieties and is also a good source of vitamin C and beta-carotene. Fresh mikan are widely available in the West, and it is also possible to buy canned, peeled whole mikan in syrup.

Aroma and flavour

Mikan has a faint citrus aroma and a sweet, juicy flavour.

Culinary uses

Apart from being eaten raw, mikan is used mainly as a dessert with kanten (agar-agar) or other fruits. After removing the flesh, the intact skin can be used as a cup in which to serve hors d'oeuvres.

ABOVE: *Japanese apples are much larger than Western types – these ones are about 10cm/4in in diameter.*

LEFT: *Kaki, the Japanese persimmon, whose arrival at market heralds the coming of autumn for the Japanese.*

NASHI

Simply meaning pear, nashi is a round, russet-coloured Japanese pear now widely available in the West. There are about ten Japanese or crossbreed varieties and popular ones include chojuro and nijusseiki. Since nashi contain 84–89 per cent water, they have a very watery, crunchy texture and are not noticeably sweet. They have an almost transparent flesh and can be used for jam but are mostly eaten raw as hors d'oeuvres or in salads.

ABOVE: *Smaller Western types of ichigo (strawberries) are now more popular in Japan than the traditional large variety.*

BIWA

The loquat originated in China, though it commonly grows in South-east Asia. The loquat is called biwa, after the guitar-like Asian instrument, which its oval shape resembles. Biwa bears yellowish orange, slightly dense fruits, the size of a small egg. and has a faintly acidic, not very sweet flavour and firm texture. When the fruit is ripe, it peels easily to reveal its smooth and shiny flesh.

In Japan, the loquat grows along the Pacific coast to Kyushu, the southern island, and is in season in early spring. It is generally consumed fresh, but because of its beautiful yellowish orange colour and small size, biwa is sometimes used decoratively as part of hors d'oeuvres trays to represent the arrival of spring. It is also sometimes used for desserts with jelly or kanten (agar-agar).

ICHIGO

First introduced by the Dutch traders in the middle of the 19th century, the strawberry is a relatively new addition to what is now a huge Japanese fruit industry. Many varieties from across the world, including the USA, England and France have been crossbred and Japan now produces various firm, sweet strawberries in differing sizes, such as Toyonoka and Joho. The huge, almost square shaped Fukuwa Ichigo, which was formerly the favourite in Japan, is now declining in popularity due to the influx of new varieties.

LEFT: *Nashi (Japanese pears) are mostly eaten raw in salads.*

UME

Also known as Japanese apricot, ume is one of the oldest fruits grown in Japan. There are about 300 varieties, which are roughly divided into two categories: flowering trees and fruit-bearing trees. Like an apricot, the pale green fruit turns yellow with reddish patterns on it when ripe. It grows to about the size of a golf ball and is harvested from June through to July. Ume is an unusual fruit since you are not supposed to eat it fresh. Not only is it too sharp to eat but the unripe fruit contains prussic acid at its core, which can cause stomach upsets. Instead, it is processed into umeboshi (salted and dried ume), jam, umeshu (ume liqueur) and is also used in confectionery.

Pickled ume or apricot

This is a simple method for pickling ume (or apricot), which retains the crunchiness of the fruit. A healthy dish, it is good eaten with rice.

MAKES ABOUT 1KG/2¼LB

1kg/2¼lb unripe ume or young small apricots

15ml/1 tbsp rice vinegar or white wine vinegar

115g/4oz/1 cup salt

shochu or brandy

1 Wash the ume or apricots and soak in plenty of water for at least 1 hour. Drain and pat dry with kitchen paper.

2 Trim the stem part using a cocktail stick (toothpick) and place the fruit in a freezer bag. Sprinkle the vinegar over the fruits, then add two-thirds of the salt. Holding the bag in one hand, roll the fruit around to distribute the salt evenly.

3 Put half of the remaining salt in a sterilized glass or other non-metallic bowl and add the contents of the freezer bag. Sprinkle the rest of the salt on top.

4 Using a cloth dampened with shochu or brandy, wipe the inside of the bowl, then cover the fruits with a shochu- or brandy-sprayed plate and place a clean 1.6kg/3½lb weight on top. Wrap the bowl, plate and weight with clear film (plastic wrap) and cover with a lid.

5 Leave to pickle for a week, during which time unwrap, take the weight off and shake the pan to spread the liquid around the fruits twice daily.

LEFT: *Ume can be salted and dried, or made into jams and liqueurs, and confectionery.*

Beans

As a major source of protein, beans have always been very important ingredients in Japanese cooking and, since the days of meat prohibition, Japanese people have developed numerous ways of cooking with them.

Daizu, known as soya bean in the West, features prominently in Japanese cuisine, as do black and green beans, which are part of the same family. Also as popular are azuki, also known as aduki, which first became known in the West as a health food. In Japan they are known as "king of the beans" and they are reputed to be good for the liver and kidneys, despite being used in cakes.

Other beans such as kidney, haricot (navy), broad (fava), Burma and lima, and peas such as green, cow, chick and pigeon, all play a part in the Japanese diet, and they can be used either fresh or dried.

SOYA BEANS

Originally from China, where they were once considered sacred, the soya bean may not play a star role in Japanese cooking, but it is the basis of the most important Japanese sauces, such as miso and shoyu, and, of course, tofu is made from it. There are numerous products all over the world that would not be the same without the use of soya beans for their flavour, texture, or simply as a binding agent.

Daizu, or soya bean, means big bean (as opposed to azuki meaning small bean), and there are three colours of the daizu family: yellow, green and black. Yellow soya beans, the most commonly used variety, are available at health food stores.

ABOVE: Two of the three colours of the soya bean family: yellow soya beans (left) and black soya beans (right).

Aroma and flavour

Soya beans have a distinctive roasted aroma, and a faint peanut-like flavour.

Culinary uses

The dried yellow beans are also called miso beans as their main use is for making miso. They are also used in the production of shoyu, natto (fermented bean) and tofu. The oil is useful for cooking, too. Soya beans can be simmered with other vegetables and chicken, or roasted to serve with drinks. Dried green beans are used for their colour in Japanese sweets (candy), and black beans are mainly used for simmered dishes.

Preparation and cooking

Except when intending to roast, dried beans should be soaked for 24 hours before cooking, then those that are still floating must be discarded.

SOYA BEAN PRODUCTS

There are numerous soya bean products, from powdered to fermented and tofu. As tofu products play an important part in Japanese cooking they are treated separately.

Kinako

This is a yellow soya bean flour, although sometimes green soya beans are used to make green kinako. Mixed with the same volume of sugar and a pinch of salt, kinako is rolled in lightly boiled, soft mochi cakes to serve as a snack. It is also used to make wagashi (Japanese cakes). This flour can usually be obtained from Japanese supermarkets.

LEFT: *Natto (fermented soya beans), packed in a straw pouch. They are normally sold, particularly in the West, in a plastic container.*

Natto

These fermented soya beans are rather smelly and slimy, and strange to the Western palate, but they go well with plain boiled rice.

AZUKI BEANS

Also known as aduki beans outside Japan, azuki (small beans) are probably the most popular Japanese variety of bean in the West. This bean has very high levels of starch (over 50 per cent), as well as protein and fibre, and some vitamin B1. It is regarded in Japan as a very healthy food.

There are various sizes of azuki beans, and they are available in a range of colours including red, green, yellow and white. Most commonly used is the red variety, mainly for cakes and desserts. The green bean (mung bean) is used to make harusame (bean vermicelli) and beansprouts are grown from it. Azuki are available at health food stores.

Aroma and flavour

Probably due to the high starch content, azuki beans have a sweet aroma and a chestnut-like flavour, so they are suitable for sweet recipes.

Culinary uses

Azuki beans can be simmered in sauce or cooked with rice to make *sekihan* (red rice) for celebrations, but they are mainly used for making *an*, which is a type of a sweet paste, for wagashi (Japanese cakes).

Preparation and cooking

Discard any damaged beans. For making sweet bean paste, soak the azuki beans in plenty of cold water for 24 hours before cooking, and discard any that remain floating. Do not soak the beans if you are making dishes where you wish to retain the shape, colour and aroma of the beans, such as for a decoration for a dessert.

EDA-MAME

In Japan, when fresh, young green beans in their hairy pods start appearing in the market, the people know summer has arrived. These beans are called eda-mame meaning branch beans as they are often sold still on the stalks. They are becoming popular outside Japan now. Fresh young green beans in the pod are delicious boiled and are often served whole as hors d'oeuvres. Keep refrigerated and use within a few days.

LEFT: *Green azuki beans, which are used to make bean vermicelli, and red azuki beans, which are used mostly in cakes and desserts.*

ABOVE: *Eda-mame (young green beans still in their pods).*

Tofu

One of the oldest processed foods of South-east Asia, tofu has become more widely appreciated in recent years due to health-conscious trends around the world. Tofu came to Japan from China in the 8th century and has been one of the most important foods ever since.

As with many other foods, the Japanese developed tofu to a more refined form, as well as producing many new by-products to suit the subtlety and delicacy of Japanese cooking. Tofu is mostly made commercially nowadays, but there are still small tofu-making businesses in many residential areas of Japan, making fresh tofu at dawn every day.

TYPES OF TOFU

Highly nutritious and low in fat and sugar, tofu is made from soya beans, which are first boiled and crushed, then the milk is separated and made into curds with the help of a coagulant. The warm curds are set in moulds for a few hours, then released into a water tank to firm and cool further. A cotton cloth is laid across the base of the moulds to retain the curds while they set and to allow excess water to drain away. Tofu made in this way often has a distinctive cloth mark on its sides and is known as regular tofu. This tofu is called momen-goshi (cotton-sieved tofu), as opposed to the more delicate, softer kinu-goshi (silk-sieved tofu – sold as silken tofu in the West), which is made with thicker milk and without draining the excess water. Both are creamy white in colour.

Japanese tofu, both fresh and in cartons, is available from Asian supermarkets in the West. There is also lightly seared tofu called yaki-dofu, which is available from Japanese shops and is mainly used in hotpot dishes. Other lesser-quality types of tofu are widely available from supermarkets.

Aroma and flavour

To the Japanese palate, little of the tofu available outside Japan has the real taste of tofu. Although some fresh tofu has a faint soya bean aroma and milky flavour, many varieties appear to be made of little more than milky water.

Culinary uses

Fresh tofu, silken tofu in particular, is best eaten as it is, cold or hot, with shoyu, chopped spring onion (scallion) and grated ginger, or in soups. The firmer cotton tofu is more suitable for cooking dishes such as *agedashi-dofu* (fried tofu in dashi sauce) and as tofu steaks. Tofu is also cooked with other vegetables, fish and meat, and used for making a white dressing for salads.

Preparation and cooking

Tofu is extremely fragile, so handle with care. Silken tofu is normally used as it is, but cotton tofu, if it is going to be fried or mashed to make a dressing, is normally pressed to squeeze out some water to make it a little firmer.

BELOW: *Clockwise from front left, soft or silken tofu, lightly seared tofu and regular, firmer tofu.*

KOYA-DOFU

Also known as kogori-dofu (frozen tofu), koya-dofu is believed to have been invented by Buddhist monks on the Koya mountain many centuries ago. It is a freeze-dried tofu, and is quite different from regular tofu in texture, colour, flavour and size.

Today, koya-dofu is often available in packets of five pieces together with a powdered soup stock in which to cook it. When purchased this way it simply requires cooking in the soup provided. This modern version is readily available.

Aroma and flavour

Koya-dofu has a much stronger soya bean aroma and richer flavour than cotton or silken tofu. The beauty of this spongy tofu is that, however long it is cooked, it does not disintegrate.

Culinary uses

Because of its spongy nature, koya-dofu absorbs flavours well, so it is used for simmering with vegetables in a rich soup.

Preparation and cooking

If the packet does not contain sachets of powdered soup, koya-dofu needs soaking in hot water for 5 minutes before cooking. However, most koya-dofu is now made so that it can be cooked immediately in the powdered soup provided in the packet.

RIGHT: *Abura-age (thin deep-fried tofu) is the most commonly used tofu in Japanese cooking and is available fresh or frozen.*

YUBA

This is the dried soya bean skin that forms on the surface of the soya bean milk during the tofu-making process. Sold in packets, it comes in various sheet forms, including flat, rolled and cut, or in thick strips, and is becoming more available from Japanese stores.

Aroma and flavour

Once cooked in soup, yuba gives out a warm soya bean aroma and has a rich, milky flavour with a crunchy texture.

Culinary uses

Yuba is used mainly in clear soups and simmered dishes. It is one of Kyoto's specialities and is often used in their version of the *kaiseki* (formal banquet).

Preparation and cooking

Soften yuba in tepid water for 5 minutes before cooking. Although it does not disintegrate, cook only very lightly.

FRIED TOFU

There are various types of fried tofu commercially produced and commonly used for home cooking in Japan. They are, like tofu, freshly made every day by neighbourhood tofu makers and sold like freshly baked bread. In the West some deep-fried tofu are also freshly made and sold refrigerated at Japanese supermarkets.

Mushrooms

The mushroom is a fungus whose developed offshoots grow in or under certain trees. In a relatively warm and wet country in which over 75 per cent of the land is covered by mountains, mushrooms grow in abundance and are used in everyday cooking.

Apart from the most popular ones, introduced below, there are the Japanese equivalents of European mushrooms such as hiratake (oyster mushroom family), maitake (hen of the wood), amigasatake (morel), amitake (boletus) and anzutake (chanterelle), as well as numerous regional seasonal varieties which are available locally.

BELOW: *Fresh shiitake mushrooms have a dark brown velvety cap and are ideal for grilling, frying or added to hotpots.*

FRESH SHIITAKE

Meaning tree (*shii*) mushroom, the shiitake is also known, incorrectly, as the Chinese mushroom, though it originated in Japan. Shiitake is a fungus that grows in the wild twice a year, in spring and autumn, under trees such as *shii* (*Pasania cuspidata*), oak and chestnut, though today it is also cultivated. It is recognized as a health food for its ability to reduce cholesterol in the blood.

Aroma and flavour

Fresh shiitake have a distinctive woody aroma and slightly acidic flavour. The mushroom has a soft, slippery texture, which adds an exquisite quality. When dried the flavour intensifies.

Culinary uses

The shiitake is one of the regular ingredients for hotpot dishes containing meat, usually beef, and vegetables, such as *shabu shabu* or *sukiyaki*. They can also be simply grilled over a barbecue or battered and fried for tempura.

Preparation and cooking

With a damp piece of kitchen paper wipe, rather than wash, off any earth and dirt, and trim off the hard part of the stem before cooking. When used whole, a decorative cross is often notched into the caps. Fresh shiitake can easily become too soft, so monitor the cooking carefully. Store fresh shiitake with the cap edges curled under, in the vegetable section of the refrigerator.

Grilled fresh shiitake with mustard

1 Wipe off the dirt from fresh shiitake with damp kitchen paper and use a small knife to trim off the hard parts of the stems.

2 Grill (broil) the mushrooms very lightly under a medium heat, or on a barbecue, for 1–2 minutes on both sides. Alternatively, heat a frying pan, add a little oil to just cover the base, and pan-fry the shiitake over a medium heat. Serve with mustard and shoyu.

Preparing dried shiitake

1 Quickly wash off any dirt from the mushrooms under running water and then soak in cold water. Dried shiitake must be soaked in tepid water for about 2–3 hours, or overnight, if you prefer. If you are short of time, you can soak for at least 45 minutes, with a little white sugar sprinkled over, before cooking.

2 Remove the shiitake from the soaking water, and gently squeeze out the water. Using your fingers or a knife, trim off the stem and then slice or chop the caps to use in cooking. Use the stems in soups. Don't discard the soaking liquid; rather drain through muslin (cheesecloth), then use in soups or for simmering.

DRIED SHIITAKE

When shiitake are dried, their aroma and flavour intensify; it is for this enriched fungus flavour, coupled with the convenience of using dried shiitake, that they are appreciated. There are many types and grades of dried shiitake available in packets, but the small, thick donko (winter mushroom) is the most highly rated. Dried shiitake last almost indefinitely if stored in an airtight plastic bag. They can also be frozen, which is a better way of retaining their flavour.

Aroma and flavour

Dried shiitake have a pleasantly strong, roasted aroma and intensified fungus flavour. The increased fibre content gives it more bite than fresh ones.

Culinary uses

In Japanese cooking, dried shiitake are usually cooked in a seasoned liquid, then used for dishes such as simmered vegetables with chicken, mixed sushi and soup noodles.

BELOW: *Various dried shiitake; on the far right are dried donko, which are considered the most flavoursome.*

ENOKITAKE

Also known as yukinoshita, meaning under the snow, this bundle of tiny berry-cap mushrooms with thin stems grows in the wild on the stumps of *enoki* (hackberry), poplar and persimmon trees in winter. Cultivated enokitake is often marketed outside Japan as a new nutritious salad ingredient to be eaten raw.

Aroma and flavour

Enokitake has a delicate, fresh flavour and a delightfully crisp texture.

Culinary uses

Enokitake are one of the regular ingredients for hotpot dishes, such as *shabu shabu*, and are also delicious in seasonal salads and in soups. They can also be eaten raw in salads.

Preparation and cooking

Cut off the spongy root of the mushroom, 2.5–5cm/1–2in from the bottom, and wash carefully. Use cooked or raw. They cook quickly, so do not overcook. Enokitake are the easiest mushroom to handle, and they give a refreshing character to dishes.

BELOW: *Cultivated enokitake.*

SHIMEJI

The shimeji is another popular Japanese mushroom and grows in autumn in bunches or in circles under trees such as *nara* (Japanese oak) and red pine. There are many varieties, but the most common has a light grey cap and grows to 2.5–10cm/1–4in in diameter. It is this variety that is most commonly available in the West from Asian supermarkets.

Shimeji keep for up to a week if stored in the vegetable compartment of the refrigerator. They can be stored dried, frozen and pickled.

ABOVE: *Shaka shimeji are a popular variety of shimeji due to their striking and distinctive appearance.*

BELOW: *Oyster mushrooms have a similar texture to shimeji, and can be substituted if the latter are not available.*

Aroma and flavour

The shimeji has little aroma and an undistinguished flavour. Rather than for its taste, the shimeji is valued for its fresh, meaty texture which is thought to be similar to that of oyster mushrooms.

Culinary uses

This mushroom's fresh and unassuming character suits most delicate Japanese cooking, such as *shimeji gohan* (rice cooked with shimeji), clear soup, and grilled (broiled) and fried dishes. It is also a popular hotpot ingredient.

Preparation and cooking

Trim off the spongy part about 2–2.5cm/¾–1in from the bottom and quickly rinse the shimeji under cold running water. Using your fingers, separate the stem and cook lightly.

Preparing shimeji

Wash or brush the mushrooms lightly with kitchen paper or a brush to remove any dirt particles. Cut off the hard base and separate any large blocks of fresh shimeji into smaller chunks with your fingers.

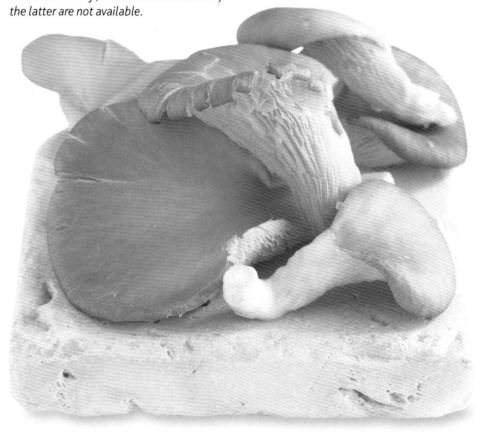

Seaweeds

The Japanese have been enjoying the bounty of their surrounding seas since ancient times, whether for fish, shellfish or seaweeds. Over 30 varieties of seaweeds plus the numerous products developed from them are regularly used in Japanese cooking. Most seaweeds contain iron, calcium, phosphorus and iodine and are rich in vitamins A and C.

KONBU

This giant kelp is an indispensable ingredient in Japanese cooking. It is used on its own and also provides a subtle flavour to numerous dishes as one of the basic ingredients of dashi (fish stock). It is rich in iodine, calcium and vegetable fibre.

Konbu grows in the northern seas off the Japanese coast, and Hokkaido, the northernmost island, is known as the biggest producer of dried konbu. There are many varieties of kelp; the size alone ranges from 5cm/2in to 30cm/12in wide and some

types of konbu grow to more than 20m/60ft long. They are all dried and graded, classified according to their uses, either for eating or for making dashi stock.

Dried konbu is also commercially processed to make numerous konbu by-products, such as cut konbu for savoury snacks and *tsukudani* (a slow-simmered savoury dish).

Aroma and flavour

Dried konbu has a distinctive ocean aroma and intense flavour. It has a pleasantly moist texture.

Culinary uses

The most important role dried konbu plays in Japanese cooking is in making dashi stock, together with katsuo-bushi (dried skipjack tuna flakes).

Preparation and cooking

Dried konbu is usually covered with a fine white powder, a natural by-product of the drying process. Do not wash or rinse off; instead, wipe with a piece of damp kitchen paper. In cooking, such as in soup or a hotpot, dried konbu sheet is made into decorative knots or rolled.

Use the konbu's soaking water in either a stock or in a soup.

LEFT: *Oboro konbu is a thin sheet that is used for wrapping rice.*

Knotting and rolling konbu

1 To knot konbu, soak a sheet of konbu in a bowl of tepid water until it is soft. Cut the softened konbu crossways into 16cm/6¼in sheets, then cut lengthways into 2–3cm/¾–1¼in wide strips. Carefully make a knot in the centre of each konbu strip and cook.

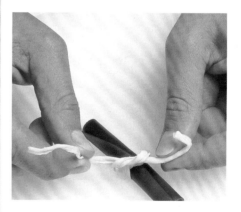

2 To roll knobu, cut a soaked konbu sheet crossways into 5cm/2in sheets and roll up tightly. A strip of carrot, an anchovy fillet, or thin strips of meat such as ham or sausage, can be rolled inside, if you wish. To secure the roll and prevent it from unravelling, tie neatly with a very thin strip of oboro konbu that has been soaked until soft.

NORI

The most famous seaweed product is nori, a dried paper-thin sheet of asakusa-nori, a laver, which is a small orange-brown, film-like marine algae. It grows up to 25cm/10in long and about 5cm/2in wide. The laver is washed in fresh water, laid in thin sheets and then sun-dried on bamboo or wooden frames.

Nori is rich in vegetable protein, vitamins and minerals. It is a packaged in a standard size of about 20 x 18cm/8 x 7in for rolling sushi, usually in packets of five or ten sheets. Mini nori sheets, about 8 x 3cm/3$\frac{1}{2}$ x 1$\frac{1}{4}$in are also available. These are used for wrapping rice, most notably served at a traditional breakfast, and some are ready-toasted or coated with a shoyu-based seasoning. Standard nori sheets are widely available from most large supermarkets and other types of nori can be found at Asian supermarkets.

Nori will keep almost indefinitely in an airtight bag placed in a container. Under no circumstances allow it to become moist.

Aroma and flavour

Although it has a light, smoky flavour, nori is mainly appreciated for its subtle ocean aroma. Dark, shiny nori has much more flavour than the cheaper reddish types.

Culinary uses

Nori is mainly used with rice for rolling sushi and wrapping *onigiri* (rice balls) and mochi (rice cakes). It can also be crumbled or shredded for use as a garnish on sushi or noodles.

Preparation and cooking

To bring out the aroma and make nori crispy, toast it on both sides before use by holding a sheet horizontally over a low heat. Move it about as you toast it so that it heats evenly. Watch it carefully as it will be very crisp within only 2–3 seconds. Do not grill (broil). One side of the nori sheet is shinier than the other, so when you make sushi, place the nori sheet shiny-side down on the makisu (sushi rolling mat) so the dull side is inside.

BELOW: *Nori sheets are ideal for making hand-rolled sushi.*

WAKAME

This is a brownish orange algae and grows up to 1–2m/3–6ft long on rocks under the sea from early winter through to early summer. Wakame is mostly dried or salted, and there are various types, sizes and grades of wakame readily available. Fresh wakame is available only in Japan, but processed wakame has been developed in recent years.

You can store dried wakame almost indefinitely in an airtight bag in a cool place away from direct sunlight.

Aroma and flavour

This seaweed has a delicate aroma and a very refreshing flavour. It is slightly slippery but has a pleasant vegetable crispness.

Culinary uses

Wakame is one of the most popular soup ingredients and is also delicious served as a salad with a vinegary dressing. It is often simmered with other vegetables.

Preparation and cooking

Dried wakame must be softened before use. If using a whole wakame with the stem intact, soak in tepid water for 15–20 minutes before cutting it out.

If using instant wakame, soak in plenty of water for about 5 minutes before use. Drain and pour boiling water over it, then immediately plunge into cold water. Some types of dried wakame can be put directly into the soup.

HIJIKI

Very popular among health-conscious eaters, hijiki is a twiggy black marine algae that grows up to 1m/3ft long all around the Japanese coast. It is full of vitamins, minerals, including calcium, and fibre, and contains no fat. Hijiki is cooked and dried, and sold in packets. It can be bought from Asian and Japanese grocery stores.

Aroma and flavour

Hijiki has little aroma and a faint ocean flavour. It also has a fairly tough texture.

Culinary uses

Hijiki is normally shallow-fried and then simmered in a shoyu-based sauce with other vegetables. It is often used with abura-age (fried thin tofu). It is also used to garnish rice dishes, such as mixed sushi and *onigiri* (rice balls), as its black, small twig-like shape provides an attractive contrast to the white rice.

Preparation and cooking

Soak dried hijiki in tepid water for 15–20 minutes until softened. It will normally expand to 7–10 times its dried volume. It goes well with oil, so it is often shallow-fried and then simmered in dashi-based soup seasoned with shoyu, mirin and sugar.

BELOW: *Hijiki seaweed can withstand vigorous cooking and it will keep well in an airtight container.*

ABOVE: *Dried and cut wakame, in a bowl. It is advisable to store dried wakame in an airtight bag in a cool place, away from direct sunlight.*

Herbs and spices

Unlike European cooking, where herbs and spices are cooked together with the main ingredients, Japanese cooking uses them mainly for additional aroma and flavour, often sprinkled on top of dishes or mixed with a dipping sauce.

Shiso, ginger and wasabi are some well-known examples, but there are also various wild plants called sansai, meaning literally mountain vegetables, which are used as herbs and spices for their unique aromas and flavours. These are, unfortunately, difficult to find outside of Japan.

SHISO
Although originally from China, Burma and the Himalayas, shiso has been cultivated in Japan for centuries, and is now used predominantly in Japanese cooking. Shiso is a member of the mint family and is also known as perilla. There are two types, green and red, and the whole shiso plant from berries to flowers is used as a herb or garnish for Japanese dishes. It is widely cultivated in the West. Green leaves in packets are sold all year round at Asian stores.

Aroma and flavour
The essential oils in shiso provide a very distinctive, pungent aroma and rich but subtly piercing flavour, which is more like basil than mint.

ABOVE: *Shiso has a pungent aroma and is perfect used as a garnish for tempura.*

Culinary uses
Normally only green shiso, with its exquisite flavour, is used as a herb and garnish for dishes such as *sashimi*, tempura and vinegared salads. Red shiso (known as the beefsteak plant in the United States) is used for making umeboshi (dried and salted Japanese apricot) and other pickles. The berries, stems and flowers of both types are also used to garnish *sashimi*, soup and sauces.

Preparation and cooking
Shiso is simply used as it is or cut into required shapes. If used for tempura, only the underside of the leaves should be battered and fried very quickly until they are crisp.

RIGHT: *Mitsuba looks similar to coriander (cilantro). The leaves are mainly used to impart a delicate flavour to clear soup or hors d'oeuvres.*

MITSUBA
This herb has three light green, coriander-like leaves (hence the name, meaning three leaves) on top of thin whitish stalks, about 15–20cm/6–8in long. A member of the parsley family, it is cultivated outside Japan and is available from Asian stores.

Aroma and flavour
Mitsuba has a relatively strong grass aroma and a faintly bitter flavour.

Culinary uses
Mitsuba is used for its unique aroma, so only a few leaves are put into clear soup, thick egg soup or used in hors d'oeuvres. It is also used for hotpot dishes and the stalks can be fried. Use the stalks to tie food – plunge into boiling water to make flexible.

Preparation and cooking
This is a very delicate herb so requires only very light par-boiling.

LEFT: Pickled thinly sliced ginger, gari, is available in packets or jars, but can also be made at home.

Culinary uses
Wasabi and raw fish are an inseparable combination and wasabi paste is always used for *sashimi* and sushi. Wasabi is also used for pickling vegetables and in salad dressings.

SHOGA
Fresh ginger, or shoga, is one of the oldest, most universal ingredients and dried root ginger is widely available all the year round. For Japanese cooking, however, only fresh ginger is used and often only the extracted juice. In addition to shoga (root ginger), so-called ha-shoga (ginger shoot), and mé-shoga (ginger sprout), are available in summer in Japan.

Aroma and flavour
Fresh ginger has a subtly pungent aroma, reminiscent of citrus, and a pleasantly sharp flavour. Young ginger is tender and mild enough to be cooked as a vegetable while older roots become fibrous and more pungent.

Culinary uses
Apart from pickled ginger to accompany sushi, root ginger is almost always grated and only the juice is used in Japanese cooking. Ginger shoot is also pickled and used as a garnish for grilled (broiled) fish dishes. Ginger sprout is mild enough to eat raw with miso, or to use for tempura.

Preparation and cooking
Always peel off the outer skin. To extract the juice, use a Japanese grater or fine cheese grater to finely grate the ginger, then squeeze out the juice. To make pickled ginger, use very fresh young root ginger,

WASABI
For over a thousand years, Japan's somewhat moderately flavoured cooking has been given an unusual pungency through the addition of wasabi. Meaning mountain hollyhock, it is sometimes introduced as the Japanese equivalent of Western horseradish, but they aren't related.

Grated fresh wasabi has a milder fragrance and less sharp pungency than horseradish. It is a rarity even in Japan and the root is more commonly used in its powdered and paste forms.

Aroma and flavour
Freshly grated wasabi has a refreshing, radish-like aroma and subtly pungent flavour. Interestingly, to give it a little more kick, white horseradish is also included, among other ingredients, to make the powders and pastes.

Making wasabi paste
Put about 5ml/1 tsp powdered wasabi in an egg cup and add the same volume of tepid water. Stir vigorously to make a firm, clay-like paste. Place the dish upside down on a board and leave to stand for at least 10 minutes before use. This will prevent the wasabi paste from drying out and at the same time helps it develop its distinctive sharp flavour.

ABOVE: The root of the wasabi is made into a powder or paste and gives a pungent flavour to many Japanese dishes.

Fish

There is no doubt that the Japanese are the world's biggest fish eaters. They deal with 3,000 kinds of fish and shellfish daily at the Tokyo fish market. Choices are far greater in Japan than anywhere else in the world and housewives go shopping for fresh fish every day.

MAGURO

A member of the mackerel family, maguro or tuna has become widely available in the West. There are several kinds of tuna: blue-fin (black tuna in Japan), big-eye, yellow-fin, long-finned and southern blue-fin. Katsuo, skipjack tuna is in the same family, but in a different group of fish.

Tuna is often sold already skinned and sliced as steaks or in chunks, which can make it sometimes difficult to tell which tuna you are buying.

In Japan, tuna is normally displayed cut into thick rectangular pieces –

BELOW: *Maguro intended for* sashimi *is classified according to which part of the fish it is from and its oiliness.*

convenient for *sashimi*. There are usually two kinds, akami and toro, depending on which part of the fish the flesh comes from. Akami, red meat, is from the main, upper part of the body and toro, oily meat, is from the lower.

Maguro is most often used for *sashimi* and sushi, salads, grilling (broiling), and *teriyaki*. Long-finned tuna is not consumed raw, but is sold canned as steaks.

ABOVE: *Fresh sake (salmon), a popular ingredient for* sashimi *in the West, and ikura (salmon caviar).*

SLICING FISH FOR *SASHIMI* AND SUSHI

Fish that can be eaten raw include tuna, skipjack tuna, salmon, mackerel, turbot, sea bass and sea bream. Use absolutely fresh fish and avoid ready-cut steaks or filleted fish. Also, do not eat defrosted frozen fish raw.

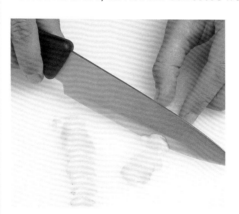

Slicing smaller or flat fish

Using a very sharp knife, fillet and skin the fish carefully, then carefully remove all the bones, including the fine bones from the fillets. If necessary use a pair of tweezers.

Using a sharp knife, cut flat fish fillets in half down the centre, then carefully slice very thinly, making sure that the blade of the knife is inserted diagonally. Do be careful not to cut your fingers.

Slicing tuna, skipjack tuna or salmon

Make sure you buy a chunky piece of fish, avoiding the part with the veins. Cut the chunk into 2–3cm/^{3}/$_4$–1^1/$_4$in thick, 6–7cm/2^1/$_2$–2^3/$_4$in wide fillets.

To cut into slices suitable for sushi, cut 5mm/^{1}/$_4$in thin slices crossways, placing the knife's blade slightly at an angle against the chopping board. For sashimi, slice 1cm/^{1}/$_2$in thick pieces, again keeping the blade slightly at an angle.

SAKE

While sake refers to salmon only, salmon and trout are categorized in the same group of fish although, rather confusingly, some salmon such as chinook (*Onorhynchus tshawytscha*), cherry (*O. masou masou*) and pink (*O. gorbuscha*) are regarded as trout in Japan. The king of salmon in Japan is chum salmon (*O. keta*), which has a perfect silvery body. It comes back to the river of its birth for spawning from September to January.

Salmon is used for *sashimi* in the West but, due to parasite infestation, not in Japan. For *sashimi*, ask the fishmonger to cut fresh from a big chunk of salmon rather than use ready-cut steaks.

In Japan, salmon is traditionally often salted and wrapped in an aramaki (straw mat). Fresh salmon is used for grilling (broiling), frying, *saka-mushi* (sake steaming), hotpots and soup dishes.

LEFT: *Whole and filleted suzuki (sea bass) is appreciated for its delicate flavour and chunky texture.*

SUZUKI

The sea bass grows to about 1m/3ft long and tastes better when over 60cm/24in. It lives around the coast and estuaries of Japan. Suzuki is a handsome fish with big round eyes, a blue-grey back and silvery white belly. The pinkish white flesh, together with the delicate flavour and the chunky texture, adds a pleasant freshness to *sashimi* and sushi. If suzuki is to be cooked, it should be done so very lightly with sauce, in soup, steamed, grilled (broiled) or in a hotpot and make sure it is not overcooked. The flesh is far too delicate to be fried.

Sea bass are available all year round, as whole fish or as fillets. They are at their best in spring and early summer, before they spawn. The tastiest specimens are wild, but farmed suzuki are acceptable if wild bass is not available.

Filleting and skinning round fish

1 Scale and gut the fish, cut off the head and wash under running water. Pat dry with kitchen paper and place the fish flat on a chopping board.

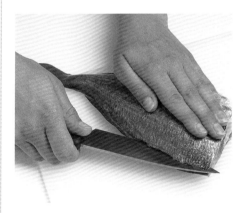

2 Insert a sharp knife as close as possible to the backbone. Cut along the back towards the tail keeping the knife flat to the bone.

3 Turn the fish over and repeat to fillet the other side. Place one fillet at a time skin-side down on the chopping board and insert the blade between the skin and meat at the tail end.

4 Press the skin firmly down with one hand and slowly push the blade, at an angle to the fish, along the skin towards the head to remove the skin. Discard the skin.

TAI

In Japanese cooking, sea bream, or tai, has a special place as a celebratory fish simply because the ending of the Japanese word for "celebration" sounds the same. The largest tai grow to 1m/3ft long but it is the 30–50cm/12–20in fish that is used whole for grilling (broiling). The flesh of tai is milky white and flaky when it is cooked so it is used for making soboro (fish flakes). It is also used for *sashimi* and sushi – such as *oshi zushi* (pressed sushi) – as well as in soups and rice dishes.

KAREI

There are more than 100 species of the karei family worldwide, including plaice, sole, halibut and flounder, and 20 of these inhabit the seas around Japan. Karei look very similar to hirame (see below) except chiefly for the location of the eyes: karei have eyes on the right-hand side of the body and hirame on the left.

BELOW: *Red and black tai (sea bream). The flavour and texture of black tai is similar to red, but not as fine.*

Depending on the species the texture and flesh can vary greatly. Sole is arguably the finest fish of the group, with a firm, delicate flesh and superb flavour. Karei are a very versatile fish and are used for *sashimi*, as well as pan-frying, simmering and also grilling (broiling).

HIRAME

A type of flounder, hirame is a flat fish with its eyes on the back. It is one of the most commonly used fish in Japanese cooking, being used for *sashimi* and sushi as well as for frying, simmering and steaming, and in vinegared vegetable dishes and dressed salads. The thin, broad chain-like frill on the edges of the fish, called *engawa*, is regarded as a delicacy and is used for *sashimi*, simmered and grilled dishes. You can substitute turbot or lemon sole, if you wish.

AJI

This is the general term for about 50 species of a group of fish ranging from horse mackerel to scad, which are now often available at good fishmongers in the West.

Very fresh aji is made into *tataki*, finely chopped flesh eaten with shoyu and grated fresh root ginger. It is also used for grilling (broiling), simmering, and in vinegared dishes. Smaller fish is good for frying whole. Aji is also famous for its dried products such as *hiraki-boshi* (the whole body is opened and dried) and *mirin-boshi* (a whole opened body dried with mirin) and *kusaya* (a strong smelling, opened dried body). Dried aji are available from Asian supermarkets.

BELOW: *Karei is a family of fish that includes plaice, sole, halibut and flounder. Aji (bottom right) is in the mackerel family.*

ANKOH

Monkfish or anglerfish, known as ankoh in Japan, is highly symbolic of winter in Japanese culinary terms. Fugu and puffer are similar winter fish.

A popular fish, ankoh is cooked in a hotpot at the table in restaurants as well as at home. It has a firm, chunky meat, not flaky even when cooked, so it is suitable for simmering, pan-frying or grilling.

In Japan all the parts of the ankoh, including the liver, stomach and ovaries, are eaten but the liver is regarded as a particular delicacy and is often compared to foie gras. The liver is normally marinated in a vinegar sauce and served as *sashimi*. Like many fish, ankoh is an excellent low-fat, low cholesterol source of protein and B vitamins.

BELOW: *The firm, chunky flesh of ankoh makes this fish ideal for most forms of cooking.*

IWASHI

Sardines, iwashi, are the most commonly used fish in Japan, and they account for 25 per cent of the total catch by the sea fisheries. Iwashi is best in winter but is available all year round.

Fresh iwashi is eaten grilled (broiled), in vinegared dishes, in mixed sushi, fried and minced (ground) into fish balls. However, it is mostly processed to make canned and numerous dried products such as niboshi, which is used for making dashi stock, and mezashi, four to six small half-dried iwashi strung together in a row with a small piece of straw.

In the past, export of these fish has been limited, but some are now produced in the West and are available from Japanese supermarkets.

SAMMA

Also known as saury, this long, narrow fish has a blue-black back and shiny silver-white belly. It inhabits the seas around North America and Russia, coming down towards Japan in autumn, the best time to eat it since by then it has acquired its maximum fat content of 20 per cent.

In autumn, samma is best grilled (broiled) or pan-fried whole and eaten with a little grated daikon and shoyu to moderate its fishy smell. Dried samma is also very popular. In other seasons when it is less oily, fresh samma is used for making vinegared salads or sushi.

Fresh samma is sold in season at high-quality fishmongers, and cooked samma in cans is often available.

BELOW: *Beheaded and gutted iwashi (sardines) are packed raw, with their backbones, in oil; the canning process cooks them. Samma (bottom left) is used for sushi, for cooking and for canning.*

Shellfish

Along with fish, shellfish have always been an indispensable ingredient in Japanese cooking, and Japan probably consumes the widest range of shellfish in the world. Most types are used for sashimi *and* sushi *as well as in other forms of cooking.*

EBI
Among the numerous kinds of shellfish used in Japanese cooking, the prawn has the largest market share. If you want to eat prawn sushi, for instance, at a sushi restaurant in Japan, you need to specify which prawn you would like from among at least five kinds likely to be available. Kuruma-ebi (tiger prawn) has a light reddish shell with brown or blue-red stripes and grows to about 20cm/8in long. Ushi-ebi (black tiger prawn) has a dark grey shell with black stripes and, along with kuruma-ebi, supposedly has the best flavour. Both are best eaten raw when very fresh but are also used for grilling (broiling), simmering, frying and in soups.

Korai-egi (Chinese prawn), also known as taisho-ebi, has a light grey shell. This prawn is used for tempura and other frying dishes, stir-frying or simmering.

Japanese shrimp, such as shiba-ebi and botan-ebi, are used mainly for cooking, and hokkoku aka-ebi, also known as ama-ebi, is a delicious sushi topping. Tenaga-ebi (freshwater shrimp) has long tentacles and is often used for simmering and frying, while even smaller shrimps, sakura-ebi, are mostly dried. Unfortunately, many of these are not available outside of Japan.

Preparation and cooking
In Japan all prawns and shrimp are available fresh, sometimes still alive, but in the West, they generally come onto the market frozen. When cooking prawns, leave them in their shells so that they won't lose too much of their flavour. When cooked, they turn bright red or pink.

Note
In the US all prawns are called shrimp, then differentiated according to size: small, medium, jumbo. The Japanese, however, use both shrimp and prawn, so US equivalents in brackets are provided, to avoid confusion.

BELOW: *Ushi-ebi (black tiger prawns) are considered the most flavoursome type of prawn of all. Cooked shrimp turn pink (right).*

ISE-EBI

The Japanese spiny lobster, ise-ebi has a brown or reddish purple shell and smaller claws than most American and European lobsters. It grows off the Pacific coast of west Japan to about 35cm/14in, though it also inhabits the seas around the Caribbean, Australia and Africa. Ise-ebi is traditionally used for celebratory meals because the red colour, when cooked, signifies happiness in Japan.

Lobsters have a uniquely firm, sweet flesh with a delicious flavour. Fresh ones are nearly always eaten as *sashimi*. At fish restaurants they are often kept in a tank and the chef makes a dish called *iki-zukuri* (live *sashimi*) from your choice of lobster in front of you.

RIGHT: *Tabara-gani (king crab) claws are extremely good to eat, especially in salads and fried dishes.*

BELOW: *Fresh ise-ebi, the Japanese spiny lobster are almost always eaten as sashimi in restaurants.*

KANI

There are about 1,000 different crabs inhabiting the seas around Japan alone. The commonest are tabara-gani (king crab), kegani (horsehair crab) and zuwai-gani (snow crab). As its intestine goes off very quickly, kani is always boiled or steamed, often as soon as it is caught on board the fishing boat, before going to market. King crabs look like gigantic spiny spiders, but are very good to eat.

The claw flesh is the main part eaten, most often fresh with citrus shoyu, in salads, in grilled (broiled) and fried dishes, or in hotpots. Crab meat is also one of the major ingredients for sushi. However, in cooked dishes canned crab meat is more usually used.

JAPANESE DELICACIES

Kani-miso Crab intestine mixture, is considered a delicacy in Japan and is most often served as part of an hors d'oeuvres tray or as an accompaniment to sake. Kani-miso is available canned.

Snow crab The sweet-tasting flesh of this crab is usually sold frozen or canned. The snow crab itself has a roundish pinkish-brown body and long legs. It is also known as the queen of the crabs.

IKA

Several types of squid are used in Japanese cooking. Taste, texture, colour and availability decide which one is used for a dish. Fresh squid is used for *sashimi* only if it is very fresh. Always cook squid lightly because overcooked squid is tough and chewy. Whole squid is also used for making *ika-zushi* (ika stuffed with sushi rice).

SQUID PRODUCTS

There are various squid products in Japan, which can increasingly be found at specialist stores in the West.

Surume

This is whole squid opened up and dried, and is one of a number of delicacies served to accompany drinks. It is normally grilled (broiled)

whole, torn crossways with the fingers into fine shreds, and eaten sprinkled with a little shoyu. Kensaki-ika (swordtip squid), with its fine, tender flesh, is the best. It is available in packets, either whole or shredded, from Japanese supermarkets.

Shiokara

This is raw squid, marinated in its own ink and salt. It is served with drinks or rice and is available in jars.

Matsumae-zuke

Another delicacy from the Kansai region, matsumae-zuke is made of surume (dried squid), konbu (kelp seaweed) and carrot shreds marinated in a mixture of mirin and shoyu. It is also served with freshly cooked rice or as an appetizer with drinks. When

BELOW: *Surume (dried squid).*

time is short, make-your-own packets, which contain all the ingredients for matsumae-zuke pre-prepared, can be bought from Japanese supermarkets.

Preparing squid

1 Rinse the squid thoroughly under cold running water. Put your fingers carefully inside the body, grab all the tentacles, together with the soft central bone and intestine, and gently pull everything out of the cavity.

2 Separate the flaps from the body so the white flesh comes away. Peel off the skin. Cut away the intestine. Cut off the tentacles and rub off the skin.

3 For *sashimi*, cut the body flesh in half lengthways and then slice each piece crossways into thin strips to reduce its chewy texture.

4 For geso (tentacle *sashimi*), divide the ten tentacles into five equal pieces or separate individually, and cut the two long feelers in half.

5 For tempura, pan-frying and grilling (broiling), make criss-cross slits on the skin side of the body of the squid then cut into several pieces.

TAKO

There are over ten types of octopus caught all over the world and their sizes vary from Idako (baby octopuses), which are less than 10cm/4in, to ones over 3m/10ft. The most common octopus are in the *ma-dako* family.

Japanese cooking uses the octopus' eight tentacles, lightly blanched, for *sashimi* and vinegared salad dishes. Octopus is also used in hotpots, oden in particular, and for making an ink-marinated delicacy to accompany drinks. Prepared tentacles are available from fish counters in Japanese stores.

HAMAGURI

Clams are one of the oldest foods in Japan as is evident from the remains of the shells found in all the prehistoric settlements excavated. They are still a very important ingredient, and many varieties are

BELOW: Large hamaguri (common hard clams) and asari (Manila clams) are just two of the many clams that are used in Japanese cooking.

used for Japanese cooking such as aka-gai (ark shell), asari (Manila clam), tori-gai (cockle), baka-gai or aoyagi (hen clam) and hokki-gai (surf clam). They are all used for sushi and *sashimi* as well as for all other methods of cooking.

HOTATE-GAI

The scallop is a very versatile shellfish because of its size and fish-like texture. There are several members of the scallop family available in Japan, including hotate-gai, the scallop most often sold in the West; itaya-gai (Japanese scallop), tsukihi-gai (saucer scallop) and hiogi-gai (noble scallop). All varieties are regular ingredients for sushi and *sashimi*. They are used for vinegared salads, or can be salt-grilled, simmered, fried or used in soups. The thin ribbon around the scallop's flesh and the red intestine are not wasted. Dried scallop is available from Asian supermarkets and some larger stores.

BELOW: Dried hotate-gai (scallops) are soaked in a little sake and steamed to make them soft and easy to handle. This process also brings out their distinctive flavour.

ABOVE: Kaki, pacific oysters, are available in Japan all year round but they are most flavoursome from November to March.

KAKI

A few Pacific oysters are available in Japan. The most common kaki (giant Pacific oyster) is oblong in shape, about 8cm/3½in long and 5cm/2in wide in contrast to the round European native oyster.

To eat oyster raw, Japanese-style, dip in a little citrus shoyu. *Kaki-fry* (fried breaded oyster) is another Japanese speciality. Oysters are also used in clear soups, hotpots and cooked with rice. Kaki are known to cause food poisoning so when eaten raw they should be as fresh as possible. Always buy fresh oysters from a reputable fishmonger.

BELOW: Fresh cockles (tori-gai) are often used for sushi.

Fish roes

The Japanese use all parts of the fish, and its eggs, in particular, are regarded as a delicacy. Since the eggs are normally heavily salted to preserve them, they go well with plain boiled rice. They are also regular ingredients in sushi and are used for making hors d'oeuvres.

TARAKO

Cod ovaries, called tarako, are available at the fish counters of supermarkets in Japan. Sold in pairs, cod ovaries are usually simply grilled (broiled) to eat with boiled rice.

IKURA

In Russia, all fish eggs are called ikura, but the name is used only for salmon eggs in Japan. Ikura is already salted to preserve it, so it normally keeps for a short time. It is mainly used for sushi, eaten with grated daikon and

hoyu, and also for making hors d'oeuvres. It is widely available in jars at supermarkets.

KAZUNOKO

Salted and dried herring ovaries, kazunoko, were once abundant but are now so scarce that they have become a rare delicacy. Soak in water overnight to soften and remove the salt before use. Kazunoko is usually eaten as it is with a little shoyu and katsuo-bushi, dried skipjack tuna flakes.

UNI

The Japanese sea urchin, or uni, is a dark spiky, round sea creature that varies in size, depending on type, from 3–4cm/1¼–1½in to over 10cm/4in in diameter. Only the ovaries of the uni are eaten. Fresh uni is one of the regular items for sushi toppings and is also used for making hors d'oeuvres. Salted uni is also available.

ABOVE: *Kazunoko (salted and dried herring ovaries).*

Look for urchins with firm spines and a tightly closed mouth (on the underside). To open, wear gloves and use a purpose-made knife, though sharp scissors can also be used. Cut into the soft tissue around the mouth and lift off the top to reveal the coral. Alternatively, slice off the top like a boiled egg. Remove the mouth and innards, which are inedible, but retain the rich juices for use in sauces. Scoop out the bright orange coral.

LEFT: *Ikura (salmon caviar).*

BELOW: *Uni (Japanese sea urchin ovaries).*

BELOW: *Tarako (cod ovaries) are usually slightly red, front. Tarako with chilli is brighter red (back).*

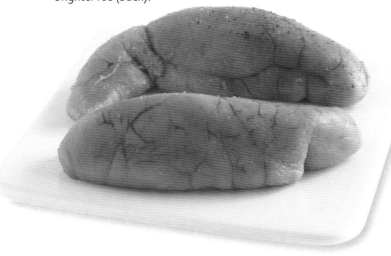

Fish products

Numerous fish products are used in Japanese cooking and many are available in the West, fresh or frozen. They are easy to use and very useful as a flavouring in home-cooking.

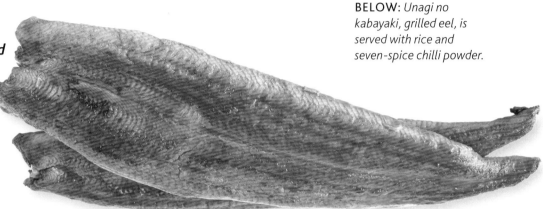

KATSUO-BUSHI

Katsuo, skipjack tuna, is cooked and dried whole to a hard block called katsuo-bushi and then shaved for use. Ready-shaved kezuri-bushi or hanagatsuo in various graded packets is widely available. This is one of the main ingredients in dashi stock and is also used for sprinkling on vegetables or fish as an additional flavouring. Mixed with a little shoyu, it makes a delicious accompaniment to hot boiled rice.

NIBOSHI

These hard, dried sardines are used for making a strong-flavoured dashi stock. In contrast to the delicate flavour of kezuri-bushi, niboshi is boiled for about 5 minutes to exude the flavour and make a more robust stock. Hence niboshi stock is used for making soups such as miso soup and the soup for soba and udon noodles.

UNAGI NO KABAYAKI

Filleted eel is steamed, then grilled (broiled) with a thick, sweet shoyu sauce. This soft fish does not resemble, or taste like, eel. It is placed on top of hot boiled rice with the accompanying sauce sprinkled with seven-spice chilli powder, or sansho. Most people buy unagi no kabayaki instead of making it themselves. It is available ready-to-eat in packets, frozen or vacuum-packed.

HIDARA

This dried cod fillet can be grilled, then torn into pieces with the fingers and eaten with rice. It is also used for making snacks to go with drinks, and is available in packets.

MEZASHI

Meaning eye-pierced, mezashi is made from half-dried whole sardines strung together, four to six at a time, by a piece of straw pierced through the eyes, hence the name. It is just lightly grilled and eaten with hot boiled rice or to accompany sake. Mezashi is sometimes available at larger Asian food stores.

SHISHAMO

This small, 10–15cm/4–6in long, narrow, pinkish silver fish is unique to the north Pacific and Atlantic oceans. Shishamo is considered one of the best Japanese delicacies to eat with sake, especially *komochi-shishamo* (shishamo with eggs), and this is priced accordingly.

CHIRIMEN-JAKO

A speciality of the Kansai region (Osaka and surrounds), these are another form of dried shirasu (white fry sardines), which have been cooked and often flavoured with shoyu. They are eaten as are and make a good accompaniment for hot rice or in *ochazuke* (cooked rice in tea). Shoyu-flavoured ones are fairly salty. They are available in packets in most Asian supermarkets.

TAZUKURI

Dried small sardines, tazukuri are lightly roasted in a small pan before serving as an accompaniment for drinks or as a snack. They have a distinctive *umami* (rich flavouring). At New Year's time they are coated in sugar and served as part of the savoury celebration hamper. Tazukuri are another fish product available outside of Japan.

Fish pastes

Numerous puréed fish products are used in Japanese cooking, among which the following are the most common. They are normally available frozen from Japanese food stores and are the main ingredients for oden *(fish pastes and vegetables cooked in dashi-based soup).*

KAMABOKO

Puréed white fish is mixed with a binding agent and made into various shapes and sizes then steamed, boiled or grilled (broiled) to produce kamaboko. The standard product is called ita-kamaboko, a small fish paste cake, about 4–5cm/1^1/$_2$–2in thick and 15cm/6in long, stuck on a wooden board. Eat kamaboko finely sliced with shoyu and mustard as an hors d'oeuvre.

SATSUMA-AGE

This is deep-fried kamaboko and is normally shaped into an oval disc measuring about 7.5 x 5cm/3 x 2in. Pour boiling water over the paste to reduce the oil before use. It can be eaten as it is with shoyu, or lightly grilled.

CHIKUWA

Puréed fish is moulded around a stick, then steamed and grilled, and the stick removed. Chikuwas normally measure about 15cm/6in long with the hole running this length. The outer skin is seared an attractive uneven brown. It can be eaten either just sliced, used for simmering with vegetables or added to hotpots.

NARUTOMAKI

This is a kind of kamaboko with a decorative pink swirling pattern inside, which is made by kneading dyed red fish meat into white meat.

Narutomaki is one of the regular ingredients for ramen, which are Chinese-style noodles, and it is also used in udon noodles and soups.

HANPEN

This puréed shark's flesh is mixed with grated yam and egg whites, shaped into a 7–8cm/3^1/$_2$–3^3/$_4$in square cake about 1cm/^{1}/$_2$in thick and then boiled. It has a light, fluffy texture and can be eaten grilled with shoyu and mustard, and is also used for hotpots and soups.

TSUMIRE

This small, greyish coloured hand-rolled fish ball is made from red meat fish such as sardines and mackerel and, though firm, has a soft texture. It is a flat disc with a "crater" in the centre so that it heats quickly and evenly. Tsumire is used in soup, *oden* and hotpot dishes and is available frozen in specialist stores.

RIGHT: *Ita-kamaboko, white fish paste on a wooden board.*

LEFT: *Clockwise from left to right; satsuma-age, narutomaki, chikuwa, and hanpen puréed fish products.*

Meat and chicken

The eating of meat was banned in Japan for many years, first due to Buddhism and later by the Shogunate for 300 years until 1868. It was only after World War II that meat, mainly beef, pork and chicken became a part of the general diet. It is still used sparingly; usually thinly sliced or shredded and cooked with vegetables, or minced (ground).

BEEF

There are four types of *wagyu* (Japanese beef): black, reddish brown, hornless and short-horned. Black beef is the most common. Matsuzaka beef, also known as Kobe beef, omi beef and yonezawa beef, are the top-quality meats. They are given beer to drink, which helps to distribute the fat. *Wagyu* is not available in the West

but you can use sirloin or fillet instead. For *sukiyaki* and *shabu shabu*, where almost transparent slices are required, choose a roasting joint without a bone, or fillet. If a joint is used, trim off the fat completely and cut into 4–5cm/1¹/₂–2in thick oblong pieces, then freeze for two or three hours. Remove to the refrigerator, leave for 1 hour to half thaw and then slice into paper-thin oblong pieces. Ready-sliced *sukiyaki* beef is generally available from stores. Trim off any excess fat, if necessary.

PORK

Since ancient times pork has been eaten, even during the period when meat was banned, and it remains popular today. It is thinly sliced, pan-fried and mixed with grated fresh root

ginger and shoyu, or else chopped and used as a flavouring in vegetable dishes. Long-simmered pork is delicious with ramen.

CHICKEN

Native regional chickens, called jidori, are popular in Japan, though there are also many mass-produced broiler chickens. *Nagoya kochin* is one such jidori, with a pinkish golden, firm meat. Minced chicken is often used for making meatballs, sauces or as a flavouring for simmered vegetables. *Yakitori* is chicken pieces threaded on a bamboo skewer, then grilled (broiled) with sweet taré sauce. Boneless chicken thighs marinated in *teriyaki* sauce and then grilled are ideal for barbecues. Chicken is also used for hotpots.

LEFT: *Chicken is used in various ways; minced for making meatballs, skewered for* teriyaki, *and the thigh for barbecuing.*

ABOVE: *Finely sliced beef for* shabu shabu *and* sukiyaki.

RIGHT: *Thinly sliced pork is often pan-fried with fresh root ginger.*

Sauces

Shoyu and miso are the two oldest and most important flavouring sauces in Japanese cooking. Their strong, distinctive flavours mean that shoyu and miso are used more as condiments for dipping or as flavourings for cooking, rather than as sauces for coating food.

LEFT: *Light and dark shoyu. Use light shoyu, left, for flavouring, such as in clear soups, and dark shoyu, above back, in simmered dishes.*

Shoyu and miso have a preservative quality and are good for marinating raw fish, meat and vegetables. The Japanese have also developed ready-mixed sauces for dishes like *sukiyaki* and *yakiniku* (barbecue), as well as Japanese vinegar and mirin, both made from rice.

ABOVE: *Light shoyu (soy sauce), right, has a lighter colour but saltier flavour than regular shoyu, left.*

SHOYU

Japan's ancient seasoning was called hishio, and consisted of a preserve of what was at that time very scarce and precious salt fermented with animal or vegetable protein and fibre. Grain hishio, fermented with grains such as rice and wheat, and also beans, was developed into miso and its exuded liquid became shoyu. (The present-day sushi is also thought to derive from the ancient fish hishio, raw fish fermented with salt and rice.)

Using new techniques, introduced from China, Japan soon developed its own type of soy sauce, shoyu, made from daizu (soya beans), wheat and salt. Shoyu is now widely available from supermarkets, but Japanese shoyu is quite different in aroma and flavour from Chinese varieties.

Aroma and flavour

Shoyu is quite salty, although less salty now than it used to be, due to recent warnings about the role of salty food in heart disease. There are basically two types: usukuchi (light), and koikuchi (dark). The usukuchi is an all-purpose shoyu, clearer but slightly saltier than koikuchi, which is used for making sauces such as taré for *teriyaki*. There are also many grades, depending on the grade of soya beans, which are priced accordingly. Tamari is made from soya beans only without wheat, so it is similar to the liquid obtained during the making of miso.

Culinary uses

Shoyu is without doubt the single most important ingredient in Japanese cuisine and is used in almost every recipe. It is often used as a dip on its own for sushi, *sashimi*, pickles and many other dishes. Tamari is a dark shoyu used for making taré sauce and is suitable for those on a wheat-free diet.

MISO

Although lifestyles are rapidly changing, for many Japanese the day still starts with a bowl of miso soup for breakfast. Miso is one of the oldest traditional Japanese ingredients – it was already being made in the 12th century – and its origin can be traced back to the ancient seasoning called hishio, a preserve of salt fermented with grains and beans.

Numerous kinds and brands of miso are available in supermarkets, even outside Japan. They are categorized into three basic grades according to strength of flavour and colour: shiro-miso (white, light and made with rice), aka-miso (red, medium and made with barley), and kuro-miso (black, strong and made with soya beans).

Aroma and flavour

Miso is quite salty and has a strong fermented bean flavour. Shiro-miso is the lightest in saltiness and flavour, aka-miso is of medium flavour, and the strongest is kuro-miso. There are less salty brands available for the health conscious.

Culinary uses

Miso is a versatile ingredient and can be simply diluted with dashi stock to make soups, including the soup for miso ramen. It is used as seasoning for simmered dishes or dipping sauces, and also as a marinade for meat and fish. Shiro-miso (white) is a speciality of Kyoto, and it is good for soups, dressings and marinades. Aka-miso (red) is good for soups and for meat marinades. Hatcho-miso, the best kuro-miso (black), is rich and salty, and is good for dipping sauces and soups. It is often used mixed with another lighter miso. It loses its subtle aroma if overcooked.

BELOW: *Clockwise from top left, aka-miso, shiro-miso, hatcho-miso and kuro-miso.*

Miso-marinated flat fish or steak

Flat fish such as plaice and turbot are used for this dish, which involves marinating the fish in shiro-miso, a kind of white miso, which is made from rice and has a light flavour.

1 On a large plate spread a thin layer of shiro-miso (use aka-miso for meat). Cover with a piece of kitchen paper and press lightly so that the miso is absorbed by the paper.

2 Place the fish fillets, flesh side down, or meat on the kitchen paper and cover with another piece of kitchen paper.

3 Using a knife, press a thin layer of miso on top of the paper so that the paste covers the fish or meat. The paste will soak through and marinate the fish or meat. Leave the fish to marinate for about 3 hours or it can be marinated overnight, if you prefer.

4 Remove the fish or meat from the marinade and grill (broil) as required in the recipe.

Ready-made sauces

A number of ready-to-use ingredients have been developed in recent years and Japanese cooking is much easier as a result. The following ready-made sauces are available in the West.

MEN-TSUYU

This is a dashi-based condensed sauce for soba and udon noodles. It is made of dashi stock, shoyu, salt, sugar and other ingredients, and is used as a dipping sauce or soup for noodles. The instructions on the packet will state how much water should be added to make a dip for soba and somen, or soup in which to cook udon and soba. Men-tsuyu is most delicious when made a few hours in advance and left to sit so that the flavours can develop. It is usual to dilute 1:1 for a dip and 1:8 for soup. Store in the refrigerator.

TONKATSU SAUCE

Pork cutlet or tonkatsu is one of the most popular dishes in Japan, and this thick brown sauce is the ideal accompaniment, together with shredded cabbage and mustard. It is made of fruits, spices and seasonings. You can easily make your own tonkatsu sauce by mixing a fruit sauce, such as ketchup, and Worcestershire sauce.

TEN-TSUYU

This tasty dipping sauce for tempura is made of dashi stock, shoyu, mirin and a number of seasonings. Ten-tsuyu is normally used undiluted together with a little grated daikon and finely shredded fresh root ginger.

PONZU

Made of citrus juice, vinegar and seasonings, ponzu is used mixed with shoyu and spices for hotpot dishes. It is very tart in flavour with a watery consistency and yellow colour.

SUKIYAKI SAUCE

This is a sweet shoyu sauce for cooking *sukiyaki*, made of dashi stock, sugar, sake and seasonings. First thinly sliced beef is pan-fried, then some of this sauce is added, together with bitesize vegetables.

YAKINIKU NO TARÉ

This Japanese version of barbecue sauce is made of shoyu, spices and various seasonings. It is slightly sweeter than the Western barbecue sauces and is very good used for griddled food.

CURRY ROUX

Japan was first introduced to curry in the middle of the 19th century, not directly from India but via England,

LEFT: *Ponzu can be mixed with shoyu and used in hotpot dishes, such as beef.*

RIGHT:
Curry roux.

where curry powder was concocted and exported. Since then, curry has become one of the most popular daily foods in Japan. The Japanese, as with many introduced ingredients, further developed the powder into an instant curry sauce roux, mixing together all the necessary ingredients such as herbs and spices, fruits, soup stock, sauces and seasonings.

Curry roux comes in the form of a soft slab, resembling

a chocolate bar, in a sectioned plastic tray. All you need to do is boil the fresh ingredients such as meat or shellfish, potato, onion and carrot, and add some of this sauce mix. There are degrees of hotness: mild, medium, hot and very hot. There are also separate roux for meat and fish. An average packet normally serves 12, but remember that a Japanese portion is very small and it really makes enough for only six to eight adult appetites, particularly if eaten on its own.

Japanese curry is quite sweet, even the very hot type, and usually contains a lot of MSG (monosodium glutamate). If you are unsure of the flavour peculiar to MSG, which can make you a little thirsty afterwards, use this product very sparingly or omit altogether from the dish.

Making simple sauces at home

Most Japanese people have a number of sauces in their repertoire that can be easily and quickly made on the day of use.

Yuan sauce This sauce gives a subtle flavour to rather bland ingredients such as white fish, and also enhances the flavours of stronger-flavoured varieties, such as salmon. To make the sauce, mix together 5 parts mirin, 3 parts shoyu to 2 parts sake and 2 parts lime juice in a small bowl. Marinate the fish in the sauce for at least 15 minutes, before frying or cooking over a barbecue.

Tonkatsu sauce This is delicious with fried pork. To make the sauce, mix together 1 part Worcestershire sauce to 5 parts tomato ketchup in a small bowl. Coat some pork slices in a little flour then in some beaten egg and deep-fry briefly until cooked. Dip the fried pork into the sauce and eat immediately.

LEFT: *The numerous types of Japanese ready-made sauces include, from left, tonkatsu sauce, sukiyaki sauce, men-tsuyu sauce, ponzu, men-tsuyu sauce for somen and yakiniku no taré.*

Vinegars
and mirin

Unlike shoyu and miso, Japanese vinegar and mirin (sweet cooking sake) are delicate tasting and good for adding subtle flavours to Japanese cooking. Both mirin and Japanese vinegar are made from rice.

RICE VINEGAR

Unless labelled yonezu (pure rice vinegar), most Japanese vinegars, called su or kokumotsu-su, normally

contain other grains besides rice. Rice vinegar, other vinegars and vinegar products are all available at Japanese supermarkets.

Japanese rice vinegar has a mild, sweet aroma and is less sharp than ordinary wine vinegar.

Vinegar has many qualities. It can be used to refresh and soften saltiness, it acts as an antiseptic, and is a coagulant for proteins. It also prevents food from discolouring, helps to wash off slimy substances from food and to soften small fish bones. It is, therefore, useful from the preparation stage of food to the final seasoning. There are numerous

vinegared dishes, such as cucumber and wakame salad, vinegar-cured raw fish, and gari (pickled ginger) to accompany sushi.

MIRIN

This amber-coloured, heavily sweetened sake is used only in cooking. It is one of Japan's ancient sake and is made from shochu (distilled sake). Shochu, mixed with steamed glutinous rice and koji (a yeast-like culture made from rice), is brewed and compressed to absorb the liquid, and then filtered.

Mirin has a faint sake aroma and syrupy texture, which adds not only a mild sweetness to food but also an attractive shiny glaze and slightly alcoholic flavour.

It is used for simmered dishes and in glazing sauces such as taré (for *yakitori*) and also for *teriyaki* sauce. Other uses include *mirin-boshi* (a mirin-coated dried fish), and daikon is pickled in mirin pulp.

Use mirin towards the end of the cooking time to add a subtle sweetness and depth to the flavour of the dish. It is not meant to be used as a sweetener, but if you must, you can use 5ml/1 tsp sugar in place of 15ml/1 tbsp mirin.

Both vinegar and mirin keep well for a long time if stored in a cool, dry place away from sunlight. It is best to use mirin within the stated time, since the flavour deteriorates.

ABOVE: *Yonezu (rice vinegar) and kokumotsu-su (grain vinegar).*

LEFT: *When buying rice vinegar, look for hon-mirin, left, rather than mirin-fuhmi, right, which is a cheap imitation.*

Dried flavourings

Ever on the look-out for delicious accompaniments to hot plain boiled rice, the Japanese have developed a number of dried flavourings. These are collectively known as tsukudani.

TSUKUDANI

Various foodstuffs, such as konbu (kelp seaweed), shiitake, matsutake, dried herring, clams, beef and even whale meat are made into tsukudani. Konbu is the most popular. It is cut into small pieces and then simmered with shoyu for a long time. It is sometimes cooked with other foods, such as shiitake or matsutake, and fish flakes. Tsukudani is fairly salty and goes well with hot plain boiled rice. Konbu tsukudani is usually available in packets from Japanese supermarkets all year round.

FURIKAKE

Consisting of various types of granulated fish and vegetable extracts, furikake are popular sprinkled on hot boiled rice. They are also used for making *onigiri* (rice balls), either mixed with rice or used as a stuffing. Various sprinkles come in packets or jars and are available from Japanese supermarkets.

OCHAZUKE NO MOTO

A favourite Japanese way of enhancing left-over rice is to pour over boiling water to which has been added a flavouring.

There are many different flavours of ochazuke no moto available, including salted salmon, cod roe, umeboshi (salted and dried Japanese apricots) and nori, and they are available from supermarkets in individual packets.

ABOVE: *Assorted furikake (seafood and vegetable granules).*

SUSHI MIX

This is a packet or jar of pre-prepared ingredients for *chirashi-zushi* (mixed sushi), which is made by stirring the packet's contents into cooked rice to make sushi rice. The garnish of shredded nori is also included in the packet. The flavour is sweet and it contains MSG (monosodium glutamate), which can leave you feeling very thirsty.

BELOW: *Ochazuke no moto (flavourings for left-over rice).*

BELOW: *Sushi mixes.*

Pickles

For the Japanese, rice and tsukemono (pickled vegetables) have gone hand in hand since ancient times. There are many varieties of tsukemono, also known as oshinko, preserved in all sorts of ways, and different regions have their own speciality.

Barrel after barrel of freshly made tsukemono are displayed in the food hall of any department store in Japan and you can sample them before buying. The Japanese do not use vinegar as a pickling agent; instead, rice bran, miso, sake or mirin pulps, mustard, koji (rice malt) or shoyu, together with salt, are used. Salting takes away the coarseness of the hard vegetables and makes them soft and digestible as well as preserving them. It also adds more character and depth to the taste and improves the nutritional content.

BELOW: *Shio-zuke (salt-pickled vegetables) can refer to a number of vegetables including, from left, aubergine, radish and cucumber.*

The following are some of the popular pickles available in packets from Japanese supermarkets and Asian grocery stores.

TAKUAN

Fresh, just harvested daikon are hung for two to three weeks, then salted and pickled in nuka (dry rice bran) and salt. It takes two or three months to mature and the end result is a soft but crunchy, delicious yellow daikon. This tsukemono is said to have been invented by the Buddhist monk Takuan in the 17th century, hence its name. Salty with a hint of sweetness, it is good on its own with hot boiled rice. It is also a regular ingredient for *nori-maki* (nori-rolled sushi) and other rice dishes. Most of the manufactured takuan has bright yellow food colouring added, so for naturally pickled daikon, look for the paler ones and check the label first.

SHIO-ZUKE

This is the general term used for all salted vegetables, and many vegetables, including cucumber, aubergine (eggplant), daikon, hakusai and mustard leaves, are used.

NARA-ZUKE

This tsukemono is a speciality of Nara, the ancient capital of Japan. The pulp that mirin is exuded from is used to pickle various vegetables, and nara-zuke (salted daikon pickled in mirin pulp) is one such pickle. It has a sweet flavour with a hint of alcohol.

NUKA-ZUKE

This is a traditional method of pickling and each household used to keep a tub of nuka-miso (rice bran mash), which resembles miso and from which it takes its name. Nuka (dry rice bran) is mixed with warm, strong brine into a mash, in which vegetables such as aubergine (eggplant), carrot, cucumber, daikon, hakusai or turnips are buried and left to pickle. It is ready to eat the next day.

This process makes the vegetables mildly sweet and enriches the flavour, but not without paying the price of its strong odour. The mash must be stirred every day, ideally with bare hands. Although long-serving dutiful wives were once fondly called nuka-miso (smelling wife), today not many wives wish to be appreciated for their smelly hands! Nuka for pickling is available from Japanese stores, although ready-pickled nuka-zuke in packets is more popular nowadays.

ABOVE: *Nara-zuke (mirin pulp pickles) is a speciality of Nara, the ancient capital of Japan and is eaten with boiled rice.*

MISO-ZUKE

The saltiness and strong flavour of miso are the two ideal qualities for making pickles, and the earliest known variety of Japanese pickle was made using miso. Red or white miso can be used on its own or often flavoured with mirin and sake to make miso-doko (miso mash). Fish and shellfish, poultry and beef can be marinated before grilling (broiling) and vegetables that have been marinated are then eaten as pickles.

All crunchy vegetables are suitable for pickling in miso but gobo (burdock root) is probably better than anything else for pickling in miso. Vegetables can be par-boiled beforehand to cut down on pickling time but the longer the vegetables rest in the miso, the more flavourful the pickle. Ready-to-eat gobo miso pickles are usually available in packets at Japanese supermarkets.

RAKKYO

To make rakkyo, spring onions (scallions) are first salted and then pickled in heavily sweetened vinegar. This is traditionally served with curry.

Making a pickled turnip flower

Serve these attractive flowers as an hors d'oeuvre or as a garnish for sushi.

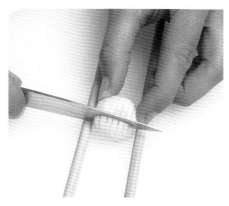

1 Trim and peel five small turnips and place, one at a time, between a pair of hashi (chopsticks) on a cutting board.

Insert a very sharp blade down into the turnip, across the hashi, and make parallel cuts until the blade touches the hashi. Turn the turnip 90 degrees, and cut across the first series of cuts.

2 Repeat with the remaining turnips, then place them in a bowl. Sprinkle with 5ml/1 tsp salt and rub in lightly. Cover with a plate, place a weight on top and leave to stand for 30 minutes.

3 Mix 250ml/8fl oz/1 cup rice vinegar with 150g/5oz/¾ cup sugar in a bowl and stir until the sugar has dissolved. Drain the turnips and pour the vinegar mixture over them. Leave to marinate and soften overnight.

Making rice bran pickles

Nuka-zuke is a traditional pickling method for vegetables such as carrot, daikon and cucumber, and is an old Japanese favourite.

1 Following the instructions on the packet of nuka, mix the water and salt in a pan and bring to the boil. Remove the pan from the heat and leave to cool. The ratio is usually 3 parts nuka to 1 part of salt mixed with 2½ parts of water.

2 Put the rice bran in a large mixing bowl, then add the salted water and mix thoroughly. Seal well or transfer the wet nuka to a large container with a tight-fitting lid. Leave the nuka to settle for 5 days, stirring well about 1–2 times a day.

3 Wash and trim the vegetables (cut big vegetables into smaller sizes), then push them into the bran bed. Softer vegetables are ready within 24 hours and harder ones, such as daikon, within 2 days. Adjust the saltiness by adding more salt or rice bran. Stir the bran well every day even when nothing is being pickled. The bran can be used indefinitely.

Index